SHUCK BEANS, STACK CAKES, AND HONEST FRIED CHICKEN

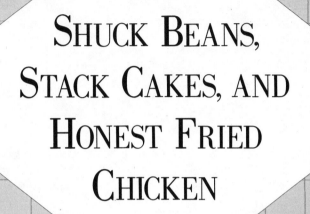

SHUCK BEANS, STACK CAKES, AND HONEST FRIED CHICKEN

The Heart and Soul of Southern Country Kitchens

RONNI LUNDY

Seasoned with Memories and Melodies from

Country Music Stars

THE ATLANTIC MONTHLY PRESS
NEW YORK
·

Published simultaneously in Canada
Printed in the United States of America

Library of Congress Cataloging-in-Publication Data

Lundy, Ronni.
Shuck beans, stack cakes, and honest fried chicken: the heart and soul of southern country kitchens: seasoned with memories and melodies from country music stars / Ronni Lundy.
Includes index.
ISBN 0-87113-517-5
1. Cookery, American—Southern style.   I. Title.
TX715.2.S68L85   1991   641.5975—dc20   91-18142

Design by Laura Hough

The Atlantic Monthly Press
19 Union Square West
New York, NY 10003

FIRST PRINTING

To

Jerry, for the love of good food;

Pap, for the love of a good story;

Pat, for the love of good writing;

and Ken and Meghan, for love.

ACKNOWLEDGMENTS

It was over a plate of satin-skinned beaten biscuits piled high with sacred slivers of two-year-old country ham that I received the word, the sum-uppance of what southern country cooking is all about.

John Egerton, dispenser of biscuits, ham, and wisdom, leaned across the kitchen table and said: "This is what southern cooking does. Southern cooking says, Come on in, get a plate. Pull it up here to the table. I'll tell you how I made this. I'll help you make it if you want to. We'll have a good time together in the kitchen, and you'll remember this for a long time."

Thank you, John. You are so right.

Southern cooking, country cooking—like country music—is indeed collaborative art. And like the cooking and the music that inspired it, this book is the result of many collaborations. I owe heartfelt thanks to those who helped bring it into being.

For everyone whose name appears in the coming pages attached to a recipe, story, or photograph, my deepest gratitude. You have taught me much—not simply about food and family, but most of all about generosity of spirit.

To the aunts and uncles, cousins and almost kin who filled the tables and made my childhood rich beyond measure, both love and thanks; and extra helpings to Aunt Rae and Uncle Charlie, Aunt Johnnie and Aunt Minnie, who gave me a second, magic home.

This book would not be were it not for Betty Fussell who dreamed it and Beth Vesel my agent, who talked me into making the dream reality. Thanks also to Betty for gentle encouragement along the way and Beth for rock-solid guidance.

To John Barstow, a damn good Yankee editor, may all your dreams of country ham, kale greens, and real cornbread come true. To Peter Knapp, bless you for good humor and good assistance.

To all the players and singers who have touched my heart, thank you for the music; but most of all, thanks to Sam, John, Courtney, Curtis, and Ebo for handing me the key.

More thanks to Vince Staten, who was too busy, and Sarah Fritschner, who never was. For good faith through the years, thanks to Greg Johnson, Maureen McNerney, Jena Monohan, Elmer Hall, and Anita Leclerc.

Thanks to Aunt Lib, Carolyn, and Loran for shuck beans.

Thank you Jane Fleishcaker, Alice Columbo, Stephen Lee, Hoppin' John Taylor, Ronna Rubin (it's my turn for dinner), Denise Stiff, Susan Niles, and Janice Azrak, who is going to make green tomato baklava for me someday.

Thanks to Joanne and Jesse Gardner for knowing that your door was always open.

Thanks, Mark Bliesener for invaluable field research; Alanna Nash; Jan Arnow; Dawghaus Photography; Bob Oermann; Mr. Peters; Tim Barnes; Dan Einstein; the good folks at the Country Music Foundation, Harry Bickel, Barry Poss, Charles Wolfe, Tracy Nelson, and Holly Gleason.

Thanks, Nap's Food Mart, for being open even when you weren't.

Thanks to the very dear friends who tasted fearlessly, suggested thoughtfully, and sustained me selflessly through the project.

And to my mother, husband, and daughter, thank you for phenomenal patience and support.

CONTENTS

INTRODUCTION

My first musical memory is of standing next to our 78 RPM record player, patting my foot to the fiddle strains and high harmonies of "Boil 'Em Cabbage Down." The record player was housed in the pull-out drawer of an old floor model radio from Sears, and I was just barely tall enough to watch the label spin as I sang:

"Boil 'em cabbage down and down.

Turn them hoecakes round and round.

The onliest song I ever did sing

Was boil 'em cabbage down."

The year was 1952 and I was about three years old, so you could say that country music and country food were linked together for me very early in life. As time went on, each was to become for me more than simple sustenance or entertainment.

I grew up in a city—Louisville, Kentucky—during the 1950s and 1960s, but many of the foods my family ate were from another place and another time. Years later in an interview about traditional crafts and their transmutation in modern times, folklorist Richard Van Kleeck would tell me that foodways are always the last art form to be corrupted, the last skill to be lost as any small culture is assimilated into a larger one. But I knew this in my childhood not as a scholarly conclusion, but as a delicious, visceral fact.

My dinners were made of the same simple, full-flavored foods my people—southern Cumberland mountain folk—had been eating for generations. And in that day and age of convenience food, peanut butter lunches, and television dinners I was one lucky, well-fed child.

No buckets of carry-out chicken or instant mashed potatoes for me. My mother fried chicken slowly but perfectly crisp in a covered cast-iron skillet just as her mother had done and her mother before her. When all the batches were fried and the platter piled with a gleaming, golden mound of drumsticks, breasts, and wings she made milk gravy in the pan to pour over the small, brown-crusted, fluff-filled biscuits in the oven. Then she mashed her potatoes to a buttery lightness first with an old-fashioned masher, then whipping and beating with a spoon.

In the coldest part of winter we were fortified by broth-rich pots of full-bodied, bronze-hued shuck beans—green beans my aunts strung on thread and hung up to dry every summer, just as their pioneer forebears had done. But while my ancestors strung their beans for survival, my aunts did it because there is nothing in the world so addictively satisfying in winter as the earthy, robust flavor of shuck beans.

The shuck beans and soup beans, too, were served with real cornbread: no sugar, no flour, but covered in a crust turned glistening brown by a well-greased and scorching hot cast-iron skillet.

My Aunt Minnie sometimes came to stay with us, and she would slow cook dried apples with dark brown sugar to fill crisp-crusted fried pies. Then she sent my daddy off to the factory where he worked with a couple in his lunch bag—just as women before her had done for their men going to the coal mines or railroad cars—or those before that for men going into the wilds to forage and hunt.

In summer we feasted on ripe fruits and vegetables. Although we had no garden of our own, there seemed to be no end to the bounties that cousins and neighbors shared. Our house would be blessed with bags and big wash pans full of tender white half-runner beans; scarlet juicy strawberries; tiny torpedo-shaped okra; red tomatoes bursting with juice; and green tomatoes full of sass and tang, just waiting to be sliced and dusted in cornmeal and fried.

Summer was also the time for vacations in Corbin, the small southeastern

Kentucky railroad town where I'd been born and many of my relatives still lived. It was time to help my aunts fill little jars with rosy hued, translucent grape jelly; to go with my daddy and my Uncle Charlie up to the country to rob the bees and bring home golden dripping cones of honey; to sit on the screened-in back porch in the twilight and lick rich globs of vanilla ice cream from the paddle of the hand-cranked ice cream freezer.

It was also the time of reunions—two each year in Levi Jackson. The dark, cool, leaf-bowered state park just north of Corbin is where Indians once roamed and settlers fought, but when I was growing up I knew it best of all as the place where my relatives from all around the country would annually gather to laugh and hug and talk and eat and eat. First, in June, it would be my mother's people, the Fores and Grinsteads; then in August, the Lundys from my father's side would come.

At each reunion, picnic tables were set end to end to form one long trencher. It was covered with black, deep, wide skillets filled to the brim with golden, buttery kernels of creamed corn; country hams aged long and sliced paper thin; green beans flecked and seasoned with slivers of rich salt pork; potato salads with dill pickles, with sweet pickles, and with no pickles at all but plenty of olives. For dessert there were apple stack cakes layered ten inches high and crammed with spicy fruit; Aunt Ariel's jam cake full of nuts and covered with caramel icing; wash tubs of ice packed with firm, round dark green watermelons and bottles of shivery cold pop.

Along with all this extraordinary food came extraordinary conversations. My family—both Mother and Daddy's sides—was filled with wonderful raconteurs and storytellers. Not yarnspinners nor tall tale-tellers, these were people who took the fabric of daily life and shaped it into wonderful vignettes and anecdotes full of humor and drama, values and history.

Settling around the park tables as reunion afternoons wore on or gathered at the round oak pedestal table in my parent's dining room at home, these relatives would joke and laugh and then "tell the one about . . ." for hours. And in the course of that time I, leaning sated and drowsy up against one of my parents as the evening grew dark, would listen and learn about people and family I'd never met, places I'd never seen, parts of myself I'd not yet discovered.

It was around these family tables that my grandparents—all of whom had died before I was born—became real to me. It was after dinner one night that my Aunt Mattie told about Frank Lundy and Alice Pillion's dramatic elopement; about the angry father who hunted them through the woods with his ax and when he couldn't find them went home and chopped his daughter's hope chest to bits.

It was over a fried-chicken feast that my mother told about the time Colonel Harland Sanders—a mean-spirited jokester back then, not the icon of commerce and Americana he's become—tried to scare her father, Bill Fore, by winding a rubber snake around the steering wheel of his truck. My grandfather—usually a sweet-natured and gentle man—unwrapped the snake, stalked back into the Colonel's Corbin restaurant and cracked a chair in two in front of him, cautioning him never to do that again.

And it was over virtually every meal that my mother prepared that I learned of my grandmother Iva's cooking prowess—for my mother assured us every time we raved over something she had made that it was nothing compared to the extraordinary way her mother could cook.

So I was bound beautifully and solidly to my past by food and by stories consumed around the family table.

"It was a charmed way to grow up," Dwight Yoakam would say to me years later, talking about his own boyhood visits to his grandparents' house in the mountains of eastern Kentucky.

But his words had a resonance for my own experience, as well, for mine was a charmed way to grow up, indeed.

Grow up I did, though, and in the process I moved far away from the dinner table, its food and stories. I traveled and lived in several places for awhile, then finally settled for some years in New Mexico. (No matter where I was, every Christmas would bring a package via my mother with shuck beans from Aunt Rae or Aunt Lib and her sister, Carolyn.)

Those were turbulent and fabulous times as my counterculture friends and I tried on new lifestyles and identities—some as colorful and free-flowing as the outrageous clothes we wore. But while many of my friends seemed to be eager to shed their pasts—childhoods that, to hear them tell it, had been spent in faceless suburbs, nourished on food from the freezer and culture from the television—I found myself wanting to reclaim my past and seal it together with my present and my future.

Music became the medium for that. Sometime not too far into the 1970s, during one of the summers when I'd settled briefly in Louisville again, I found my way to a little storefront bar and restaurant on Bardstown Road. Behind the bar was a smiling woman, Sheila Pyle, dishing up bowls of rich brown pinto beans with golden triangles of cornbread and a green onion laid to the side, just as it ought to be.

Up on the stage was a wiry boy in ridiculously flared bell-bottomed jeans, a mass of golden curls tumbling to his shoulders, chopping furiously on a mandolin as if life depended on it. He was singing the music of Bill Monroe (father of bluegrass, and the exact same age as my father) in a perfect hillbilly twang but playing licks from Jimi Hendrix and Eric Clapton with the rocking revivalist furor of Little Richard and Jerry Lee Lewis.

It was Sam Bush and the New Grass Revival and what none of us knew at the time is that they were creating a new form of music, progressive bluegrass. What I did know, though, was that that boy and his band were singing my life. I was entranced with the music—a combination of an old, old culture and an original new one that seemed to mirror my own life.

As my interest grew and I began to explore the traditional bluegrass and old-time country music that was at the Revival's roots, I found more connections to my own experience. As far back as you care to look, the heart of traditional country music has been about the struggle to bring an old life and a new one together in an intense embrace. The sadness that permeates it comes from a loss of place and time. For the early settlers in the mountains, it was their Irish, Scottish, and English homelands. For my father and mother's generation, it was the small-town warmth they had to leave behind to make a living in the city. For me, it was a family way of life that couldn't keep pace in modern times.

The best of country music has always given voice to that sense of longing and loss. But it is also distinguished by its compelling power. And that strength comes from its ability to weld the most vital elements of its past with the most promising ones of the present: Monroe's mix of Pentecostal harmonies, black blues and a personal, furious rhythm that would later show up in rock and roll; Hank Williams's blend of raw roots aching with cool cowboy swing; Bush's mix of bluegrass precision and acid-rock invention; Emmylou Harris's and Dwight Yoakam's melding of classic country vocals with sizzling contemporary instrumentation. At its very best, country music accepts the promise and change of the new while holding on fiercely to the parts of the past that nourish it. That's just what I wanted to do with my own life.

*   *   *

In time, I began to want not just to listen to the music, but to write about it—to ask the musicians where it came from within them, what they thought it meant, and to tell others about it.

By 1980 my husband, Ken, and I had moved back to Louisville to raise our daughter, Meghan. I began to write about music for the newspapers here, the *Louisville Times* and the *Courier-Journal,* and eventually for magazines ranging from the small, cultish *Bluegrass Unlimited* to *Esquire.*

I also began to write about food—somehow the two just seemed to go together.

In fact, food often cropped up in my interviews with country and bluegrass musicians—most of whom, I discovered, had childhood culinary experiences similar to mine. Talking about those experiences often created a communion that no amount of abstract musical discussion could establish.

With Bill Monroe it was an apple stack cake I baked for him that seemed to break the barrier of restraint that marked our initial interview but was missing from later ones. And I remain convinced that one reason Chet Atkins returns my calls is because I knew how to make real cornbread when he asked.

The first interview I had with John Prine was over the telephone. He was on the road, in a hotel somewhere, and heating up a can of corned-beef hash on a hot plate. In no time we were rhapsodizing about the amazing hashes our mothers could make from nothing more than cheap beef and onions, and that somehow evolved into a discussion of independence of spirit and the plunge he was contemplating: setting up his own record label.

The first time I spoke with Emmylou Harris we cautiously and politely discussed her current project, then got sidetracked onto a lip-smacking conversation about salt-pork-flavored, simmered-forever, southern green beans. That turned into a discussion of the visceral power of old-time music and finally became a truly memorable talk about the spiritual, healing grace of sounds.

And when Dwight Yoakam first hit the big time, a score of skeptical rock and roll writers wanted to know if he was just making up those stories about eating squirrel down at Granny's house in Betsy Layne, Kentucky. I just wanted to know how his grandmother cooked the squirrel, though, and if anyone had had to tell him a whopper to get him to eat it as my Uncle Charlie had told me. From those food-centered conversations we discovered a common childhood few of our peers had shared. And from that came long discussions about the real roots of Yoakam's music and its power.

* * *

Without realizing it, I'd begun to write this book years before the idea was even suggested to me. That happened in 1988 when Beth Vesel, now my literary agent, called on the recommendation of my friend, Vince Staten.

Beth had been talking with her friend and colleague, food writer Betty Fussell, who was fascinated with what she saw as a growing desire among Americans to rediscover and embrace their roots. Betty saw that desire expressed in a movement away from new and exotic cuisine and back to the more simple, home-cooked foods of America. Beth thought she saw a similar feeling being expressed in the resurgent popularity of country music. And together they thought that a cookbook combining those two elements—a book of authentic home-cooking recipes gathered around performers' memories of home and food—would be an excellent way to reestablish connections to the past and rediscover the flavors and experiences of earlier times.

I agreed, and from those early conversations and later ones with my editor John Barstow, this book was born.

From the outset we were determined that this not be a "celebrity" cookbook: one of those collections of supposedly favorite recipes of the stars which are, in fact, seldom more than collections of recipes picked from other cookbooks and magazines by press agents.

Instead, the recipes were to be real ones of foods remembered from the past—both mine and the performers'. And, echoing the spirit of the new traditionalist movement in country music, the book would also include some new variations on older themes. The recipes were to be chosen solely for their flavor and quality. And they were to come from good southern, country cooks wherever I might find them.

I didn't have to look far. The favorite foods of most of the performers I talked to were those made by their mothers and grandmothers. And when I began making calls to the source to find out what made Naomi Judd swear the potato salad that her mother, Polly Rideout, makes is the world's best; or Brenda Lee go into raptures over the way her mother, Grace Rainwater, fries chicken, I was greeted again and again by gracious and generous cooks more than willing to share their recipes and stories. Likewise, my own mother, aunts, and cousins were willing to rack their memories and empty their recipe boxes so that I might recreate some of the tastiest moments of my childhood.

And so began the nearly two years of interviewing, translating, reconstructing, and testing that yielded the more than 180 recipes in this book. It was an extraordinary experience.

The people you will meet in this book invited me both figuratively and often literally to join them at the supper table. They shared their food with me, and their stories and memories and triumphs and sorrows as well. They told me tales that were hilarious and stories that were shaded with subtle meanings. They fed me recipes for foods that were every bit as delicious and unforgettable as the ones that I had grown up eating. And in many ways, the experience I had researching and writing this book was much like the communion of stories and food that I had been nourished on as a child.

I had feared initially that the performers might be too busy to talk for a book that is, after all, primarily about food, not music. Or that the cooks might be reluctant to share their secrets and treasured recipes with a stranger.

Instead I encountered folks who took to the project with remarkable warmth and enthusiasm: musicians willing to juggle busy schedules to spend time reminiscing about grandparents and gardens, cold watermelon and hot cobbler, sausage frying and biscuits baking. And I found cooks who not only let me rifle through their recipe boxes, but were willing to reconstruct the process of cooking certain foods so they could tell me not only what they put in, but exactly how they did it—more often than not the real secret in turning a simple country dish into something sublime.

I experienced southern hospitality and country generosity at its finest. Eugenia Harris, Emmylou's mother, wrote out all her recipes in delicate script, and then sent me a pear cake by mail so I could taste it and see if it was worth the effort before I tried to bake it. (It was. You'll find the recipe on page 306.) Polly Rideout cooked a luncheon feast for my daughter and me and while we ate, she sifted through the voluminous notebook of recipes she'd collected during her time as an Ohio River barge cook. Amy O'Brien, Tim and Mollie's mother, met me at one of her children's performances bringing cookies, a Wheeling, West Virginia, corn scraper, and a notebook with her mouth-watering recipes. And Ruth Ann Rankey, Dwight Yoakam's mother, served home-baked muffins, tea, and memories the first time I visited her in Columbus, Ohio, then insisted on taking both my photographer and me to lunch the next.

Women I had never met—Grace Rainwater; John Prine's mother, Verna—were willing to spend an hour or more on the phone talking about the best ways to make a hash or cook up a head of cabbage.

My aunts Lib and Rae, and cousins Billy, Helen, and Jo Ann pulled recipes from their files and their recollections. And my mother not only took my phone calls day and night, answering questions about techniques and ingredients, but recreated a number of dishes with me hovering at her elbow, noting her every move.

Restaurateurs—some old friends, others who didn't know me from Adam—told me the secrets to some of the best dishes in the house. Even folks I'd not thought to ask volunteered when they heard of the project.

What I found again and again were people convinced, as I am, that the food they'd grown up with—simple country cooking, for years scorned by food snobs and unjustly ignored by culinarians—was some of the best eating ever. They were folks who would soundly second Huck Finn, who once said of the likes of corn dodgers with buttermilk, pork, cabbage and greens: ". . . there ain't nothing in the world so good when it's cooked right."

Of course, few of us eat these foods the way we once did, on a daily basis and in trencherman spreads like this one Emmylou Harris recalled from days at her grandmother's house down in Birmingham: ". . . both fried chicken and pork chops, creamed corn and green beans with potatoes cooked down 'til they were shiny with the bacon seasoning, cornbread and homemade rolls, mashed potatoes and sometimes rice pudding or cake and always a cobbler on the back of the stove from whatever fruit was in season. And that was just lunch."

Few of us labor all day out of doors the way those who partook of such midday meals once did. And people are now too aware and concerned about the effects of cholesterol and fat to consume such feasts every day. But many of the recipes gathered here respond to that concern. Whenever possible, canola or olive oil replaces the highly saturated fats that were used in the past. I also recommend margarines made with buttermilk as a delicious substitute for butter. In addition, I've reduced the amount of salt called for originally in many recipes with little loss of flavor. And there are some new variations (like the healthy Killed Lettuce on page 206 created by my friend Lenore Crenshaw) that offer all the flavor of the old recipes with none of the sin.

There are also plenty of wonderful old recipes, like stack cakes made with dried fruit and just enough sugar to sweeten them, or simple salads, that are as healthy as anything you can find in today's diet-conscious cuisine.

But there are also recipes here that require bacon or ham for the fullest, finest flavor. There are some truly decadent dishes and desserts. And there are foods that just must be eaten together in a traditional feast to be relished completely. Fried chicken, for instance, simply isn't honest fried chicken without hot, flaky biscuits, cream gravy, and buttery mashed potatoes to go with it.

Such sins are not unforgivable ones, I'm inclined to believe, when committed on occasion and in the context of a regular diet that is well balanced and healthy.

As my friend and fellow southern food writer John Egerton said: "Moderation is the key. Not to swear off those wonderful foods completely, but to indulge them and then balance with others—that seems to be the way to a satisfying but healthy life. Besides, I'm not convinced that any life without country ham and biscuits would be worth living."

The people in this book would be among the first to agree with Egerton, and to add to his list such delicacies as good greens and pot likker, red velvet cake, biscuits with just a kiss of bacon grease, steaming grits, pan-fried oysters, sweet potato casserole, stewed beef and cornmeal dumplings . . . all of which you will find here.

Just reciting the litany to someone who grew up with these foods can spark fires of delight and desire in their eyes. And to those who didn't share such blessed childhoods, experiencing these flavors for the first time is like discovering a rustic treasure trove. I know from the times I tested things like green tomato casserole and pie, shuck beans, stack cake, and cornbread dressing on dubious Yankee friends who became believers at first bite.

But now the testing is over and the cooking is done. The book is ready and in it, the family and friends are gathered around the big oak pedestal table with all the leaves added to accommodate us. We're ready to share our food and stories and through them find the links between our present and past.

Won't you all stay a while and have something to eat with us?

POULTRY

HONEST FRIED CHICKEN

GRACE RAINWATER'S BUTTERMILK CHICKEN

CREAM GRAVY

NOT BARBECUE CHICKEN

SOUTH CAROLINA MARINADE

MEMPHIS TRIPLE PEPPER MARINADE

SOUTHWEST MARINADE

CLAY-POT CHICKEN

CHICKEN COBBLER

THANKSGIVING TURKEY

CORNBREAD DRESSING

NANNY'S OYSTER DRESSING

HOT BROWN

HONEST FRIED CHICKEN

I was born in the state of Kentucky and Colonel Harland D. Sanders was not, so you can believe me when I say that I, not the Colonel, know the secret to making honest fried chicken.

Honest fried chicken does not come tricked out with countless secret herbs and spices. It is not quick fricasseed under pressure and will not improve in taste if left to languish under hot lamps that would be more at home in a tanning salon than in a kitchen.

Proper fried chicken deserves to be served hot from the skillet, heaped high on a platter, hovered over by steamy, golden, tantalizing wisps of aroma. Honest fried chicken has a crust that is at once crisp and tender. When your teeth sink through it, the meat they find inside should be firm but succulent, bursting with hot juice and rich chicken flavor. One bite of chicken fried with proper attention to time and technique and you will never, ever be seduced by an impostor in a bucket again.

Time is the secret to making genuinely delicious fried chicken, and that is one reason you will seldom encounter the real thing in a restaurant. Most restaurant chicken is deep fried fast at high temperatures that produce crisp, hard crust and dry, flaky meat.

Chicken cooked the way my mother taught me, and the way her mother had been taught by her mother before her, is slow fried in shallow oil in a heavy skillet that is tightly covered so the juices stay in the meat. The crust is crisp to the bite, but in the mouth becomes meltingly tender. Achieving such a crust around flavorful but fall-from-the-bone-tender chicken takes approximately 30 to 35 minutes of frying. That's just enough time to make a crisp, green salad and whip up a batch of scratch biscuits to be smothered in gravy, the only accompaniments you need for a fried chicken feast.

The other secret to perfect chicken is in the final "crisping." This is accomplished by taking the lid off the skillet and letting the pieces cook in the open for a few minutes after the chicken is done. I'm not sure why this works; I only know it does and that chicken served straight from the covered skillet without that crisping time will have a crust that is flavorful but mushy.

Some southern cooks swear by a skillet known as a chicken frying pan. It is usually made of cast iron, is at least 10 inches wide, and the inside of

"Take a chicken and you kill it
And you put it in a skillet
And you fry it 'til it's golden brown.
That's southern cooking
And it tastes mighty nice."
"Kentucky Means Paradise" by Merle Travis

the lid is studded with nipples that gather and drip the cooking juices back onto the meat making chicken fried in such a pan juicier—or so its champions claim.

I have such a pan and it makes wonderful fried chicken; but so does my extra-heavy aluminum skillet with a smooth-surfaced lid and I prefer to use it because it's easier to clean. In any case, you need a heavy skillet with straight sides—not a rounded omelet-style pan—and a tight-fitting lid.

I have made only one change in my mother's chicken frying technique. Like most women of her generation, she favored melted vegetable shortening for the frying medium because it was healthier than the lard favored by her mother's generation. I, in turn, have adopted canola oil. Not all vegetable oils will produce the desired crust during frying and some, like olive or peanut oil, impart their distinctive and unsuitable flavor to the chicken. But canola oil works just fine and contains 20 per cent less saturated fat than shortening.

That's not to suggest that my fried chicken qualifies as health food. It's still probably a cholesterol sin to eat it; but oh, what a lip-smacking, soul-satisfying wicked delight it is.

2 pounds cut-up chicken

1/2 cup flour

1/2 teaspoon salt

1/4 teaspoon freshly ground pepper

canola oil, 1/2 inch deep in pan

Wash chicken pieces and trim visible clumps of fat. Put flour, salt, and pepper in a clean plastic or paper sack and shake to mix. Put skillet on a high flame and add canola oil 1/2 inch deep.

As the oil heats, shake each piece of chicken—one or two pieces at a time—in the bag of flour until coated. Lay chicken in the hot oil, with the skin side down. (If you are frying mixed pieces of chicken instead of all breasts or thighs, put the largest pieces in the pan first.) You can nest the pieces fairly close together. When the skillet is full, turn heat down to medium and let chicken fry until it's just golden and crispy, then turn and let the second side get just golden.

Reduce heat to low, cover, and cook 25 minutes. (Check occasionally to make sure the heat is not too high and the chicken browning too fast or burning.) Remove lid and turn pieces over once more. Turn heat up a bit—but

Four Way Fried Chicken

Memphis is the home of Sun Records and the place where the raunch and rhythm of blues got mixed up with Hank Williams's whine and Bill Monroe's overdrive to make rock and roll. This is the town where tradition was turned on its ear, and to pretty fine end at that. So it's appropriate that Memphis is also the only place I've ever eaten restaurant chicken as wonderful as my mother's pan-fried. And that chicken was made in a deep fryer.

The Four Way Grill is an unimposing brick storefront with wrought-iron bars on the windows. Inside, the atmosphere is warm and welcoming. Mrs. Irene Cleaves, who opened the restaurant with her husband in 1947, will come to your table to greet you and make you feel at home.

The chicken will make you feel even better. It comes with a perfect, deep, crackly crust and the meat is so juicy it squirts as you bite.

Mrs. Cleaves is as generous with advice as she is with portions. She says they get the chicken to its perfect state in vegetable oil kept at an even 300 degrees in a deep-fat fryer.

"When you start it off, your grease has to be real hot, but not smoking—just piping hot," she said.

They don't dip the chicken in batter at the Four Way, but just wash each piece well and then "dust it good" in flour, salt, and enough pepper for a little taste, but not enough so it will be showing up on the chicken.

Then each piece is dropped into the deep-fat fryer basket. "You just let each piece fry a while—just until it floats. When it floats, it's done."

not too high—and cook a few minutes longer until crust is crisped all around. (If crust on the sides of the breasts is still soft and mushy, turn those pieces on their side in the oil for a minute or two so they can fry up crisp.)

Remove chicken from pan and drain on paper towels, then put on warm serving plate while you make Cream Gravy (page 8). Serve with Buttermilk Biscuits (page 258), or Chicken Fixings (page 246) and a crisp fresh salad. Homemade Apple Butter (page 345) is great alongside fried chicken and biscuits. *Serves 4.*

If you're frying chicken for a crowd, you may want to fry in two skillets at the same time. If not, keep the finished pieces in a barely warm oven while you fry the second skilletful. You may want to fry up two skilletsful even if you're not having company for supper since leftover refrigerated fried chicken is delicious the next day with Mine and Mama's Potato Salad (page 213).

Variation: In the mountains of the southeastern United States, one delicious variation is to coat the chicken in cornmeal instead of flour. The cornmeal gives the chicken a rich taste and the drippings make an extraordinary, flavorful gravy. To fry chicken this way, use the recipe above substituting 1/2 cup white, fine-ground cornmeal for the flour (but add one tablespoon of flour to the mix to make it adhere better).

The meal crust on this chicken is more delicate than a flour crust, so be especially careful when turning the pieces not to tear the crust off. I use a fork and a small metal spatula, sliding the spatula under the chicken and crust so it doesn't stick to the pan, and using the fork on top of the piece to steady and guide it as I turn.

Slingshot

Brenda Lee remembers her daddy hunting regularly for squirrel and rabbit when she was growing up in Lathonia, Georgia, in the late 1940s and '50s. But he hunted them with a twist.

"He didn't use a gun," she said. "He hunted just with a slingshot. Yeah, he shot a mean slingshot. And he must have been pretty successful with it because I remember we ate rabbit a lot."

GRACE RAINWATER'S BUTTERMILK CHICKEN

Most southerners wouldn't be caught dead skinning a chicken before frying it. In fact, most country cooks will tell you that it's the skin that keeps the meat moist in the frying process.

But Georgia-born-and-fed Brenda Lee begs to differ.

"I don't like skin on my fried chicken. Don't like it at all," she told me emphatically. And when I made a skilletful of chicken the way her mother, Grace Rainwater, does it—coating the chicken in thick buttermilk first—I understood. The result is exquisite—tender, juicy chicken in a crunchy, tangy crust.

6 chicken breasts, bone in

1/2 cup low fat buttermilk

1 1/2 cups flour

1/2 teaspoon white pepper

1 teaspoon salt

canola oil, 1/2 inch deep in skillet

This chicken is fried exactly like Honest Fried Chicken (page 3); but its preparation is slightly different. Wash chicken breasts and remove skin and all visible fat, leaving the bone. Pat dry with paper towel.

Pour buttermilk in a shallow bowl. In a second shallow bowl, mix flour, pepper, and salt.

Before coating chicken, put the skillet on high heat and add canola oil 1/2 inch deep.

Dip each breast in the buttermilk, making sure it is completely coated.

Dip in the bowl of flour, turning to thoroughly coat both sides. Shake each piece ever so slightly to remove any really loose flour, then lay it in the hot oil, fleshy side down. You can nest the pieces fairly close together. When the skillet is full, turn heat down to medium and let chicken fry until it's just golden and crispy, then turn and let the second side get just golden. Be very careful when turning not to break the buttermilk crust.

Reduce heat to low, cover, and cook 25 minutes. (Check occasionally to make sure the heat is not too high and the chicken browning too fast or burning.)

Remove lid and turn pieces over once more. Turn heat up a bit—but not too high—and cook a few minutes longer until crust is crisped all around. (If crust on the sides of the breasts is still soft and mushy, turn those pieces on their side in the oil for a minute or two so they can fry up crisp.) *Serves 6.*

CREAM GRAVY

Fried chicken drippings make a rich, golden-flavored cream gravy. Served over hot biscuits with a drumstick on the side, it's good enough to bring even the most petulant Papa down from the housetop and into the kitchen for dinner.

But chicken drippings aren't the only basis you can use to make delicious cream gravy for bread or biscuits. Green tomatoes fried in cornmeal leave dregs that make a tangy sauce, and sausage gravy is a breakfast delicacy prized in country kitchens.

You make cream gravy right in the pan that the meat or tomatoes was fried in. Drain off all but about two tablespoons of fat, but leave all the little pieces of crust and crumbs in the pan to give the gravy flavoring. Use a metal spatula to gently scrape them from the bottom and sides of the pan so they don't burn. Sprinkle a tablespoon of flour over the drippings and cook over low heat until browned, stirring constantly to keep flour from lumping. It takes a minute or two.

Slowly stir 1 cup of milk into browned flour. Although it's called "cream" gravy in the country, I never really knew anyone to make this gravy from real cream. And I've found that low fat, 2 per cent milk works just fine and is supremely tasty.

Stir gravy constantly. Using a small wire whisk to stir will minimize the chance the mixture will lump. (If it does despite your best efforts, remove pan from heat and whip it with the whisk briefly until smooth.) When the milk and flour are smooth, turn the heat to high and bring to a boil, still stirring constantly. It will take a minute or two for the gravy to come to the desired thickness. Taste and add salt or pepper, then serve. *Makes about 1 cup.*

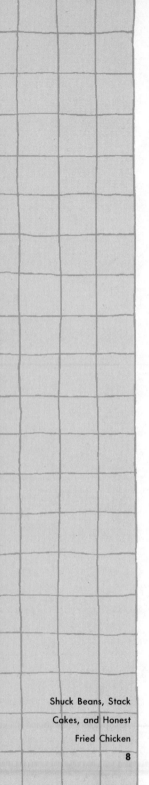

Shuck Beans, Stack
Cakes, and Honest
Fried Chicken

8

NOT BARBECUE CHICKEN

For folks who take their barbecue seriously (and that is most anyone born south of the Mason-Dixon line) "Barbecue Chicken" is an oxymoron. That's because the essence of barbecue is not some secret sauce slapped on a slab of meat cooked out on a grill. The essence of barbecue is in very, very slow smoking in an enclosed pit. And while such cooking turns pork into paradise, makes mutton respectable, and gives plain old American beef an aura of exotic mystery, all it does to chicken is make it fall apart.

But although chicken doesn't cotton to long-term hickory pit cooking, it's the perfect meat to grill over coals in the backyard. It's also an excellent meat to marinate and it takes quite naturally to soaking in some of the regional-style sauces that folks like to put on their real barbecue from time to time.

What follows are recipes for three marinades. There's a tomato-less, mustard-based tangy sauce like the ones you're apt to be served on barbecued pork in South Carolina. There's a hot tomato sauce such as those you might be served in Memphis. (Then again, you might be shot in Memphis if you asked for such a sauce on barbecue made with a dry rub. The city is divided between those who sauce, and those who rub and deem sauce heresy.) Finally, there's a southwestern-style, chili-lime sauce with an acidic, fiery pungency.

Each is in a quantity suitable for soaking a dozen small, skinned chicken breasts—enough for 6 people. (Not only are the skinned breasts better for you, but they soak up the marinade more readily. Small ones will grill up quickly and they can be eaten with one hand while holding in the other a paper plate full of Country Cooked Green Beans (page 153), potato salad (Polly's, page 211 or Mine and Mama's, page 213), and Polly Rideout's Yeast Rolls (page 256).

Lard Times

"I started fooling around in the kitchen when I was ten or eleven years old," says Verna Prine, mother of singer/songwriter John and his three brothers.

The Hamms, Verna's family, lived in Muhlenburg County, Kentucky, in a small German farming community "where everybody was cousins, even my schoolteacher. And cousins and folks lived with you, even folks who weren't related. If they showed up at the house and looked hungry or tired, my father would have them come in and share whatever we had. That's just the way he was and the way it was done. One woman, wasn't even a relative, showed up for dinner once and ended up living with us for two years.

"And back then you cooked with what you had. I mean, you'd kill the old red rooster in my day and time and there was nothing better than the flavor of that old, fat bird.

"And back in my time we cooked with lard and I still say there's nothing like it for frying a chicken in. Nothing can make that taste. And we kept the lard in a big bucket in the kitchen and when it came time to use some, you just scooped your hand in there and got a handful to put in the frying pan or the biscuits. For God's sake, I used my hand to measure for years before we ever had measuring cups or such. And I still don't use them or measure stuff out when I cook to this day."

South Carolina Marinade

1/4 cup light brown sugar, firmly packed

1/2 cup warm water

1 cup honest mustard

1/2 cup apple cider vinegar

1 teaspoon celery salt

1/2 teaspoon white pepper

1 teaspoon Worcestershire sauce

For this marinade, you want a tawny-colored mustard without any fancy gourmet ingredients—but not a ballpark yellow one. I use Gulden's.

In a medium bowl, dissolve brown sugar in warm tap water. Add other ingredients and mix until well blended.

Memphis Triple Pepper Marinade

14 1/2-ounce can whole tomatoes

3 tablespoons minced onion

1 tablespoon Worcestershire sauce

1 teaspoon allspice

1/4 teaspoon salt

1 teaspoon freshly ground black pepper

1/2 teaspoon cayenne pepper

12 ounces Dr. Pepper

Blend tomatoes until smooth, then put in a small saucepan with all the ingredients except Dr. Pepper. Bring to a boil, then simmer for five minutes, stirring occasionally to keep from sticking. Remove from heat, add Dr. Pepper, and mix well before using as marinade.

SOUTHWEST MARINADE

juice of 5 limes

1/8 cup ground red chili

1 teaspoon ground cumin

2 cloves garlic, crushed

1/2 teaspoon salt

See information on ground chili (page 142). Mix all ingredients together well, then slather on chicken, rubbing the marinade lightly into the flesh.

Marinate skinned, rinsed, and dried chicken pieces in the sauce you choose in a nonmetal covered container in the refrigerator for 2–4 hours before grilling.

Half an hour before you're ready to start cooking, light charcoal in a covered, kettle-style grill. When the coals are ready, spread them out evenly in a single layer. (The coals are ready when a gray ash covers them.)

Oil or grease the rack for grilling and place it 3 to 4 inches above the coals. Remove chicken from marinade and place on rack with the fleshiest side down. Let brown, then turn the chicken pieces over and grill covered for 20–25 minutes. You may want to turn them again and baste frequently with any leftover marinade. If chicken begins to char, raise the rack higher from the fire.

If you're using the South Carolina or Memphis marinade you may want to use any remaining as table sauce. To do so, just before chicken is done, put remaining marinade in a small saucepan, heat to the boiling point, turn down, and simmer for about 5 minutes before serving.

Serve chicken as soon as it comes off the fire and soak up all the lavish praise your guests might want to heap on your pungent grilled chicken. But don't be calling it barbecue.

CLAY-POT CHICKEN

Nothing makes a house smell like a home more than a plump hen baking up in the oven. But unless proper attention is paid to the bird through the process, chances are that hen will come out of the oven smelling far·more succulent than it tastes. There's an art to making sure a fowl cooks done before it cooks dry.

Not all cooks agree on exactly what that art requires. Some recommend frequent basting while others argue that opening the oven door repeatedly to do so dries the bird out. Some cooks swath a hen's breasts in grease-drenched cheesecloth—moving the cloth through the baking process as need arises.

Whether or not these methods produce the required results, they're not apt to be attractive to cooks who want meals with maximum flavor in minimum time—and that describes many of us in this harried age.

Into this dilemma comes a piece of ancient wisdom: the terra cotta pot.

Let me confess right here that I did not grow up seeing clay pots used in my mother's or my aunts' kitchens. The tradition of clay-pot cooking hails from ancient Etruscan culture, not rural American.

Nor do I usually recommend purchasing special cooking equipment, having been raised with an almost superstitious belief that making do with whatever you already have will almost always lead to surprising and delicious results. But I was given a clay pot ten years ago and have become a fervent advocate of them since. So fervent that should the kitchen catch fire, the clay pot may be the second thing I'd grab right after the cast-iron skillets. (Or perhaps I should leave the skillets in the fire for a little extra seasoning?)

Food cooked in a clay pot emerges riddled with savory flavors and dripping with succulence. The unglazed terra cotta is porous, so when the lid is on the pot it becomes a self-enclosed, moist but breathing oven. Food cooked in it tastes neither steamed nor dry roasted but like some aromatic and tender missing link in between.

To cook in a clay pot you must follow three important rules:

1. You must submerge the pot in water for at least 15 minutes before you put in the food and pop it in the oven.

2. The oven must be stone-cold at the start.

3. You must clean the clay pot only with clear, hot water and a wire brush.

"C—That's the way to begin

H—That's the next letter in

I—That is the third

C—That's the season to the bird

K—Fill it in

E—Gettin' near the end

C-H-I-C-K-E-N

That is the way to spell chicken."

"Chicken," Tin Pan Alley Song

Poultry

13

Never use detergent, which fills the pores and causes all your food to taste like dish soap in the future.

Clay-pot recipes call for higher temperatures and longer cooking times than conventional oven recipes, but once you've popped this bird in the oven, you can almost ignore it until it's ready to serve. "Almost" because the marvelous aroma wafting from your oven as the bird bakes will hardly let you forget it completely.

There are a few other clay-pot recipes scattered throughout this book. (For more recipes for clay-pot cooking, I highly recommend *The Clay-Pot Cookbook* by Georgia MacLeod Sales and Grover Sales, Atheneum, 1982.) If you want to adapt these clay-pot recipes to conventional baking methods the rule of thumb is to subtract 100 degrees from the given oven temperature and 30 minutes from the cooking time—and preheat the oven. But I can guarantee that the flavor you get will not be as complex or satisfying as it would be if cooked in clay.

Proof? Both my mother and Aunt Lib swear that never in their combined 130 plus years have they tasted chicken as magnificent as that roasted in my clay pot.

My clay pot has a capacity of two quarts, and the interior of its bottom is glazed.

4 medium unpeeled potatoes, quartered

2 chopped green onions

1 3-pound chicken

1 teaspoon rosemary

1 teaspoon salt

1/2 teaspoon freshly ground pepper

12 medium carrots, peeled and trimmed

Soak top and bottom of a 2-quart clay pot in water for 15 minutes. Place potatoes with the cut side up on the bottom and sprinkle green onions over them. Rinse and dry chicken well. Crush rosemary with salt and pepper and rub the bird inside and out, then place on top of potatoes. Place carrots on the sides and on top of the bird. (They will come out with a sweet, fresh carroty taste and texture—not the stewed taste of carrots roasted the conventional way with meats.)

Put water-soaked lid on the pot and put the pot into a cold oven on the center shelf. Turn heat to 425 degrees and bake for 1 1/2 hours. You may want to check the chicken after an hour and fifteen minutes since roasting time varies. The chicken will brown nicely in the clay pot, but if you want a crisper skin on it, you may want to remove the carrots and return the chicken to the oven, uncovered, for the last 10 minutes.

Remove chicken to a serving platter.

Pour drippings into a wide-mouthed glass jar or measuring cup and let settle until grease has risen to the top (about one minute). Skim off grease and discard. Transfer juices to a gravy boat and serve with chicken. *Serves 4 heartily.*

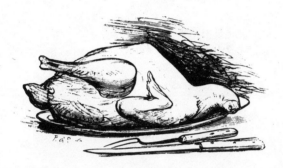

CHICKEN COBBLER

Chicken Cobbler tastes like a cross between a chicken pot pie and chicken stewed with dumplings, but the dough for it is both easier to work with and lower in fat than the conventional shortening-laden doughs of its cousins.

It is a marvelous dish for taking to potluck suppers or serving buffet style to guests who will savor both its fresh, rosemary flavor and the comforting, homey memories it evokes. The proportions here are "company" size and will generously serve 10. I bake my cobbler in a round, wide, shallow, 4-quart capacity glazed earthenware pan, but you can divide the recipe in half and bake in a 2-quart shallow casserole.

This recipe is for cobbler from scratch, but you can also make it with leftover chicken and frozen broth.

3-pound chicken

1 small onion

4 stalks celery

2 carrots

3 medium potatoes, cubed

1 pound carrots, sliced

10-ounce package frozen peas

4 cups chicken broth

1/4 teaspoon freshly ground pepper

2 teaspoons crushed rosemary

1 teaspoon salt

3 cups flour

1 1/2 teaspoons salt

1 cup buttermilk

1/2 cup canola oil

1 cup low fat milk

1 tablespoon cornstarch

Rinse chicken and giblets. Put in a kettle with lid, add peeled onions, celery, and 2 peeled carrots. Cover with water, turn heat on high and bring to a boil. Turn heat down, cover, and simmer for 45 minutes.

Remove chicken from pot and let cool until it can be handled. Separate meat from bones and skin. Break or cut meat into bite-sized pieces, then refrigerate. Return bones and skin to the pot and simmer for at least an hour.

Wash potatoes and cut into bite-sized cubes. Peel and slice carrots. (These quantities should make approximately 3 cups each of cut potatoes and carrots.) Put in a large pot along with frozen peas. Add 4 cups of strained chicken broth and seasonings. Bring to a boil, then simmer for 15 minutes.

While vegetables are simmering, make pastry. In a mixing bowl, sift together flour and salt. Combine buttermilk and oil, then add all at once to the dry ingredients. Stir until dough holds together. Knead in bowl 10 times, then divide into 2 equal balls. Roll the first out on a floured board and cut into strips about 3/4 of an inch wide.

Mix cornstarch with low fat milk. When blended, add to vegetables and broth, stir well, bring to a boil, and then simmer and stir for 5 minutes. Add the chicken and mix well. Pour half the mixture into a large, lightly oiled casserole. Lay strips of pastry across the top.

Roll and cut the second ball of pastry. Pour the rest of the chicken-vegetable mix into the casserole and top with strips of pastry.

Put in preheated 350 degree oven for 45 minutes. Check and raise temperature to 375 for the last 15 minutes if the top pastry isn't browning. Goes well with Ambrosia (page 225). *Serves 10.*

Nanny's Piece

"I spent many Christmases and most of my summers with my mother's parents, Nanny and DeDa down in Alabama," Emmylou Harris recalls.

"Just a typical Sunday lunch at Nanny's would be fried chicken, pork chops, creamed corn, green beans, cornbread, rolls. And the green beans would have bacon and potatoes in them; and we'd have mashed potatoes, too. And then all those desserts!

"Of course, Nanny had a piece of chicken and it was her piece of chicken. And it was the back, which nobody else wanted.

"One story that I always loved to hear was about when my aunt's husband—who wasn't her husband yet—was courting and came over for one of Nanny's dinners the first time.

"J.D. was just the sweetest, kindest person: very laid back; very 'Yes, ma'am' and 'No Ma'am,' and wanting to make a good impression.

"And there was this big platter of chicken for dinner, and of course it was passed to J.D. first. And he's thinking: 'Okay, well, I'm going to take the one piece that nobody wants.'

"It wasn't the piece that he wanted, of course, but he was going to be real polite. And so he reaches for the back . . .

"And my grandfather hollers: 'That's Mama's piece!'

"And it nearly scared J.D. to death! Oh, poor J.D.! He turned as red as tomatoes."

THANKSGIVING TURKEY

Roasting that first holiday turkey is something of a rite of passage for home cooks.

"My mother would let me into the kitchen—even when I was little I'd go in and cook," Eugenia Harris, Emmylou's mother, told me. "But I remember vividly that the first full meal I cooked was one Thanksgiving in my teens when I made the whole dinner including the turkey."

Her mother had suddenly taken ill right at Thanksgiving, Mrs. Harris said, but they'd already bought everything for the dinner, so her father gave her permission to put it all together.

"Well, I did cook the old turkey until he just sort of fell off the bone. But it was good, and after that Thanksgiving, I knew I was a cook for sure."

Southern cooks often roast their turkeys unstuffed and then serve alongside a big pan of dressing, flavored with stock or drippings from the bird and made with eggs and sometimes cream. And if the bird is the symbol of the holiday celebration, it's the dressing that is its true justification.

As to the turkey, I like roasting mine with a couple of cut-up apples and a few stalks of celery tucked in the cavity. They give the kitchen a delectable holiday fragrance and add to the bird's moistness. You may omit the celery and apple, and roast the bird lightly greased inside and out. To determine how large a turkey you want, estimate 1/2 pound for each person to be served.

> 1 turkey
>
> 2 medium, tart green apples
>
> 2 stalks of celery
>
> butter or oil

If your turkey is frozen, you need to defrost it thoroughly before roasting. For an 8–10 pound bird, this takes about 2 days in the refrigerator, 3 days for a larger turkey. Or you can defrost a bird in 5–6 hours if you submerge it in cold water. It can be dangerous, though, to defrost a turkey by leaving it out of the fridge at room temperature for several hours since bacteria can form in the areas that warm up first.

When you're ready to roast, heat the oven to 450 degrees. Remove the neck and giblets from the cavity. (Rinse them and, after turkey is in the oven, pop them in a large saucepan along with a peeled onion, a carrot, and a couple of stalks of celery. Cover with water and simmer while the turkey roasts, adding more water as necessary, to make stock to be used for gravy and dressing.)

Rinse the turkey well inside and out. Drain and pat dry with paper towels. Rub the outside of the turkey all over with butter, or lightly brush with oil. (I like to use the butter wrappers I've saved for just such greasing jobs to rub the turkey down. Country singer Bobby Bare says he gets a terrific turkey by rubbing it with a good, rich olive oil.)

Place on a lightly greased roasting rack, breast side up, in a roasting pan that is about 2 inches deep.

Wash apples and cut in half. Wash and trim celery. Put half an apple in the neck cavity (cut to size if cavity is too small) and the rest along with the celery in the body cavity. Bind legs together with metal brace or string. Tuck neck skin flap over opening. Some people tuck the wings under the bird's back to keep them from browning too much, but I never do. I let them get crispy brown and toss them in the stock pot after dinner to give my homemade broth a rich, roasty flavor.

Pop the turkey in the 450 degree oven and immediately turn the heat down to 350 degrees. Some people say the high heat "seals" the meat, keeping it juicy, and I agree.

Roast the turkey for about 18 minutes per pound for a bird under 6 pounds, 15 minutes a pound for a larger one. Some birds roast faster, so you can begin testing as early as 13 minutes per pound. After turkey has roasted about a third of the allotted time, baste with pan juices. After it's reached the two-thirds mark, remove pan from oven and, using oven mitts and being careful not to drop it or splash, turn turkey over and put back in pan backside up.

Flipping the turkey in this way browns the bottom beautifully and, I think, yields a juicier breast—although it's not essential to baking a tasty bird.

A perfectly cooked turkey measures 180 degrees on a meat thermometer that has been inserted in the thickest part of the thigh. Without a thermometer, you can check for doneness by piercing the thigh. If juices run clear, and the flesh of thigh and drumstick feels soft, the bird is done.

Remove from oven, and place breast side up on serving platter. Allow to cool at least 15–25 minutes before carving, and remember to remove the apples and celery before placing on the table.

"Turkey in the straw, haw, haw, haw. Turkey in the hay, what do you say? Roll him up and twist him up—a high tuck a-haw And hit 'em up a tune called 'Turkey in the Straw.'"

"Turkey in the Straw," Traditional

Make gravy for the turkey by putting 3 tablespoons of pan drippings (a mix of grease and juices that is best heavier on the juices) in a saucepan over medium heat. Stir in 1–2 tablespoons of flour, blending smooth with a wire whisk. Gradually add 1–2 cups of stock made from giblets, stirring constantly as you do, until thickened. Add salt and pepper to taste and serve hot.

Turkey trimmings at our house always include one of the dressing recipes that follow, Mashed Potatoes (page 179), and Christmas Fruit Salad (page 223). Yammy Pudding (page 184) is also fast becoming a family tradition.

CORNBREAD DRESSING

My mother's dressing was made with cornbread and delicious enough that one school friend would trade me all the cookies from her lunch bag for the leftover slices of dressing my mother packed for me.

> **6 cups cornbread**
>
> **(1/2 cup cracker or bread crumbs, optional)**
>
> **1 cup chopped celery**
>
> **1 cup chopped onion**
>
> **2 eggs**
>
> **1 cup turkey broth**
>
> **1 cup roast turkey drippings**

Crumble cornbread into large bowl, making sure to break up all the lumps. The recipe for Real Cornbread (page 235) should make enough cornbread for 6 cups of crumbs, but you can fill the quota out if you need to with up to 1/2 cup of crushed crackers or bread crumbs.

Chop celery by splitting large ribs in quarters along the length and chopping pieces about 1/4 inch long. My mother and I both favor the taste of plenty of celery, but some folks may find this a bit much. You can use as little as half a cup and still have a good flavor and the necessary crunch in the texture.

Chop onion finely and mix together well with celery and cornbread. Break two eggs into the bowl and mix thoroughly. Mix in 1 cup of turkey broth and

1 cup of drippings from the turkey's roasting pan, trying to get as much juice and as little grease as possible. Add salt and pepper to taste if you want. I don't use pepper in my dressing and usually find my cornbread and drippings make the dressing salty enough without adding more, but your tastes may differ.

Pour dressing into a greased baking pan (approximately 11 by 7 inches) and bake for 20 minutes in 400 degree oven, until dressing is "set" but not at all dry. I usually pop the dressing in the oven when I take the turkey out. That gives the turkey just about enough time to cool for slicing.

This makes enough for 6 big servings. You can double or triple the proportions to make more.

Dressing will reheat well the next day and is especially good warmed up with pieces of turkey laid over the top, and leftover gravy or broth poured over that. It will also freeze.

You can also add a handful of crushed dried sage to the recipe if you like.

Nanny's Oyster Dressing

Eugenia Harris's mother made cornbread dressing, too, but hers was laced with butter and cream and spiked with the rich flavor of oysters. It's a grand accompaniment for the holiday bird, but I've also made it with double the oysters and served it as a main dish with a green salad, or as an appetizer.

6 cups cornbread

4 cups soft white bread crumbs

2 cups chopped onions

2 cups chopped celery

2 teaspoons salt

1 teaspoon black pepper

1 1/2 cups melted butter

6 beaten eggs

1 12-ounce can evaporated milk

1 cup turkey broth

1 pint fresh oysters and liquid (double if serving as a main dish)

Crumble cornbread and white bread crumbs together, add celery, onion, and seasonings and toss until well mixed. Drizzle butter over crumb mixture, then add beaten eggs, milk, and broth and mix lightly, but well. Add oysters with their liquid and mix lightly again until oysters are evenly distributed. Turn into a lightly greased, deep 3-quart pan and bake at 400 degrees for 45 minutes–1 hour, or until mixture is firm and browned around the edges. *Serves 1 dozen.*

HOT BROWN

What's a sandwich created at a cosmopolitan downtown hotel doing in a book about country cooking?

Well, if someone tells you how to roast a giant turkey for the holidays it seems they would also be morally obliged to offer you at least one good recipe for using up the leftovers. And the Hot Brown sandwich, purportedly invented at the Brown Hotel in Louisville, Kentucky, in the late 1920s, is without question the best one I know.

Besides, the version here uses a down-home delicacy—thin slivers of country ham—to create a Hot Brown with a slightly backwoods and thoroughly delicious accent. If you don't have ham, however, you can make the Hot Brown the traditional way by criss-crossing strips of crisp bacon over the top after broiling.

4 sandwich-sized, not-too-thick slices of turkey breast

4 pieces of country ham the same span, but sliced ultra thin

4 pieces of good white bread

1 tablespoon butter

2 tablespoons flour

1 cup milk

1 cup turkey broth

salt

white pepper

3 tablespoons grated Parmesan cheese

1 egg, beaten

1 cup grated Gruyère cheese

Both turkey and ham need to be room temperature when you begin. Toast the bread, trim the crusts, and lay each slice on a separate ovenproof plate with sides an inch deep to accommodate cream sauce. Cover first with ham, then top with turkey.

Melt butter in a heavy saucepan over medium heat and stir in flour to combine evenly. Slowly add milk and then turkey broth, stirring constantly to keep it from lumping. (If you don't have turkey broth, or want a very mild cheese sauce, use 3 cups of milk, omitting the broth.)

When the sauce begins to thicken, add a pinch of salt and white pepper and then stir in the grated Parmesan. When the cheese is melted, remove sauce from heat and stir into the beaten egg very, very slowly and beating all the while so the egg doesn't curdle.

Ladle the sauce evenly over the turkey sandwiches, then sprinkle the grated Gruyère over that. Place under the broiler until the top is browned and bubbling. *Serves 4.*

For years musicians playing the bluegrass circuit have enjoyed the bountiful home-cooked dinners provided after shows by fans. Here John Hartford ties into some honest fried chicken after a performance in Cuba, Missouri, in 1958. Note the pad and pen—John says he was probably writing down lyrics to a song as he ate.

MEATS

Country Ham, Country Style

Quilted Country Ham

Quiltless Country Ham

Easter Ham with Kale

Fried Country Ham and Red Eye Gravy

Baked Garlic Chops

Real Barbecued Pork Shoulder

Country Rib Dinner

Butter Beans and Sausage

Pork Roast for a German Afternoon

Fresh Boudin

GRILLED BLUE TENDERLOIN

LIVER AND ONIONS

LIVER POMMERY

MOTHER'S ROAST AND GOOD BROWN GRAVY

MOTHER'S HASH

VERNA PRINE'S HASH

POLLY'S MEAT LOAF

MOTHER'S MEAT LOAF

COUNTRY FRIED STEAK

SWISS STEAK

CHIPPED BEEF AND GRAVY

FRIED SQUIRREL

FRICASSEED RABBIT

PAN-FRIED RABBIT PRUDHOMME

COUNTRY HAM, COUNTRY STYLE

Pork is a staple food in plenty of cultures around the world, but nobody loves a pig like a southern country cook.

Bacon drippings, ham, and salt pork season any number of traditional down-home dishes from fresh-snapped, long-cooked green beans to real cornbread. And nearly every part of the pig's corpulent carcass has been turned into something good to eat—from pickled pig's feet to pork brains with scrambled eggs. Why, in St. Louis, displaced country boys line up at barbecue stands in droves for that regional soul-food delicacy: deep-fried pig snoots.

But the pièce de résistance of rural American pork cuisine is the magnificent, traditional dry salt cured, slow smoked country ham—which you just about can't find anymore.

Yes, it's true that you can find any number of hams labeled "country" in the marketplace these days—most of which have been cured with the aid of shortcuts such as brine soaking or injection, liquid smoke, and heating and cooling techniques that can shorten the traditional curing time from nine months to as little as 90 days.

These hams meet the standards imposed by the United States Department of Agriculture for curing, but they don't meet with approval from real country ham connoisseurs who find them much too briny and tough.

Real country hams have a far richer flavor than those cured quickly—a taste more smoky than salty that resonates. Real country hams also have a deeper reddish color and—if cooked properly—a tender texture. They get this way from being cured for about five weeks in dry salt, then smoked from two weeks to two months with green hickory or other hardwood that smolders and then hung up to age au naturel through the warmer months—particularly during what old-timers like to refer to as the "July and August sweats."

You won't find these hams down at the corner chain supermarket, but if you're lucky, you can find them in stores and sometimes from distributors in certain areas of Virginia, Kentucky, Tennessee, North Carolina, Georgia, Alabama, and Arkansas.

Most everyone agrees that the Smithfield area of Virginia is where southern country ham was first refined into an art form.

Legend has it that in Colonial times pigs raised there were fattened on

"I got a pig
Home in a pen
Corn to feed him on.
All I need's
A pretty little gal
Feed him when I'm
    gone."

"Pig in a Pen," Old-time fiddle song

Meats

27

peanuts, giving the hams deeper color and a distinctive oily flavor. Tradition also has it that Smithfield hams are cured with a thick coating of black pepper. But there's some argument among ham hawkers as to whether Smithfield hams are still the best—or if their commercial popularity has induced producers to rely on too many shortcuts.

Truth is, every region has its own ham champions, and being a born-and-bred Kentuckian, I'll hold for those produced down Cadiz way in Trigg County where the locals celebrate this endangered art with an annual festival each October. It's said that Trigg County hams owe part of their distinction to a tradition curers in those parts are said to practice: throwing a stalk of tobacco on the fire during smoking to give the hams a deeper brown color. Alben Barkley touted these hams around Washington, D.C., when the Kentucky statesman was vice-president under Harry Truman, and they often found their way to the dining room of the White House.

If you want information on ordering a Trigg County ham, write to County Agricultural Extension Agent John Fourquarean, Box 271, Cadiz, KY 42211.

If you find yourself lucky enough to come into the possession of a genuine, slow-cured country ham, this is a method of preparing it that will allow you to literally steep it in tradition.

QUILTED COUNTRY HAM

First thoroughly wash the ham with clear water, using a wire brush to remove any mold. (The mold is harmless and is a sign of age and distinction.) Put the ham in a metal container big enough to hold it and then some. Folks in the country usually used a lard can, but a great big stock pot will do as well.

Cover the ham with water and let it come to a boil, then drain the water. Cover with fresh water again and bring to a boil again, this time letting it boil for 30 minutes. Remove the pot from heat (don't drain the water this time!) and cover with a snug lid.

And now comes the fun part where you let the ham steep overnight in its own warm juices, wrapped up cozily in a quilt. One modern theory is that this slow steeping allows the ham to rehydrate, replacing some of the liquid lost in the curing process. Old-timers, though, will tell you that it just makes a ham taste good.

To steep the ham the traditional way, you need a great big old box or a tub and an old, clean quilt. (Actually, any kind of blanket will do just fine, but a quilt is more in keeping with tradition.) You line the box or tub with the quilt or blanket, leaving its edges hanging over the sides.

Set the pot into the box on the quilt. (You might ask for help doing this since the pot, filled with the ham and the liquid it's been cooked in, can be quite heavy.) Wrap several layers of newspapers around the pot to insulate it. Then pull edges of the quilt up around the newspapers snugly to hold them in place and stack a couple of blankets over that. Let the quilted ham "set" for 24 hours.

When you unwrap the ham the next day, it should still be warm. Take it out of the pot and water and you should be able to remove the hock with a good sharp knife. You can freeze the hock for seasoning soup beans later.

Wipe the ham dry and refrigerate until it's cool. Slice it very, very thinly and serve the slices stacked high in very, very hot biscuits. Slices can be rewarmed briefly, but be careful not to overcook. Country ham is excellent as an accent to cold chicken or turkey sandwiches and in Jambalaya (page 131) or the Hot Brown (page 22).

Country hams range in size from about 12 to 20 pounds. Estimate that you can serve 3 people with each pound.

QUILTLESS COUNTRY HAM

Maybe the only quilt you own is a $2,000 showpiece hanging in the living room. Or maybe you want to slice off part of your ham for frying. If so, here's another excellent (albeit less dramatic) method for preparing country ham.

Ask a butcher to saw off the hock for you and while he's at it, have him cut it into rounds an inch or so thick, which is just perfect for cooking with greens later. You can freeze the hocks.

Then ask the butcher to cut 6 to a dozen slices of ham from the hock end, no more than 1/4 inch thick each. You can prepare these according to

Hollis Carr's Ham

Hollis Carr began curing hams with his daddy around Cadiz, Kentucky, about 60 years ago and he's still curing them today.

He rubs his with black and red pepper and then smokes them over hickory sawdust for 15 days "to give it a good color and aroma. Sometimes sassafras is good on the fire, too. We generally put a little tobacco or tobacco stalk on the last day to keep off the skippers."

When his hams are ready, along about late November, he ships them off to folks who've ordered them from around the country. But he always keeps one for himself. His own ham he takes to the butcher and has the skin cut off, the bone taken out and the ham sliced thick for frying. The slices will keep in the freezer until his wife, Myra Dean, takes a notion to pull a couple out and fry them up with red eye gravy (the Carrs make theirs with coffee).

Sometimes they boil and "bake" the whole ham the old fashioned way, wrapped in quilts. That's appropriate since Myra Dean has been president of the local quilting society for some time.

Carr advises: "About the shank end, around here people generally trim that off and an inch or two at the other end to season beans and such with, because it's not as sweet or good as the part more in the middle."

In the time they've been curing and cooking hams, you'd think the Carrs might have come up with a few recipes for using up the leftovers.

But Mr. Carr said: "Generally around here it don't last too long. Not long enough to be leftovers, anyway."

Just in case you have some, however, Hot Brown (page 22) and Jambalaya (page 131) make good use of leftover country ham.

the recipe for Fried Country Ham and Red Eye Gravy (page 35). If you trim the rind and some fat from them, they'll keep in the refrigerator for a couple of weeks—or can be frozen for 3 months.

Before you leave the butcher's, have him weigh the rest of the ham so you'll know how long to cook it. When you get home, wash the ham in fresh water, use a wire brush to scrub off mold and a sharp knife to pare away hard edges, then cover in clear water and soak overnight.

When you're ready to cook, drain ham and put in a large roasting pan, skin side down. Cover with water that has 1 tablespoon of brown sugar added for every pound of ham. Bring water to a boil, then cover, turn down and simmer for 20 minutes per pound.

Remove from heat, but leave the ham covered and let it sit in the water overnight. After it has cooled, remove from the water and pare away the skin and some fat, leaving a layer about 1/2 inch thick. Pat a mixture of brown sugar with fresh ground black pepper into the fat, then pop the ham into a 400 degree oven for 15 minutes to set the glaze. Let it cool completely and slice very, very thinly to serve. Make a feast of it with Cheese Grits (page 169); Yammy Pudding (page 184) and Country Cooked Green Beans (page 153).

Because you've had slices removed, this ham will weigh less than a full country ham—that's why you want to have it weighed *after* cutting. *Estimate that you can serve 3 people with each pound of ham.*

EASTER HAM WITH KALE

Once upon a time there was a woman who always baked her Easter ham by cutting off a couple of inches of meat from both ends before popping it in the roasting pan.

"Why do you do that?" her husband asked curiously.

"Because that's the way my mother made the ham and hers was the best in the world," she said with conviction.

Next Easter, the family was at the mother's house for dinner and the baked ham was served with a few inches missing from either end.

"Why do you do that?" the son-in-law asked with a bit of a plaintive edge coming into his voice.

"Because that's the way my mother made the ham and hers was the best in the world," his mother-in-law replied with pride.

Soon the bewildered husband found himself sitting next to the grand-mother in the rocking chair.

"You know your Easter hams, the best ones in the world? Well, why do you bake them with a couple of inches of ham cut off each end?" he implored.

"Why, honey," she answered, "my roasting pan was always too small to take a whole ham, so I had to cut those ends off just to make it fit. Pretty near ruined the ham, too, I always thought."

There are, of course, much finer, more sensible and tastier ham traditions. One of my favorites is the country ham served stuffed with fresh spring kale greens at Easter time in the mid-South. The greens make a gorgeous visual contrast to the deep pink of country ham, and the perfect complement to its taste. You can also stuff a regular ham in this way and it's good although it neither looks nor tastes quite so unusual.

12–15 pound country ham

1 ham hock piece

4 cups water

2 1/2 to 3 pounds kale

1 dozen green onions

1 cup light brown sugar

2 cups bread crumbs

Prepare ham according to the Quiltless Ham recipe for Country Ham, Country Style (page 29); but after it has baked, remove it from the stock instead of letting it sit in it overnight. Let ham cool until you can handle it—but not too much since it should still be warm during the next steps.

While ham is cooling, rinse ham hock and put in a big saucepan with water, bring to a boil and then turn heat down and let simmer, covered, while you work with the ham.

Remove skin and trim fat from the back of the ham, then remove bone. Use a sharp knife with a long thin blade to cut several 1-inch plugs from the meat, inserting knife in the fat side of the meat and piercing ham through.

Wash greens thoroughly and tear into pieces. Put in the pan with the water and ham hock. Simmer covered until greens are nice and tender but still a bright green, not the darker khaki of traditional southern-style greens.

Hog Butchering in Kentucky

Helping his granddaddy, Luther Tibbs, butcher a hog is an experience singer/songwriter Dwight Yoakam says gave him "a piece of America that a lot of my peers have never seen and will never understand . . . a verbal palette to work with that has hues other people don't have."

It was the fall of 1967, the year Yoakam turned 11, and he and his family had come down from their suburban house in Columbus, Ohio, to spend the weekend with his mother's parents in rural Betsy Layne, Kentucky.

"I remember I was real keyed up. We got up early in the morning—my brother Ronnie and me—and it was real cold, a November morning. My brother and I carried big warsh tubs of scalding water, which we managed to get on ourselves more than once, up the hill. But we got up that hill with those tubs.

"And it was breathtaking when I think back about that experience, you know. Out there in the wilds in southeast Kentucky. In this cold. You can see your breath as you walk up the hill in the early November morning.

"And we used butcher knives, Ronnie and me. We scalded the butcher knife by sticking it in that scalding water and we scraped the slaughtered hog.

"You know, hogs—unlike the pictures you see of pigs in barnyard drawings—they have hair all over them, hogs do. So we scraped for a couple of hours; scraped that hair off the hog with those butcher knives. I don't know how much my brother and I really helped to achieve that end, but we scraped as long as the men scraped.

"And I've always thought that was a pretty amazing thing to be a part of—particularly for an eleven-year-old who'd been away from that most of his life."

Drain, remove hock, and season lightly with salt and pepper, remembering that country ham is salty, too, and will flavor the greens as they bake together.

Chop green onions very fine and mix with the cooked greens, then pack the plug holes and the bone cavity of the ham with them.

Real Coffee

"Daddy is the best coffee maker in the world," Emmylou Harris said. "In the morning his coffee just walks right out of the pot and into your cup."

Bucky Harris makes his famous coffee in a Farberware electric percolator and uses a percolator grind vacuum pack coffee—one well-rounded, standard coffee measure for each cup.

The true secrets to making excellent coffee, he said, are an immaculately clean pot and fresh water.

"The first principle is clean your pot and I mean clean it. I wash mine with dish soap and a little mop every time I use it. And about every third or fourth time, I run a baking soda solution through. I just add some baking soda to clear water and let it perk. Then you rinse the pot real well to get all the soda out and you have to let the pot cool completely before you make coffee in it. You've always got to start with a cold pot and cold water."

You also always have to have the freshest water possible and to that end, Harris lets the water run out of the tap for a bit before he measures it into his coffee pot.

"You don't want water that's been standing in the pipes all night. It just won't taste quite right. In fact, you may not want to put this in, but when I get up in the morning, I make sure to flush both the toilets first thing just to get the water moving through the plumbing in the house. Then I run the water a good bit in the kitchen just to make sure what I use in my coffee is as fresh as I can get. And if you do all that, you'll have a good cup of coffee every time."

Mix sugar and bread crumbs together and press them into the fatted side of the ham to form a crust. Tightly wrap the ham with cheesecloth and bake in an open roasting pan for an hour at 350 degrees. Let the ham cool completely before unwrapping and slicing. Sliced thinly, it will serve 30–40 on Easter Sunday. Deviled Eggs (page 220) should be among the trimmings.

FRIED COUNTRY HAM AND RED EYE GRAVY

One of the most pressing questions in country kitchens concerns that traditional accompaniment for fried country ham—Red Eye Gravy: Do you make it with coffee or not?

John Egerton, country-ham savant and author of the splendid book *Southern Food,* says not, recommending simply ham juices and perhaps a little clear water because "if the ham is real ham, coffee won't be necessary."

But I find myself on the coffee side of this question, believing that any elixir christened "red eye" ought to be potent enough to pop them wide open—and a spot of caffeine is the kick that's required.

Just as the ham should be real ham, the coffee should be real and really strong. As Bucky Harris, Emmylou's father, says, "If you can't walk on it, it's not strong enough."

It should also be fresh, so brew your coffee while the ham fries.

2 slices country ham, 1/4 inch thick

1/4–1/2 cup strong, fresh black coffee

Place ham slices in a large cast-iron skillet and turn the flame low. Cook each side for about 5 minutes until the ham is sizzling. Move to warm plates and pour the coffee into the skillet, scraping the crusty ham remains from the pan and stirring as you let it simmer for about 3 minutes. Serve with fried eggs, the gravy on the side to be spooned over Good Grits (page 167) and/or Buttermilk Biscuits (page 258). *Serves 2.*

Real Bad Coffee

Chet Atkins, dean of country guitarists, left his eastern Tennessee home and started his professional picking career in his teens. It put him on the road and at the mercy of roadside coffee pots at a tender and impressionable age.

"On the road out of Knoxville I remember a lot of bad food, but the worst of it was the coffee," he recalled. "Some of the restaurants, you could smell the coffee urn for a block away. They had those big old urns about this high and yea big around. And I guess they were hard to clean, but they sure didn't clean them often so the coffee had that terrible old burned kind of taste."

My daddy drove a truck around that same region about the same time Atkins was on the road, and he drank his share of bad restaurant coffee, too. But one place near New Haven, Kentucky, had coffee so bad he could hardly believe it. So the next time my mother went on a trip with him, he drove 50 miles out of his way just so she could taste it.

"It was the worst I ever had and all they had was canned milk to go in it," she said. "But you know, I think your Daddy went back there several more times when he was working up that way. I don't think he could ever quite convince himself that coffee could be as awful as it was."

Baked Garlic Chops

When I was growing up in Louisville during the 1950s, steak was the essence of the modern American dream—a fat, sizzling T-bone served up on a platter the ultimate symbol that one had arrived. But I would have cheerfully traded a whole grill full of T-bones for a skillet of my mother's pan-fried pork chops.

She coated her 1/2-inch-thick chops in flour, salt, and pepper (shaking them in a bag), browned them on both sides in hot oil in a heavy skillet, then turned the flame down and let them simmer covered for about 25 minutes—much as she made her fried chicken. And like fried chicken, her pork chops were served with cream gravy, mashed potatoes, and biscuits.

I loved those chops, would eat every meaty bite and then contentedly gnaw and suck on the flavorful, crusty bone until my father shot me that look that let me know my manners had crossed the acceptable line.

These days breaded, pan-fried pork chops (especially served, as they must be, with gravy and buttery potatoes) cross the line that divides sensible eating from deep, dreadful indulgence. But the flavor is so wonderful that such a dinner is still worth a once-in-a-great-while indulgence.

Nevertheless, pork has such a fine, enticing flavor that there are a number of other, hearty home-style ways to make it that will satisfy the taste buds without endangering the heart. The recipe here is a garlic-redolent version of a baked pork chop dish my mother used to make and which I still make and savor with impunity. With extra fat trimmed from the chop, it's a lean but wickedly tasty dish.

2 medium cloves garlic, peeled and crushed
1/2 teaspoon salt
1/8 teaspoon white pepper
4 pork chops, 1 inch thick
1 tablespoon olive oil
2 large Idaho potatoes
1 large white onion
1/2 cup water

Early on the day when you want to serve the chops, peel and crush the garlic in a small, sturdy bowl. Add the salt and pepper and use the back of a wooden spoon to mash them together to make a paste.

Trim excess fat from the chops. Rub each chop on both sides with the garlic paste, put in a covered glass or ceramic container, and refrigerate for at least 4 hours.

When you're ready to cook, begin by preheating oven to 350 degrees. While oven is warming up, heat a heavy Dutch oven or similar deep, covered

"Pork chop, pork chop

Three, four, five.

We eat pork chops

To keep alive.

We play football.

We play soccer.

We keep pork chops

In our locker."

Baltimore high school cheer

roasting pot on a burner set to medium. Add olive oil to the pan and then brown the chops on both sides.

While they're browning, wash potatoes and cut in half lengthwise. Peel onion and cut into four thick rounds.

Remove chops from pan and put potatoes in, cut side down. When they are slightly browned, remove pan from heat and potatoes from pan. Add water to pan and scrape all the browned drippings from the bottom of the pan, mixing with the water. Put potatoes back in the pan, skin side down now; lay an onion on top of each potato and a chop on top of each onion. Cover and bake in the oven for one hour. *Serves 4.*

Real Barbecued Pork Shoulder

Any barbecue devotee knows that Real Barbecue is a subject worthy of a book all its own, and luckily it's already been written by two friends of mine, Greg Johnson and Vince Staten. Their *Real Barbecue: The Only Barbecue Book You'll Ever Need* (Harper and Row, 1988) not only surveys the hundred best barbecue joints across the United States, but explores the spiritual relationship of barbecue and the meaning of life; offers information on buying, building, or jerry-rigging your very own backyard smoker; and includes directions for barbecuing various cuts of meat, plus recipes for "secret" sauces and appropriate barbecue sides.

About the only thing it doesn't have is a Wet-nap in the sleeve and a recipe for covered-grill-smoked pork shoulder the way Mr. Vince once fixed it for a bunch of us one fine warm Saturday in June a couple of years ago.

That pork shoulder made an instant barbecue convert out of my nine-year-old who still recalls it with misty eyes and salivating chops. But that's not the reason why the recipe is here.

It's here because it illustrates the fundamental truth that although sauce is nice, Real Barbecue has very little to do with what's slopped on it. Instead, Real Barbecue is defined by how it's cooked: long and lovingly over hardwood or the coals thereof until the meat is crusted on the outside, fall-off-the-bone tender inside, and permeated with the sweet, sucking moisture of its own juices mingled with the dusky tang of the smoke. This recipe yields pork shoulder that is Real Barbecue to its very bone. And although you are welcome to enjoy your own favorite barbecue sauce on it (or you can make sauces out of either the South Carolina or Memphis Triple Pepper marinades with Not Barbecue Chicken, page 11), you will find that none is really necessary.

This recipe is also here because it is one for Real Barbecue that can be produced on a standard-sized covered grill right in your own backyard. Here's what you do.

aromatic wood chips for grilling

hardwood or mesquite charcoal

4-pound U.S. No. 1 grade pork shoulder, with bone

3 tablespoons black pepper

3 tablespoons white pepper

3 tablespoons cayenne

3 tablespoons paprika

You need a standard-sized, covered kettle-style grill with smoke holes in the lid.

Bags of wood chips for grilling are available at many places that sell grills and charcoal or also at good butchers. The chips can be from hickory, apple, oak, or any number of woods. The kind doesn't matter so much as the size. Johnson says, "the chunkier the better because you don't want them to burn up that fast, you want them to linger and smoke." To aid in that process, soak the wood chips in water overnight.

The next day, about nine hours before you want to serve your barbecue, mix spices together and then massage into the surface of the pork shoulder. Staten and Johnson say that when you're using a dry rub such as this one the meat needs to bask at room temperature for at least a half an hour before it hits the fire.

While your shoulder is basking, pile hardwood or mesquite charcoal briquettes in a mound in your grill and light as you normally do. Some barbecue savants firmly refuse to use charcoal lighting fuel saying it imparts a faint petro-chemical taste. Others say that by the time the meat gets to the fire, all the lighting fluid and its vapors have long since burned away. You decide which camp you belong to. At our house we light the charcoal using a metal, charcoal-lighting chimney—but for ecological reasons, not matters of taste.

When the coals are white hot, shovel them to one side of the grill. On the other side, put a tin plate or pan (an aluminum pie pan is what Vince uses) filled with water.

Sprinkle a good handful of soaked wood chips over the coals. Put the grate on the grill and the meat on the grate, fat side down, over the plate with water. Put the grill lid on, making sure that the smoke holes are open. Cook meat with the fat side down for one hour, then turn. The shoulder will cook the rest of the time with the fat on top so it can drip down into the meat, flavoring it.

The smoking process takes about 8 hours and during that time you'll add more soaked wood chips as needed. You can tell they're needed when smoke stops coming out of the smoke holes. You can add them to the fire by dropping them through the bars of the grill.

Shuck Beans, Stack
Cakes, and Honest
Fried Chicken

40

You will also need to occasionally add more charcoal. You can just add unlit briquettes to the burning ones, but Vince says that the best way to add charcoal is to have an auxiliary grill where you preheat them so you can maintain even heat. He uses a little metal fire-bucket as his auxiliary, but some folks use an inexpensive small grill. Light about a dozen briquettes and let them get white hot, then transfer to the smoker with a little shovel or tongs.

Check the meat frequently in the last hour because it may get done earlier. You'll know it's done because the meat will separate from the bone. Lift it carefully off the grill and into a big metal pan.

Using a knife, fork, and fingers pull pieces of the meat from the shoulder. Vince uses the knife and fork for big chunks, but says fingers work best as you get in closer to the bone.

"You're going to burn your fingers a little, but it's worth it," he says.

Chop the meat to a texture you like and then pile on the best buns you can find. Add warmed sauce if you want and pass big slices of onion and pickles on the side. Macaroni Salad (page 215) and Deviled Eggs (page 220) are essential side dishes. Summer Corn Pudding (page 162) is also superb. *Makes about a dozen barbecue sandwiches.*

The hearty eating country dinners provoke can wear a body out. Here my father, Pap Lundy (foreground), conserves energy as he dines at a 1949 Lundy family reunion with my cousins Mitch Dunn (left) and Tommy Lundy (right).

COUNTRY RIB DINNER

Country ribs are meatier than spareribs, the ones we usually barbecue. Be sure to ask your butcher for country-style ribs for this dish. And be sure to serve it to friends who aren't bashful about digging in to juicy food with fingers as well as forks.

The sweet potatoes absorb most of the molasses and apple flavor in the cooking and are wonderfully moist and sweet, just the perfect accompaniment to the hearty meat.

3 1/2 pounds country-style ribs

1 tablespoon olive oil

1 garlic clove

1 tablespoon flour

1 1/2 cups apple juice

1 1/2 cups warm water

1 tablespoon molasses

1 teaspoon rosemary

1 teaspoon salt

1/2 teaspoon black pepper

4 medium unpeeled sweet potatoes, halved

1 medium peeled onion, quartered

Trim excess fat from the ribs, but not so much that you lose any of the meat. Heat a heavy Dutch oven—preferably cast iron—over a medium flame, then add olive oil and the peeled garlic clove split in half. Shake clove in pan (so it doesn't burn) until it's light brown and the oil is well scented with garlic. Remove clove and set aside. Brown ribs a few at a time in the oil, then set aside, returning any drippings to the pan.

Turn flame to low and brown the tablespoon of flour in the drippings, adding a bit more oil if necessary. Slowly stir in apple juice to make a smooth gravy.

Dissolve molasses in warm water and add to the gravy.

Add rosemary, salt, and pepper and stir well. Lay halved, unpeeled sweet potatoes in the sauce along with onions and garlic clove, then lay ribs over the top.

Bake in 350 degree oven for one hour. Remove ribs and potatoes to serving plate and reduce sauce over medium flame, stirring constantly, until thick enough to lightly coat a spoon. The sauce is great for dipping the ribs in, or spooned over slabs of hot cornbread. Speckled Butter Beans (page 174) and Jerry's Slaw (page 217) are tasty accompaniments. *Serves 4 substantially.*

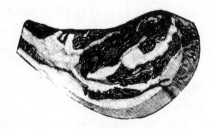

BUTTER BEANS AND SAUSAGE

I grew up reading cookbooks as if they were literature. My mother and I would talk about techniques and ingredients the way my college professors later discussed plot and character.

Were things necessary to the progression of the recipe or primarily symbolic? What if you changed just a few parts around? Would it come out right in the end? Would it be better?

I especially loved old cookbooks that sometimes gave strange directions and ingredients—as exotic and enchanting to me as the descriptions of time and place in my favorite Louisa May Alcott books. At their best, cookbooks aren't just introductions to food, but windows opening on to a time and its people.

For instance, one of my favorites is the 1885 *La Cuisine Creole,* redolent of Louisiana spices and reeking of male chauvinism.

"Cooking is in great measure a chemical process, and the ingredients of certain dishes should be as carefully weighed and tested as though emanating from the laboratory," its introduction proclaims.

"Few female cooks think of this, but men with their superior instinctive reasoning power are more governed by law and abide more closely to the rule; therefore are better cooks, and command higher prices for services."

After I stopped rolling my eyes over this comment, it occurred to me that the distinction it makes (although not the conclusion as to who is better) could also be applied to modern urban cooks vs. traditional rural ones. If you can run right out to a convenience store for a missing ingredient or a gourmet market for an exotic one, it is easier to stick to a recipe explicitly than if you are forced to make do with whatever is on hand.

But making do—as so many country cooks learned to do at their mama's knee—can often make a recipe so much better. And while the authors of *La Cuisine Creole* preferred strict adherence to the scientific approach, I'm inclined to favor the serendipitous one instead.

This recipe started out in a South Carolina cookbook calling for dried lima beans and catsup among its ingredients. But I can't abide dried limas and so substituted their creamy little southern cousins, speckled butter beans, which I keep stocked in my freezer.

And as to the catsup, well, we were fresh out. But I had a nice little jar of country dijon mustard on hand and after a little adjusting and doctoring, came up with the recipe that follows. And I must say I can't imagine anything tasting nicer on a cold winter evening, no matter how scientifically constructed.

2 cups water

16-ounce package frozen speckled butter beans

1/2 teaspoon salt

1/2 cup country dijon mustard

1 tablespoon butter

1 tablespoon milk

12 links breakfast sausage

1 medium Vidalia onion

2 green cooking apples

1/2 cup brown sugar

Heat water to boiling in a medium saucepan and add butter beans. Break frozen beans apart and spread evenly through the water as you bring it to a boil again. Cover, turn heat to low, and let simmer for 25 minutes, adding water if absolutely necessary.

While beans are cooking, fry sausage links until just brown. Remove skillet from heat and cut sausage into bite-sized chunks. Remove sausage from skillet leaving drippings in the pan. Chop Vidalia—or other sweet, white onion—into bite-sized pieces and put in sausage drippings over very low heat. Stir occasionally to keep from browning too quickly. Core and slice apples into the skillet and stir them with the onions until all are coated lightly with the sausage drippings. Sprinkle brown sugar over the top and stir until it is melted. Turn the heat up to medium and let the sugar thicken, stirring occasionally to keep it from burning. When the sugar gets thick and syrupy and clings to the apples, remove from heat.

When beans are cooked, add salt, mustard, butter, and milk and mix well. Turn into a lightly oiled 2-quart baking dish, lay sausage pieces over the top, and then spread apple/onion mixture over that.

Bake at 350 degrees for 30 minutes. *Serves 4 with cornbread.*

John Prine's First Trip to the Opry

Singer/songwriter John Prine's family is from Muhlenberg County, Kentucky, and although Prine was born and raised in Chicago, he says at heart he's always been a Kentuckian.

"It's like I'm from there, but just wasn't actually born there. When my mother was carrying me—about eight months along—they came down to Kentucky and the Smokies and the grand Ole Opry, so I was nearly born down south. Hell, I'd already been to the Opry in 1946, before I was even born."

Prine grew up hearing his father tell about that Opry trip. They hadn't bought tickets in advance and when they got to the door, it was sold out. But his dad pointed out his very pregnant wife and said how they'd driven all the way from Chicago.

"My dad said: 'We've got to see the Opry. Why, every Saturday night I sit at my kitchen table and point my radio to the south just to hear it.' "

His father thought he got better reception if the radio was facing Nashville, Prine said.

And sure enough, the ticket-taker, swayed by such dedication, relented and let the Prines in.

"The way we were raised in Chicago was as if when my dad's ship came in we were all going to go back to Kentucky. He escaped Kentucky because he didn't want to work in the mines. But he never lost that longing to go back there and he always thought it was his home."

Pork Roast for a German Afternoon

John Prine says he likes all kinds of food, but the country food his Kentucky-born mother and grandmother made is his favorite. When he cooks that's the premise he starts with. But like his grandpa, Prine's also an improviser and inventor of sorts. One of his best culinary inventions is a simple, country pork roast with a twist.

Prine rubs the roast with lots and lots of pepper and a little salt, puts it in a paper roasting bag, adds sweet German wine, and lets it roast slowly to make good juices. He cooks pork chops the same way.

I'm not a fan of bag baking. I guess I'm afraid the paper will drink up the juices when I'm not looking. But I discovered that Prine's technique is perfect for the clay pot—and I bet you'll think so, too.

The name of this dish, by the way, comes from Prine's wonderful, bluegrass-flavored 1986 album, "German Afternoons."

"I had this guy explain to me once that a German afternoon is like you go into town with some errands to run and stuff to do but then you run into an old buddy you haven't seen. And you drop into a bar for just a minute and start to talk. And next thing you know it's already evening and you've just spent a German afternoon."

This roast is the right incentive for such a German afternoon. Call a friend over, pop it in the oven, and enjoy the rest of the wine and good conversation while the roast fills your house with its sweet, heady fragrance.

4-pound pork loin roast

2 teaspoons freshly ground black pepper (tellicherry recommended)

1 teaspoon salt

1 cup Riesling

1 tablespoon flour

Soak clay pot top and bottom in water for 15 minutes. (See Clay-Pot Chicken on page 13 for more information on this cooking vessel.)

Trim excess fat from the pork roast. Mix salt and pepper together. (Any good black pepper, freshly ground, will do, but the tellicherry has a fragrance that goes especially well with the wine.) Rub salt and pepper into the roast all around. Pour wine into the bottom of the clay pot then place roast in wine, bone side down. Insert a meat thermometer into the thickest part of the roast, being careful not to touch the bone.

Put cover on and place pot into stone-cold oven. Turn heat to 425 degrees. Roast for 1 1/2 hours or until the thermometer registers 185 degrees. Remove roast to serving plate; degrease the juices. Put a tablespoon of the grease in a small, heavy saucepan on medium heat and add the flour, stirring to make smooth paste. Pour the degreased juices into this, still stirring to smooth and let thicken. Serve gravy on the side. Tomato Pie (page 189) is delicious with this. *This makes enough to feed 6 for dinner, but it's better served to 4 or fewer with some left over for pork roast sandwiches the next day.*

FRESH BOUDIN

Stuffing fresh sausage of any kind—but especially the spicy pork-and-liver-blended boudin—is without doubt the most visceral kitchen experience I've ever had. I don't recommend it to just anyone, particularly casual or squeamish cooks. After all, it requires the laying on of hands to about 50 feet of raw and pungent pig intestines.

On the other hand, if you relish rich, meaty, spicy country eating, there is nothing to match a link of fresh, steamed boudin split open and into a crusty French bun. These sandwiches are served religiously in the tiny Cajun/country dance halls that speckle southwest Louisiana, which is why the musicians who play fiddle, accordion, triangle, and frottoir in them have dubbed the clubs "the boudin circuit."

I learned to make boudin under the tutelage of Ronnie and Dianne Comeaux, who make and serve 500 links or so each week at their little grocery, Comeaux' Cajun Corner in Lafayette, Louisiana. Ronnie's recipe is based on his father's and it has a secret ingredient that he refuses to divulge. *But the recipe here, scaled down from Ronnie's usual 230-pound version and with a twist or two of its own, will make enough sinfully rich filling to stuff about 2 dozen 10-inch links, which is enough to stuff about 2 dozen hungry folks.*

If you make these, you must have a party and serve them with a big bottle of Tabasco on the side, a bucket of cold beer, and records by D. L. Menard (called "the Hank Williams of Cajun music"), Zachary Richard, Wayne Toups, and Beausoleil on the turntable.

50 feet of pig intestines

2 1/2 pounds of pork shoulder

3/4 pound pork liver

1 tablespoon salt

1/2 tablespoon paprika

1/2 tablespoon cayenne pepper

1/2 tablespoon black pepper

1 large onion

4 celery stalks, chopped coarsely

1 large green pepper, chopped coarsely

1 pound raw, medium grain white rice

6 green onions

handful of parsley

Ask the butcher if the intestines were packed in salt and, if so, soak them in water for 2–3 hours. If not, rinse lightly.

Chop pork shoulder into stew-sized chunks and put it and liver in a heavy stock pot and cover with water. Add salt, paprika, red and black peppers, onion, and coarsely chopped celery and green pepper. Bring to a boil, then simmer about 45 minutes.

Remove meat and reserve the liquid. Cook rice according to package directions, substituting spicy meat broth for about 1 cup of water.

While the rice is cooking, grind the meat in small batches in a food processor or food grinder with chopped green onions and parsley. Make sure each small batch has liver, onion, and parsley with the pork.

When the rice is ready and meat is ground, mix the two together in a big mixing bowl thoroughly but lightly. Add enough broth while you do this to make the mix very moist, but not soupy. The amount will vary according to the absorbency of rice and meat—you want something that is moist enough to cling together when you pack it, but not runny. Taste the mixture and adjust seasonings. More pepper is always allowed.

To stuff the boudin, drain intestines from their soak or rinse, then grab an end in one hand and rub it between your fingers until the casing opens. When it's stretched, insert a long-necked funnel with a neck about 1 inch wide

"I got a pig

Home in a pen

Corn to feed him on.

All I need's

A pretty little gal

Feed him when I'm

gone."

"Pig in a Pen," Old-time fiddle song

into the casing, and slide as much of the casing as you can onto the funnel neck without tearing. Tie off the end with a piece of string.

Hold the casing on the funnel neck lightly with one hand while you use the other to fill the funnel mouth with the stuffing. Use your hand to gently force the filling through the funnel mouth and into the casing. You want to hold the casing back just a bit as you fill it to prevent air bubbles. A firm, smooth sausage should roll off the end of the funnel.

Fill casing to within about an inch of the end, then tie off. Grasp end with one hand and pinch the sausage about 10 inches down the casing and gently spin toward you to form a link. When you make the next link, spin the sausage in the opposite direction, and continue down alternating the direction of the spin until all the links have been made. Repeat process until all the filling is used up, then lay the links out on a baking rack to cure for an hour or so.

Cooking or Dressing Up?

Sonny Aymond, son of Enola Prudhomme and nephew of the famous K-Paul, is an impressive Cajun cook in his own right, heading up the kitchen in his mother's Carencro, Louisiana, restaurant, Prudhomme's Cajun Cafe.

Sonny likes things simple but delicious and the dishes he creates are usually new spins on the foods he grew up eating. They've won him international renown and more than a few cooking contests. But he said he's started to lose interest in competitions lately because how well you cook doesn't necessarily relate to how well you finish.

"Shoot, I entered one a while back for Louisiana chefs and I took first prize in the cooking category," Sonny said in his rich Acadian accent.

"But I lost the Grand Prize and the guy who won it won it because he got 20 points more than me for his garnish.

"Do you believe that? Garnish!

"So I told 'em: 'If you wanna cook, let's cook. If you wanna look pretty, let's dress up.' "

(This is a good time—with all these feral sausage links spread around—to invite in friends to marvel at your macho cooking skills.)

When casings are dried, you should refrigerate the links (they'll keep up to seven days) or freeze them (good for two months). (If you refrigerate the boudin before the casing is dried, it will develop a slimy surface.)

When you are ready to serve, steam links on a rack above simmering water for 10 minutes—or a little longer if they've been frozen. Warm a small French baguette for each boudin sandwich. (If you can't get small ones a little longer than a hot dog bun, then buy longer baguettes and cut them into boudin-sized lengths.) Split the boudin casing open and spill the contents into the roll, packing it firmly into the bread. Serve Tabasco and thinly sliced raw onions with it. If you want more classic Cajun goodies, serve chilled Cajun Potatoes (page 184).

GRILLED BLUE TENDERLOIN

This is the perfect meat to prepare for the last cookout in autumn when the air is crisp and golden and the markets are full of a variety of tart cooking apples. Although this recipe is hardly traditional, it absolutely must be served with the best of all old fashioned fruit dishes, Fried Apples (page 194). You need a covered barbecue grill to cook this thoroughly and well. The leftover smoke-kissed meat is delicious sliced thick and served on rye bread with mayonnaise and mustard the following day.

> 2 pounds pork tenderloin
> 1 cup crumbled good blue cheese
> 4 green onions, chopped

Light charcoal in grill and while you're waiting for it to get to the right stage for grilling (a light, white ash over all the pieces) prepare pork. Make a deep gash in the tenderloin, splitting it lengthwise, but not cutting all the way through. With your hand, mix blue cheese with the green onions to make a thick paste, then pat this into the gash in the tenderloin. Tie up well, enclosing the cheese—I fold the loin over on itself so the gash is totally closed up.

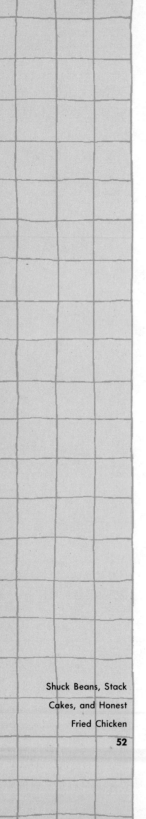

Lightly grease the grill and place it about four inches above the coals. Put loin on the rack and put cover over the grill. Turn every ten minutes so all sides brown. Roast for 45–60 minutes, until meat is no longer pink inside. If meat begins to char or brown too quickly, mist coals with water to turn the heat down. Serve with Fried Apples. *Serves 6.*

LIVER AND ONIONS

Country folk swear by liver—either with religious devotion or a passionate aversion that borders on the superstitious. But Polly Rideout, mother and grandmother, respectively, of country singers Naomi and Wynonna Judd, has been a culinary evangelist on the subject, making converts out of nonbelievers with her simple but delicious preparation of liver and onions.

"When I was cook on the river barges, I'd fry liver my way and I'd have fellas come up and tell me they'd never eaten liver in their life, but they just couldn't get enough of it the way I fixed it," she said.

Polly says the secret is to fry the liver fast in very hot bacon grease which gives it a crisp, flavorful crust but a creamy, tender center.

"The problem is most people just cook liver to death," she said.

Of course, the problem with Polly's recipe is, it's so good you can eat it to death.

> 1 pound calf or beef liver, sliced 1/2 inch thick
>
> 1 cup flour
>
> 1/2 teaspoon salt
>
> pepper
>
> bacon grease
>
> 5 medium onions, sliced thick

Remove thin outer membrane and veins from the liver.

Put enough bacon grease into the skillet so that the grease, when melted, comes halfway up the side of the liver. (In a large-sized skillet, that's about two hefty tablespoons.) Heat the grease on high until it sizzles when a speck of flour hits it.

While grease is heating, mix flour with salt and dredge each piece of liver. Add pepper to taste. Put the pieces of liver in the grease without crowding. (You will probably need to fry in batches and you may need to add more bacon grease as you go along.)

Fry until golden brown on each side, turning only once. Pay close attention since it takes only a minute or two for each side, and the secret of this liver is not to overcook it. Place cooked pieces of liver on a warmed plate until all are fried.

Turn heat to medium high and put sliced onions in the pan. Turn and stir the onions while frying to keep them from sticking or burning, but do it gently so they don't get all broken. Cook until they are brown and soft. This seems like a lot of onions when you start, but they cook way down. Top liver with cooked onions and serve it with Mashed Potatoes (page 179) and Polly Rideout's Yeast Rolls (page 256). *Serves 4.*

LIVER POMMERY

Mike Driskell, one of Louisville's most popular young chefs, calls this dish "a kind of country version of liver gone uptown." I call it my favorite liver recipe in the world. It's named after the brand of mustard Mike prefers to use, but any good quality grainy dijon will do.

> **2 onions**
>
> **8 tablespoons butter**
>
> **8 ounces beef liver in four thin slices**
>
> **1/2 cup flour**
>
> **1/4 teaspoon salt**
>
> **1/8 teaspoon black pepper**
>
> **4 tablespoons grainy dijon mustard**
>
> **1 cup heavy cream**

This dish is served with caramelized onions and they take a long time, so begin them first. Cut onions in half and slice very thin. Melt 4 tablespoons of the butter in a heavy skillet over low heat and add the onions.

Cook, uncovered, over very low heat for 45 minutes, stirring occasionally to keep them from sticking, but being careful not to break too many onions in the process. You cannot turn the heat up to speed along this process or the sugar from the onions will scorch instead of caramelize. But believe me, the flavor is worth the patience.

When onions are ready—or very nearly so—make the mustard sauce for the liver by whisking mustard and cream together in a heavy saucepan, then cooking down over medium heat—stirring constantly—until very thick.

To cook the liver, heat the rest of the butter on medium in another heavy skillet. Make sure liver is clean of all membranes and gristle.

Mix flour, salt, and pepper and dust each piece of liver lightly with this. Sauté the liver in the butter. Mike says to cook the first side until blood droplets begin to form on the top of the liver, then you turn and cook that side until they form again, then you turn a third time and cook for just a minute longer. The whole process takes about five minutes.

Remove liver to warm plate, pour mustard sauce over it, and serve with caramelized onions on the side. When Mike serves this in his restaurant, he garnishes it with crisp bacon and slices of fresh green apple. Home Fries (page 182) make a nice down-home accent. *Serves 2.*

MOTHER'S ROAST AND GOOD BROWN GRAVY

Rare roast beef was a rare item indeed in my mother's kitchen. In fact, I don't believe I tasted rare beef until I was well into my 20s and moved away from home. That's because my mother's roast was not a prime rib like those brought to the table by a beaming Donna Reed or June Cleaver on television. My mother's roast was instead a much cheaper cut of meat, the chuck or blade roast, which she cooked slowly and thoroughly until it was a deep mahogany color with crispy, flavorful edges moistened in dark brown natural gravy.

To be sure, it had a firm, chewy texture not prized at all among rare beef epicures, but the flavor of the crust of my mother's roast was darker and richer than anything I've eaten since. And the gravy—well, that was the whole point of having roast for dinner, it seemed to me. We drizzled it over the roasted potatoes my mother usually served on the side, or poured it on cut-open slabs of steamy Real Cornbread (page 235). (But we never put it on her sacred mashed potatoes, which were too rich and buttery on their own to be touched by any gravy—no matter how good.)

Slow, long cooking was developed, of course, to tenderize more inexpensive cuts of meat. My mother favors the blade, which, she says "is about the cheapest you can buy and it also makes the best brown gravy. Now a shoulder roast—I can't stand the meat from one and it doesn't make brown gravy worth a hoot."

"You can have the best roast in the world, but if you haven't got no gravy, bud, you've got nothing. And if you can make the best gravy in the world, you can pour it over a shoe and people love it. That's what my grandma and mother knew about cooking."
—John Prine

Meats

55

4-pound blade roast with the bone

salt

pepper

6 medium potatoes

2 cups water

2 tablespoons cornstarch

1/4 cup water

Trim fat from the edges of the beef, cut into inch-sized chunks, and render over high heat in a heavy roasting pot (with lid) until you have about 2 tablespoons of grease. Discard the fat. (If there isn't enough fat to yield 2 tablespoons, make up the difference with vegetable oil.)

Put meat in the fat, turn down heat to medium, and brown well on both sides. When the meat is browned, sprinkle salt and pepper on both sides. If you've got a good heavy pan and the lid fits nice and snug, my mother says the roast will make its own juice without any water. But you can, if you want to, add about 1/4 cup water to the bottom of the pan.

Pop the roast into a preheated 300 degree oven and leave it for 2 1/2 hours—give or take a half hour or so. The edges of the roast and the drippings will be a rich, brown mahogany color and the roast itself will have not even a hint of pink inside.

"Now what makes the good brown gravy is cooking it for a long, slow time. And you want your gravy to look like it's come to the point of almost being burned, it's that brown. But you don't want it to burn, because that would make it bitter," my mother says.

She also says that while some people like to cook potatoes and carrots with a roast, she doesn't because "that ruins your gravy. It just takes something out of it."

Instead she browns her potatoes with the roast drippings separately.

To do this, wash, peel, and quarter potatoes and boil them in water to cover until they're tender, but not mushy—about 15 minutes. When you take the finished roast out of the oven remove about 2 tablespoons fat from the drippings. Drain boiled potatoes, put them on a cookie sheet, drizzle the reserved fat over them, and pop them under a broiler for a couple of minutes until they are browned, turning to get them browned all over. Serve them on the platter with the roast.

While potatoes are browning, make the gravy. Set the roasting pan with the rest of the drippings over a medium flame, add 2 cups of water and stir and scrape to get all the crusty browned bits loose from the bottom of the pan and mixed with the water.

Mix cornstarch with 1/4 cup cold water until smooth. Drizzle into the juices in the pan and while you do, Mother says, "stir it like the devil." When cornstarch is blended in, turn heat up, bring to a boil and boil for about a minute, stirring constantly, until gravy is slightly thickened. This is a thin gravy. Serve on the side. Jerry's Slaw (page 216) and the Lone Oak Squash Casserole (page 175) are especially nice with this roast. And although lots of people like yeast rolls or the like with beef, my mother always served Real Cornbread (page 235) so we could split the slices open and drench them with good brown gravy.

The roast here will feed 6–8, but I suggest you cook it for a smaller group so that you'll have enough meat, gravy (and cold cornbread) left over to make Mother's Hash (recipe follows) the next day.

MOTHER'S HASH

Some meals are so good you hate to see them end, but I never minded the finish of a dinner with my mother's Roast and Good Brown Gravy. That's because as soon as it was over I could start looking forward to the next day's meal of hash from the leftovers.

This recipe for hash and the one that follows from John Prine's mother, Verna, are deceptively simple. There are no fancy ingredients, but the secret to their flavor is in how they are made.

My mother says that the most important thing in her recipe is to sauté the onions first.

"Some people like to dump the onions, meat, and potatoes all into the pan at the same time. But that's not how my mother did it and that's not how I do it, and it's just not as good if you do," she says.

Because this hash is made from whatever meat and gravy is left over from Mother's Roast and Good Brown Gravy (page 55), regard the measurements of ingredients here as a guide, increasing or decreasing the amount of onions and potatoes to match the amount of meat you actually have.

2 cups shredded cooked beef

1 cup finely chopped onion

2 tablespoons grease

2 medium potatoes, peeled and finely chopped

leftover gravy

water

salt

pepper

Use your fingers or a fork to pull meat apart in shreds. This takes a little longer and is a little messier than just cutting little chunks of beef from the roast with a knife, but I think it makes a better textured hash.

Measure meat and for every 2 cups, chop 1 cup of onion finely.

Skim off any grease that may have settled on the top of leftover gravy while it was refrigerated and put the grease in a large skillet (with a lid) on medium heat. Add enough oil to make 2 tablespoons. Add the onions and sauté, stirring occasionally, until translucent.

(If there's no grease on the gravy, just use oil to sauté the onions and when they begin to get soft, add about a teaspoonful of gravy to the skillet to flavor them.)

For every 2 cups of meat, peel 2 medium-sized potatoes and chop them into pieces about the size of a thumbnail and 1/8 inch thick.

When onions are soft and translucent, add potatoes to the skillet and stir until coated. Then add the meat and every bit of leftover gravy that you have. (If you don't have any gravy, you can still make good hash with just water, although it's not quite as tasty.) Add enough water to cover meat and potatoes and turn the heat to high.

Stir as you let the mixture come to a boil. Lower heat to medium, cover the pan, and let cook for 30 minutes, stirring frequently. The hash should be bubbly while it cooks, but not rapidly boiling. Turn down the heat if it's cooking too rapidly. You want the liquid to thicken, but not evaporate. Add salt and pepper to taste.

Hash is great for breakfast, lunch, or dinner served over leftover corn-bread that's been split open and toasted, or on biscuits, especially the Grit Biscuits (page 262). Fried Apples (page 194) are all you need with it.

This hash, made with 2 cups of meat, will make enough to feed 4.

VERNA PRINE'S HASH

The country cook's ability to make magnificence from meager stores is nowhere displayed so well as in a hash. Carved from the skimpy leavings of the previous day's roast, dressed up only with onion and maybe a few diced potatoes, then poured over plain toast or a biscuit, this humble hash can, nevertheless, have a most addictive flavor.

John Prine's mother, Verna, learned to make hash from her mother-in-law, Idell Prine. "I had four boys to feed and a husband and hash was one real good way to do it."

So good that her husband sometimes brought home a six-pound blade roast and said, "I don't want nobody touching this for anything else. I want it to be hash."

So good that Prine says when he goes to visit his mother in Chicago these days, she sends him back to Nashville ". . . with Tupperware on the airplanes—big Tupperware things of hash. She asks me what I want for birthdays and Christmas: I say, 'Ten pounds of hash.'

Pot Without a Handle

"I cook my pot roast in a cast-iron thing called a waterless cooker," Verna Prine says.

"When I was growing up they'd always say, 'You can cook a pot roast as long as you've got a pot to cook it in and a window to throw it out of.'

"That pot I use has a lid fits real tight. It had a handle at one time, but it just wore off. My God, I guess it was one of the first things I got when my husband and I got married. And I have to use pot holders now to move it around and cover and uncover it. I'm about the only one in the family can use it. And my boys sometimes say, 'Ma, you just keep that thing because you're the only one can work it.'

"But I keep it because nothing tastes so good as a pot roast cooked in old cast iron. In fact, I have several pieces of cast iron for my cooking and to me there's just nothing like it."

"And I say, 'I couldn't think of a better present, Ma, 'cause every time I eat it, I think of you.' "

4-pound blade roast with bone

salt

pepper

1 onion, sliced

1 onion chopped very, very finely

Be sure to get the blade with bone when you're buying your meat, Verna Prine says, because that's what gives both roast and hash its flavor. In fact,

Hash as Muse

Some people cook to eat, but sometimes John Prine cooks to write.

"In order to write songs, I need to get my mind somewhere else. I can't have my total concentration on my writing. So I write when I'm driving, when I'm cooking. I very rarely write behind the guitar. Cooking's one of the best times for me to write.

"So I was in the kitchen a while back working on making some hash like my mom does. And it was the week that the Berlin Wall came down, you know. And they had these TV shows with people dancing on the wall and stuff. So I wrote me a song right then called 'Dancing on the Berlin Wall.' And it starts out:

'I want your East German kisses on my West German face

Let's hang old Gorby's picture up above the fireplace

Tell all the friends and neighbors and bring Grandma in her shawl

Tonight we're going dancing on the wall.'

"Anyway this song just came out pretty fast and I liked it. And I think—yeah, I'm pretty sure that batch of hash came out pretty good, too."

she puts the bone in the pan with the hash while it cooks to give it more flavor, and you will too if you know what's good.

Trim fat from the outside of the roast and render it in a heavy cast-iron pot (one with a snug-fitting cover) over medium heat. Remove fat, leaving hot grease, and brown roast on both sides in it. Salt and pepper both sides liberally after they are browned. Sprinkle sliced onion over top of meat, cover with lid, and roast in 300 degree oven for 2 hours. If roast doesn't yield enough juice when it's browned, add 1/2 cup water before roasting.

When roast is done, take it out of the pot and let it cool at least enough to handle. It's really best, though, if refrigerated overnight. Refrigerate drippings separately so the grease will rise to the top and can be easily skimmed off.

When you're ready to make the hash, cut meat into thin, small pieces—about the size of a thumbnail—and put in a heavy skillet with a lid. Add the degreased roast juices and enough water—if necessary—to just cover the meat. Chop an onion very finely and add to the meat.

"I don't know if that makes a difference in the flavor, but I had to chop my onions real fine because my kids—when they were little—if they found a piece of onion in something, they wouldn't eat it," Verna Prine said.

Lay the big bone from the blade roast in the middle of the hash and then cover and simmer for about an hour. Taste and season with more salt and pepper bearing in mind that the Prines are all "great ones for pepper."

Remove the bone from the pot before serving. Verna said she sometimes served her hash on hot biscuits, but most of the time she just served it on the plate like a thick stew with mashed potatoes on the side.

"I had one boy, not Johnny, who used to like to eat his hash on his mashed potatoes and then catsup on top of that," she said. But I wouldn't recommend it, since the flavor is too good for such doctoring.

This will feed a mom, dad, and four hungry boys.

"No corn in the crib, no chicks in the yard. No meat in the smokehouse, no tubs full of lard. No cream in the pitcher, no honey in the mug. No butter on the table, no 'lasses in the jug."

" 'Leven Cent Cotton, Forty Cent Meat" by Bob Miller and Emma Denver

POLLY'S MEAT LOAF

The meat loaf Polly Judd Rideout makes is so delicious and well known in Ashland, Kentucky, that when her daughter, country singer Naomi Judd, was growing up there she and her siblings could take Polly's meat loaf sandwiches to school and trade for anything that the other kids had in their lunch sacks.

And when Polly started cooking on a towboat for an Ohio River barge line after her children were grown and gone away from home, it was this legendary meat loaf that solved the most vexing problem of her new career.

Barge crews, including the cook, work two-week stints on the river followed by two weeks off at home. The new schedule suited Polly fine except she worried who would take care of her yard and beautiful flowerbeds.

"No problem," said a long-time friend of Polly's son Mark. "All you have to do is make me a meat loaf every time you come home and I'll be glad to be your yardman." And that's exactly what she did.

Here's Polly's recipe for meat loaf: good for paying yardmen, plumbers, and accountants but, most of all, delicious in sandwiches. This will make enough for 4 to eat heartily at dinner with plenty left over for big sandwiches the next day. At our house, we make the sandwiches on thin rye bread with plenty of mayonnaise, and serve Deane's Brown Sugar Bread 'n' Butter Pickles (page 340) on the side.

> 2 pounds lean ground beef
>
> 1/2 pound breakfast sausage
>
> 1 large egg
>
> 1 package Saltines, crushed (40 single crackers)
>
> 2 medium onions, chopped
>
> 1 green pepper, minced
>
> 1/3 cup Worcestershire sauce
>
> 3/4 cup catsup
>
> 1/2 teaspoon ground pepper
>
> 1 teaspoon salt

Because the proper way to mix this meat loaf is to squoosh it thoroughly with your hands, and that means getting your hands thoroughly covered in

When Naomi Judd (front) comes home to her mother, Polly Rideout, in Ashland, Kentucky, their favorite hangout is the kitchen. And their favorite dishes are Polly's Meat Loaf (page 62), Polly's Potato Salad (page 211), and Polly's Chocolate Pie with No-Weep, No-Shrink Meringue (page 284).

meat loaf, you'll want to get everything set up to toss in before you start.

Turn the oven to 325 degrees and get out a shallow baking pan, about 9 by 12 inches.

Put the meat and egg in a large bowl. Crush the crackers finely. Polly puts them in a plastic bag and rolls them with a rolling pin to do this. Chop onions. Mince green pepper a bit finer than the onions. Pour 1/3 cup Worcestershire sauce in one measuring cup and pour 1/2 cup of catsup in another. (You'll use the other 1/4 cup later.) Now you're ready.

Sprinkle pepper and salt over the meat and start squeezing and kneading it to mix well. When the sausage is pretty well distributed through the beef, sprinkle the saltines on and squeeze and knead them until well mixed. Dump onions and green peppers over this and mix and knead so they're not all in a clump, then add catsup and Worcestershire and go to it with both hands again.

Polly says to mix and mix until the mixture has the same texture and ingredients throughout: "The way you do it is to squeeze that meat."

The way you know it's ready is that it will hold together somewhat like bread dough when you knead it. And you'll want to knead it several times to make it stick together good and firmly.

Then slap it into the pan and shape it into an oblong loaf. Pat it and slap it into shape, firming it as you do.

When you've slapped to satisfaction and the loaf is firm and proud, put it into the oven and bake at 325 degrees until it forms a crust—usually in about 45 minutes. When it's formed the crust, pull it out and slather the rest of the catsup down its crest. Put it back and bake it for about 45 minutes more. Let it cool just a bit before slicing. Meat loaf just about has to be served with Mashed Potatoes (page 179) and if you make up a double batch, you'll have plenty left over to make Cold Tater Cakes (page 181) the next day with your meat loaf sandwiches.

Enough for 4 and sandwiches the next day.

MOTHER'S MEAT LOAF

"After I get meat loaf mixed and shaped right, I always slap it real good a few times," Polly Rideout told me.

When I told that to my mother, her eyes lit up with born-again fervor. You see, when I was growing up, she used to make one of the best meat loafs around these parts. But a few years back she stopped making them altogether because she said, "they just don't do right anymore."

But Polly's mention of slapping was all the inspiration it took to get her back in the kitchen.

"That's it! That's what I was forgetting," she nearly hollered.

Sure enough, a few days later she served me a meat loaf sandwich that tasted as good as in the old days.

"I kneaded that meat loaf just like it was bread dough and then I slapped the devil out of it. That's all it was needing to make it right," she said.

2 hot dog buns

5 ounces evaporated milk

2 finely chopped medium onions

2 cups chopped dill gherkins

2 beaten eggs

1 teaspoon salt

1/2 teaspoon pepper

2 pounds ground beef

1/2 pound ground pork

Break the hot dog buns into 8–10 pieces in a large bowl. Pour evaporated milk over and let soak while you chop the onions and pickles. (My mother uses crust cut from pieces of white bread, but I always worried what to do with the rest of the bread afterwards. The hot dog buns give you the same crusty flavor but with no waste.)

Peel 2 medium onions and chop very finely so the pieces will permeate the meat loaf with flavor.

Use the crispest, tastiest small dill gherkins you can find, and slice each in half lengthwise. Then slice thin chips about 1/8 of an inch thick from the halves, enough to make 2 cups. (Don't try to shortcut this step with dill relish. The pieces in it are lots smaller and when the meat loaf is chilled and sliced for sandwiches, the flavor won't be as pungently dilled.)

Toss onions and pickles with the soaked bread to mix.

Beat 2 eggs and add. Sprinkle salt and pepper over all and then add the meat. Roll up your sleeves and use your hands to work all the ingredients together. After the ingredients are well mixed, squoosh the meat loaf mix through your fingers, then pat it back together, working it like this until the meat is smooth and the mixture holds together like bread dough.

Pat the meat into a loaf shape in the bowl and "slap the dickens out of it" half a dozen times top and bottom to firm it up. Lift it into a large loaf pan, pat it soundly into place, and then smack the pan a time or two on the counter for good measure. All this slapping and pounding will make a firm loaf that holds together when you slice it.

Put in preheated 350 degree oven and bake for 90 minutes. Remove from oven and carefully drain all the grease. Let cool for 20 minutes before slicing.

Serve with Tomato Pie (page 189) or Green Tomato Casserole (page 187) and Summer or Winter Corn Pudding (page 162 or 163), but be sure to save some meat loaf for sandwiches.

Serves 4 with leftovers.

COUNTRY FRIED STEAK

Emmylou Harris doesn't really relish the road trips that her career as one of the most popular new traditionalist country performers requires. But the Alabama-born singer confesses that one of the small pleasures of being on the road is the excuse it gives her "to stop at a roadside diner and tie into a real nice piece of country fried steak and cream gravy. Of course, that's not something you can eat all the time, but every once in a while, it's awfully good. And eating it almost feels like being back home."

Country Fried or Chicken Fried Steak shows up on the menus of most roadside restaurants, especially in the South; but these days what you're served is apt to be an over-processed beef pattie slathered in a too spicy breading and deep fried quickly before being topped with a gelatinous glop masquerading as gravy.

That is not how my mother or Emmy's made Country Fried Steak. And it's not what you should be eating if you want to know what makes otherwise sensible women swoon over such humble food. Here's a recipe for real Country Fried Steak. This is especially good served with biscuits for breakfast.

1 pound round steak

1/2 cup flour

1/2 teaspoon salt

1/4 teaspoon pepper

2 tablespoons bacon grease or canola oil

2 tablespoons flour

2 cups milk

Trim visible fat from the meat and cut into 4 serving pieces about the size of your hand. Now you want to beat the steak a bit to tenderize it and some folks use a kitchen mallet to do this. My mother, though, uses the edge of her potato masher and so do I because it textures the meat nicely.

When meat is pounded, mix flour, salt, and pepper in a shallow, wide bowl and dredge each piece of meat in it, coating it well on both sides. Heat grease or oil until it's hot but not smoking in a heavy, wide skillet with a lid. My mother always used bacon grease and it does flavor the steak subtly, but canola oil is much better for the heart and it will fry the meat well.

Brown each piece of meat on both sides, turn heat down a bit, cover and let the steak fry like chicken for 15–20 minutes. Remove cover and let it crisp for about 5 minutes; then take the steak from the pan and drain.

Leave about 2 tablespoons of drippings and all the browned flecks of crust in the pan. Turn heat a bit lower, sprinkle flour into the drippings, and stir to keep it from lumping while you let it get tasty and brown. (You can use the salted and peppered flour left over from breading the meat if you want.)

Slowly add about 2 cups of milk, stirring all the while. Let it cook for 3–5 minutes until thick. Taste and add seasonings, if needed. (If you've used the breading flour, you probably won't need any. If it's a tad too salty, a pinch of white sugar added will temper that.) Serve gravy on the side. It's particularly good ladled over thick, meaty slices of garden red tomatoes.

Serves 4.

SWISS STEAK

Prime cuts of beef didn't show up very often in country kitchens in the South but the women who cooked in those kitchens were adept at slow-cooking, tenderizing recipes that made prime eating out of the less expensive cuts. Probably because they are less expensive, many of these dishes show up with regularity on the menus of diners and cafeterias in the South—but rarely are they prepared as carefully (nor do they taste so delicious) as the ones our mothers made at home. This is my mother's recipe for Swiss Steak, a dish I can't abide outside of her kitchen. But made her way, it has a special savory richness particularly when served with her Mashed Potatoes (page 179).

3 pounds round steak, about 1/2 inch thick

1/2 cup flour

1/2 teaspoon salt

1/4 teaspoon freshly ground black pepper

1 14 1/2-ounce can whole tomatoes

3 small cloves garlic

1 teaspoon Worcestershire sauce

1 teaspoon dried mustard

1 teaspoon brown sugar

1/2 teaspoon celery salt

1 tablespoon bacon grease

1 large onion, chopped

1 green pepper, chopped

Trim meat of excess fat and cut into hand-sized pieces. Mix flour, salt, and pepper together and dredge each piece of meat in flour covering both sides. Pound flour into meat, using a maul or some heavy utensil. My mother uses the side of her potato masher and I like to do the same. Rub flour in after each pounding and pound again.

Put tomatoes, including juice, into blender and add garlic, Worcestershire, mustard, sugar, and celery salt. Blend until smooth.

Heat bacon grease in a heavy roasting pan with a lid, like a Dutch oven. Brown the meat on each side. Layer meat with onions and green peppers. Pour sauce over all, cover and place in 300 degree oven for 1 1/2 hours. Succotash (page 173) or Winter Corn Pudding (page 163) are good choices for a side dish. *Serves 6.*

Better Gravy

"Any kind of gravy you make is better to me if it's cooked a long time," my mother says.

"I like to make gravy almost like you add more milk than you mean to, and then you have to let it just cook down slow until it gets the consistency you want, stirring all the while."

CHIPPED BEEF AND GRAVY

My father worked the swing shift when I was growing up which meant that he slept odd hours through the week and we often ate odd meals at odd times. My favorites were the late-night breakfasts my mother would fix for him before he went off to the midnight shift—and for me, his little companion who would eat along to keep him company at the table. We'd sit at the small white porcelain-topped table in the tiny kitchen with the cold black night wrapped around it. Inside, though, it was warm with the yellow glow of the little lamps hung above the sink and table, and the fragrance of biscuits or toast and other savory aromas coming from the stove.

I still like sausage and eggs with fresh tomatoes as a supper dish, but my favorite of all the late-night breakfasts was when mother would make Chipped Beef and Gravy.

When I grew up and went out into the world of school cafeterias where cream gravy is some viscous white stuff plopped out of a can or reconstituted from powder, I discovered that others did not regard Chipped Beef with the same tender esteem I did. In fact, after trying one or two versions of this gelatinous mess on cold toast, I quickly grasped why friends who'd served in the armed services had christened it S.O.S.

But the way my mother made her Chipped Beef—nurturing the bacon-flavored gravy along slowly, the scrape of her metal spoon in the pan the only sound in the cool hush of the night—it was comfort food of the very first order. Salty, creamy, and warm, it was just the ticket to soothe the spirits of a little girl sending her daddy off into the night.

2 tablespoons bacon grease

2 tablespoons flour

2 cups of milk

2 1/2 ounces dried beef

pepper

The chipped beef my mother used came in small glass jars with tiny little stars embossed around the rim which we then used for juice glasses. These days dried beef comes in a resealable vacuum bag and is usually found in the section of the grocery where canned hams and other tinned meats are. That's what you want. There is a type of dried beef stocked in the cooler section with lunch meats, but my mother warns that it "is not fit to eat."

In several other recipes I recommend you substitute canola or olive oil for the traditional bacon grease, but in this one, the flavor of the bacon is essential.

In a heavy skillet, melt the grease over medium-low heat. Sprinkle 2 tablespoons of flour in the grease, and stir it to keep from lumping while it froths and bubbles. When flour is well seasoned, slowly add milk while stirring. You want this mixture to cook and thicken slowly over medium-low heat and you need to keep stirring as it does.

When it's the consistency of a thick cream sauce (but not so thick that the gravy "sets up" the way it does when this dish is served in restaurants) tear the slices of dried beef into two or three pieces each and drop into the gravy. Stir them in well and let them simmer in the gravy for a few minutes to let the flavors mingle. You don't rinse the beef before dropping it in the gravy, and the salt from it will be more than sufficient to flavor the dish. Add pepper to taste, then serve on Earlene's Biscuits (page 259). *Serves 4.*

FRIED SQUIRREL

Dwight Yoakam says that one of the great pleasures of summer trips to visit his grandparents, Luther and Earlene Tibbs, in Kentucky was the squirrel dinners his granny made.

"There was nothing like my granny's squirrel dinners back home in Columbus. And when I'd go back home to Ohio and tell my friends what we ate—well, this was in the 1960s in the city, you know, and a lot of them didn't know whether to believe me or not," Yoakam said.

Real woodland, country-bred squirrels such as the ones Dwight Yoakam's granny cooked aren't so easy to come by these days. But just in case you have a hunter friend who comes home with a couple of plump ones someday, here's what you do to fry them up mountain style.

Uncle Charlie and the Squirrel

I had my first taste of squirrel on a summer trip down to Corbin, Kentucky. My great-uncle Charlie had to tell one wonderful whopper to convince this then four-year-old girl that eating a fluffy squirrel wouldn't be a sin.

"Now let me tell you," Charlie said, his clear blue eyes sparkling with mischief. "I was just out there walking through the woods, minding my own business, enjoying the sound of the birds and the colors of the trees. And there right up in one of them trees, I saw the saddest little old squirrel you ever have seen. Oh, he was crying big alligator tears. They were falling down like raindrops.

"And I said, 'Squirrel, what's wrong with you? Why are you so sad on a pretty day like this one?'

"And he said, 'Mister, I'm just an old squirrel, a real old squirrel. I'm so old, well, I'm nearly ready to die. And I'm so sad that I won't be no good to nobody when I'm gone. I just don't know what to do. I sure wish I could be dinner to some pretty little girl tonight, soon as I've died.'

"And I said, 'Do you think that would make you happy?'

"And he said, 'Yes, I believe it would.' "

And Charlie told me then he told that squirrel all about me and how he'd fry him up in a big skillet for me that night. And that old squirrel, he said, got such a big smile on his face and fell right out of that tree into Charlie's arms dead as a doornail, but twice as happy.

And of course, I ate every bite that Charlie put on my plate that night. And I was awful glad to do that squirrel the favor, because I'm telling you the truth, he tasted mighty good.

2 squirrels

1 cup flour

1/2 teaspoon each salt and pepper

1 tablespoon bacon grease

shortening

2 tablespoons browned flour

1 1/2 cups milk

Dress the squirrels and cut into pieces as you would rabbit. Cover with salt water and soak in refrigerator overnight. Dry when ready to cook.

In a big, heavy cast-iron skillet with a lid, on medium-high heat, melt bacon grease plus enough shortening to stand 1/2 inch deep in the pan.

Put flour, salt, and pepper in a strong paper or plastic bag and shake to mix. Add the squirrel, a piece at a time, shake until coated and lay in the skillet. The grease should be hot enough to crackle when you do.

Brown squirrel pieces on both sides, then turn the heat low and cover with lid. Cook for 30 minutes. When crust is brown and meat is tender, remove from pan and place in warming oven.

A Tablespoon of Brain

"My father was a very clean hunter, cleaned his game really well," recalled Ruth Ann Rankey, Dwight Yoakam's mother.

"With a squirrel, he'd skin the head and take the eyes out and clean it just like the rest of the body and we'd cook the head along with everything else in the squirrel stew.

"And what you did was you cracked the head open after it was cooked and scooped out the squirrel's brains to eat them. I guess it was probably about a tablespoon's worth. We usually cooked two or three squirrels at a time and lucky for me not everybody liked the brains so we never did have fights over them. And if you liked them, it was something of a delicacy to eat. It was very smooth and almost like a custard and it tasted just wonderful."

Pour off all but about 3 tablespoons of fat, and gently scrape browned bits from bottom of the pan into it. Turn heat low and sprinkle browned flour over the drippings, stirring to make a paste. Slowly add milk, stirring constantly until it makes a gravy. *Serves 4 with Earlene's Biscuits (page 259).*

FRICASSEED RABBIT

Rabbit was favorite game for backwoods hunters and often, like the protagonist in Charlie Monroe's song "Have a Feast Here Tonight," they'd cook their catch right out in the woods where they'd caught him. But better yet was to take the rabbit home where butter, cream, and some spices could enhance the

"I'll build me a fire
And I'll cook that old
     hare.
Roll him in my blaze
     and make him brown.
(Cook him well!)
Have a feast here
     tonight
While the moon is
     shining bright.
Just find a level place
     to lie down."

"Have a Feast Here Tonight" by Charlie Monroe

Meats

73

game in a fricassee. This recipe is adapted from a traditional one from the 1800s and is a simple but tasty way to cook the fresh rabbit available from some butchers. You can also use frozen rabbit, found in most grocery stores. If you use frozen, thaw it first according to package directions.

2 rabbits, cleaned and cut up

1/2 teaspoon salt

1/8 teaspoon cayenne pepper

1/8 teaspoon mace

2 tablespoons olive oil

2 cups chicken broth

2 tablespoons butter

2 tablespoons flour

1/2 cup half and half

1/8 teaspoon nutmeg

The Ferret and the Rabbit

When Dwight Yoakam's mother, Ruth Ann Rankey, was growing up in the coal towns around Pike County, Kentucky, in the 1940s, it was her daddy's skill with a shotgun and her mother's diligence in the garden that kept their stomachs full.

"My daddy was a coal miner and worked hard all of his life. But even when you work hard, you can't count on the mines. When the coal fields play out or the price goes too low, the companies will close down and the miners will be out of work and luck," she said.

"Even so, we always ate well. My mother raised a big garden every year, and dried and canned. And my daddy was an excellent hunter. But there was one time my mother sure got the best of him."

Her daddy, Luther Tibbs, had gone out hunting in the morning. Ruth Ann and her mother, Earlene, were working around the house when they heard a dog barking and prowling around their property—and so they went out to run it off.

"While we were out, Mom saw a rabbit running into its hole. She got a real big smile.

Rinse and dry rabbits. If yours are wild ones, you may want to soak them in vinegar overnight to tenderize them, rinsing them well the next day.

Mix salt, cayenne pepper, and mace and rub into the flesh of the rabbit evenly and well.

Heat olive oil on medium flame in a heavy pan with a lid, add the rabbit pieces and brown well on each side. When all pieces are browned, pour the chicken broth over it, cover and let simmer for an hour.

Using your fingers, blend butter and flour together as if you were making pastry. Form into small balls and when the hour is up, uncover the rabbit and drop the balls of butter and flour in the broth, spread evenly around the pan. Let this simmer for about 15 minutes, then mix nutmeg into half and half and add to the juices in the rabbit pan. Turn heat low and let these simmer together, uncovered, for another 10 minutes, being careful not to let it get so hot the milk curdles. *This makes a feast for 6. It's very nice served with couscous on the side.*

"My daddy used to keep a ferret at the house for hunting, so Mom got the ferret and a big cloth sack. She set the ferret into the rabbit's hole, and when the ferret went in that rabbit came running out and into the sack.

"She pulled the rabbit out by its ears and cracked its neck with the side of her hand. Killed it on the spot. Then she went straight home to skin it and cut it up.

"When my dad came home, he hadn't been able to get anything and he was looking kind of downcast. But she had her rabbit on, already stewing it for supper and she had that smile all over her face. I think that was the best rabbit she ever made."

Ruth Ann remembers her mother stewed her cut-up rabbit in water with just salt and pepper for seasoning. When it was good and tender, after about an hour or hour and a half, she would remove the rabbit, add flour mixed with 3/4 cup water for thickening, and 2 cups of milk. She cooked this until it made a thick broth, then poured that over the rabbit to serve.

PAN-FRIED RABBIT PRUDHOMME

The first time I entered Enola Prudhomme's Cajun Cafe in south-central Louisiana, I felt like I'd walked into the dining room of a long-lost relative. She, her husband, Shelton Prater, and her son, Sonny Aymond, adopted our family at first sight. Enola filled our table with amply piled plates of the food we'd ordered plus loads of little dishes of "lagniappe." In Cajun country, the word means "a little something extra." In Enola's vocabulary, it means anything tasty she's cooked up that day that you forgot to order but still might like to try.

Enola is the sister of famous New Orleans chef Paul Prudhomme and they learned their Cajun cooking skills in the same family kitchen. Sonny has worked with Paul in New Orleans also and a lot of the recipes the Cajun country Prudhommes served are based on Paul's. But as Enola says: "A chef always changes a recipe a little to suit his or her own taste." And that's the case with this rabbit dish, one of the most delectable I've ever tasted.

"Rabbit is a must on our menu in this part of the country," Enola says. "If you debone your own rabbit, be sure to reserve the bones to make a rich stock. Also, the front legs make a terrific sauce piquant or stew."

6 ounces uncooked rotini pasta

3/4 cup peanut oil

2 tablespoons Chef Paul Prudhomme's Louisiana Cajun Magic for Pork and Veal

4 boneless rabbit hindlegs, pounded 1/4 inch thick

2 cups all-purpose flour

1 cup buttermilk

2 cups fine dried bread crumbs

2 tablespoons unsalted butter

1/2 cup beef stock or water

2 cups whipping cream

1/2 cup grated fresh Parmesan cheese

Cook rotini according to package directions, drain and set aside.

In a heavy skillet, heat oil on high until very hot. While oil is heating, sprinkle 1 tablespoon of the Cajun Magic seasoning on both sides of the meat, dredge through flour, dip in buttermilk, and then dredge in bread crumbs. Carefully put in hot oil and fry 5–8 minutes until golden brown on each side, turning a couple of times so as not to burn the meat. Remove from skillet and let drain on paper towels.

In a large skillet bring butter, stock, and remaining seasoning to a boil. Add the cooked pasta, turn down to a lively simmer, and cook for 10 minutes. Add cream and cook, stirring, for 10 minutes more or until sauce thickens. Add cheese, stirring until it's melted. Remove from heat, and serve immediately with pan-fried rabbit over hot pasta. *Makes 4 servings.*

FISH

GREEN RIVER STYLE FISH SANDWICH

TROUT DURBIN

FISH BEIGNET

VACATION FISH

LOW COUNTRY SHRIMP AND HOMINY

BARBECUED SHRIMP

SHRIMP JOCELYN

PICKLED SHRIMP

MARYLAND CRAB CAKES

GULF SHORES CRAB CLAWS

OYSTER FRY

COBBLER ROCKEFELLER

Green River Style Fish Sandwich

I grew up in Louisville a block away from one of the best fish fries in the world: the Suburban Social Club. It was in a long, low cinder-block building right next to the Cozy Theater and every Saturday in the summer the members would gather in the wee hours of the morning and start breading hundreds of pounds of fish for the weekly fry.

In the late 1950s, I would walk up to the corner a little before noon on Saturday and for a dollar get a fish sandwich, bottle of icy orange pop, kid's ticket to the Cozy's matinee double feature, and a small box of Milk Duds. What a life!

The Cozy's gone now, but Suburban still fries at the corner of Third Street and Central Avenue (just two blocks from Churchill Downs) each Saturday (including Derby Day) from April through November. The sandwich will cost you more than a quarter, but it's worth it. The filets are thin, deep fried with a pungent, peppery crust and served with slivers of onion marinated in vinegar.

The sign out front says the fish is cooked Green River Style, but when I asked the head of the social club once if this was indeed how fish is made down along Kentucky's Green River he just laughed and said: "Nah. I think we just started calling it that a long time ago because it sounded so good."

He also laughed when I asked him to tell me the secret to the recipe. But after several attempts in my own kitchen, I think I've finally come close.

To do this right, I recommend you get a deep fat thermometer to gauge when the oil is at precisely the right temperature—375 degrees F. If you get it hotter, the crust will burn up before the fish is done. And if you don't get it hot enough, too much oil will be absorbed in the frying. When the fish is fried at the right temperature though, not only does it taste great, but it absorbs very little oil.

The filets you want should be about the span of a hand or smaller and only 3/4 of an inch deep at their thickest. A nice, firm white fish is what you want, whatever is freshest. My brother-in-law, Dave Fryrear, a trophy-winning bass fisherman and a darn good fish fryer, says the secret to really good, flaky fried fish is to get the fish itself cold first. He refrigerates his filets for at least six hours before frying, and I suggest you do the same.

"Fish and whistle,
  whistle and fish.
Eat everything that
  they put on your dish
When we get through
  we'll make a big
  wish
That we never have to
  do this again."
"Fish and Whistle" by John Prine

Fish

81

In my family, we eat our fish sandwiches on thinly sliced rye bread with a little mayonnaise and plenty of the vinegar onions piled on top.

1 medium white onion

1 cup rice vinegar

4 filets

2 cups white cornmeal

2 teaspoons salt

2 teaspoons white pepper

1 cup buttermilk

canola oil for deep frying

A few hours before you're ready to fry the fish, peel onion, cut in half and slice thinly. Cover with rice vinegar in a container that has a snug-fitting lid. If necessary, gently push the slices down into the vinegar until submerged. Cover with the lid and refrigerate until ready to serve. Onions will keep for several days.

When you're ready to fry, pour oil to fill the frying pan no more than halfway. You can use a deep fryer if you have one, but if not, a large, heavy saucepan or a deep skillet will do fine—just make sure you don't fill it so full that the oil bubbles over when you add the fish.

Mix cornmeal, salt, and pepper well in a wide, shallow dish. Pour buttermilk into another. Coat each filet with buttermilk, then dredge in the cornmeal mix.

When oil has reached 375 degrees, place a couple of the breaded filets in it being careful not to overcrowd. Fry until a deep golden color on both sides, about 3–4 minutes. (Use a long-handled slotted spoon to turn the filets if necessary, but be very careful not to break or pierce the crust.)

When golden and crispy, remove and let drain on paper towels or brown paper sack. Make sure the oil comes back to 375 degrees before starting the next batch. Serve immediately on rye bread and let everyone pile on onions, catsup or mayonnaise to taste.

My mother almost always makes Jerry's Slaw (page 216) to eat with fish sandwiches, but I like Macaroni Salad (page 215). *Makes 4 sandwiches.*

Caterpillar Pets

My Uncle Charlie of fried squirrel fame introduced me to the pleasures of fishing. When I was just old enough to walk he'd load me into his old gray Buick along with his wife, Aunt Rae; her sister, Aunt Johnnie; and their sun hats and cane poles and we'd all head out to the Laurel River.

They'd settle on a good bank—each in a different spot—and it was my job to run back and forth toting the little metal bucket full of bait. It was hard for a natural chatterbox child to keep her own counsel the way grown-ups wanted you to on a fishing day, but I could be bought off by icy bottles of pop from the cooler. And then there were the caterpillars.

Charlie let me dip into the bait bucket to pick out the best possible caterpillar each time he needed to replenish a hook. I liked to pull out the little fuzz-covered, black squiggles and let them inch around my fingers and nose a while to make sure they were "good and lively" before I passed them on to Charlie. I thought they were furry and funny and perfect little pets. I swear it never dawned on me until much later that I was handing my little friends over into a piercing, soaking death.

I'm not even sure it occurred to me until much later that "fishing" is what you did to get fish on the table for supper. Instead it seemed like a singular mix of social and spiritual rite—one part solitary contemplation and one part laugh-filled conversation during a lunch break on the cold chicken, pickles, salads, and sandwiches my aunts would pack. It was simply an added, benevolent perk that such a fine activity also put tasty bluegills, catfish, and bass on the dinner table.

Steamboat Fishing

John Hartford wrote "Gentle on My Mind," one of the most recorded songs in history. But while he's known as a songwriter and unique entertainer—one who plays concerts in a black bowler hat and makes music with a banjo, fiddle, and piece of plywood which he amplifies and then dances on to create a live rhythm track—Hartford's real avocation is that of riverboat man. Hartford, who is a licensed captain, said he fell in love with the Mississippi River as a boy in St. Louis:

"I had a schoolteacher who put the pilot house from an old wrecked steamboat in the schoolyard when I was a kid, and I think that started my longing. By the time I was 15 or 16 years old, I'd signed on to work on the *Delta Queen*—a big old beautiful steamboat that still runs the Mississippi and Ohio rivers today.

"We'd started out in Cincinnati that first day and come down the Ohio River and the tradition was that on the first night out the boat landed at a place called Sugar Creek. And the engineer, he'd go down and fish there with a bit of bread wrapped around some lunch meat for his bait. He'd catch 'em like crazy. He could have caught those fish with anything, I guess, because the wash from the boat would push the fish in toward the bank and then they'd get stuck there between the boat and the shore. He probably could have put a plain hook in and pulled fish out of that place.

"The main thing I remember about the engineer was he smoked Ibold cigars. And the main thing I remember about the fish, well, I don't think I've ever had fish that tasted as good as those he caught my first night on the *Delta Queen*."

TROUT DURBIN

Lon Durbin and Sam Bush were young altar boys together down in Bowling Green, Kentucky. Bush grew up to be a progenitor of the progressive bluegrass movement—a mandolin/fiddle playing innovator who took one of the most tradition-bound styles of country music and added twists, turns, and flavors to create a brand new sound so stunning it can raise goosebumps on your arms.

Likewise, Durbin has made his name as a chef who deals in fresh improvisations on traditional food themes. Trout Durbin—Lon's variation of a classic French dish—is a good example, and the most popular menu item at his Bowling Green, Kentucky, restaurant, the Parakeet.

The fishing gene seems to be dominant in country music families. Here's four-year-old Polly Rideout in the early 1930s, posing on a pier with her catch from a Kentucky lake; here too is Polly's granddaughter Wynonna Judd, with her catch some four decades later.

2 whole trout, about 1 1/2 pounds each

1/2 cup flour

1/4 teaspoon salt

1/8 teaspoon white pepper

1/4 teaspoon paprika

6–8 tablespoons clarified butter

1 1/2 cups sliced mushrooms

4 whole canned artichokes, quartered

juice of 1/2 fresh lemon

2 tablespoons chopped fresh parsley

Trot Line Running on the Laurel River

My daddy and Uncle Jack used to fish using a trot line—a long, small-linked metal chain or fishing line that they would tie to a bush or limb then run underwater across the river and tie on the other side. Down the length of the trot line, about every foot or so, they'd hang a stringer of fishing line, each with its own hook and bait.

In the summers we'd vacation for a week on the Laurel River down by Noe's Dock. Daddy and Jack would put out their line as soon as we got to the river and then twice a day—usually early morning or late evening—we'd go run the trot line.

Jack would troll the boat down the side of the river until Daddy found the right landmarks and the right tie-off branch. When they found it, Jack would cut off the motor and we'd begin to inch our way across the river with Daddy and Jack pulling along the line.

There was always an air of mystery and stealth about this enterprise. I think trot lines were probably illegal—and I know that Daddy and Jack were always worried another fisherman floating by might suss out where theirs was and pick it clean sometime before they got to it. Consequently, any time a boat approached, they'd drop their hands down in the river still holding the line, but keeping it underwater so prying eyes couldn't follow

Clean and bone the trout, remove head and tail if you are squeamish, and open flat. Mix flour, salt, white pepper, and paprika well, then dredge the trout in the seasoned flour, coating both sides.

In a large cast-iron skillet, heat 4 tablespoons clarified butter over medium heat, then sauté the mushroom slices about 2 minutes. Add the artichokes and toss until warmed. Remove from skillet.

Add 2 tablespoons more of clarified butter, turn heat just a smidgen higher than medium, and cook trout about 2 minutes on each side until golden. Remove to warmed plate. (If your skillet isn't wide enough to accommodate both trout at once, do one at a time, adding more butter for the second trout if necessary.)

it to its source. And my cousin Larry and I would sit in the middle of the little metal boat trying to look casual and feeling a little afraid but very excited.

If something was caught, you could usually feel its weight and any movement for a while before you got to it on the line. And part of the fun of running the trot line was listening to Daddy and Jack speculate about just what they might have caught and where along the line it was going to show up as they moved along its length. They caught a fair share of evil-whiskered, gray catfish for dinner—and also a fair share of branches and debris carried into their trot line by the river's current.

Uncle Jack wasn't much of a worm man when it came to bait. It seemed like every year he'd heard of something new that the fish were just crazy for like crickets or a certain kind of lunch meat. My favorite was the year he got into dough balls made from corn flakes and bright pink cream soda. He'd sit at the kitchen table in the morning mixing the two together, then rolling the batter into bite-sized balls. Larry and I got to share whatever pop was left in the last bottle, and it seemed like the cupboard was full of cornflakes and cream sodas all vacation long. I still like the bubble-gum taste of that pop with fried fish.

"Have you ever seen them put the kids in the car
After work on Friday night?
Pull up in a holler about 2 A.M.
See a light still shining bright?
Those mountain folks set up that late
Just to hold those little grandkids
In their arms—in their arms.
And I'm proud to say that I've been
blessed and touched
By their sweet hillbilly charms."
"Readin', 'Rightin', Route 23" by Dwight Yoakam

Fish

Toss mushrooms and artichokes back into skillet and add fresh lemon juice and parsley. Mix and heat until just warmed, then spoon over trout and serve immediately.

If you're feeling really extravagant, fire up the grill and make Roast Corn with Bacon (page 164) and Grilled Asparagus (page 171) to go along.

Trout will serve 2.

FISH BEIGNET

The first time I ate Fish Beignet was at the Olde N'Awlins Cookery on Conti Street in the French Quarter in 1987. Up until that time I'd thought all beignets were sweet, but our waiter assured us that the word was frequently used to mean any truly tasty little fried morsel.

The first time I made Fish Beignet was a few months later when long-lost friends showed up starving on our doorstep just as we were about to make our dinner on a small slab of swordfish. In the tradition taught me by my mother, I decided I'd have to come up with something to stretch that fish, and beignet was the answer. And although the pepper does make them a little homely, that didn't stop us from eating them as fast as we could and wishing there'd been just a few more.

Those first beignet were made with just the pepper in the flour—and our friends found them tasty. But they hardly registered on the hell-fire-and-brimstone meter that my husband keeps in his mouth. So now we add Tabasco to the egg to make them even more potent—and wonderful.

Cool Cucumber Sauce is the perfect antidote (page 340).

1 pound swordfish, 1 inch thick

1 cup flour

1 teaspoon salt

1 tablespoon black pepper

1 tablespoon cayenne

1 tablespoon white pepper

2 eggs, beaten

6 drops Tabasco

canola oil for frying

Cut swordfish into cubes about an inch square. Mix flour, salt, and peppers well in a bowl. Blend Tabasco into eggs in another. Pour oil about 1/2 inch high in a deep skillet and heat to 375 degrees.

While oil is heating, dip cubes of fish in egg and then roll in peppered flour, then dip a second time in egg and flour.

Drop double-dipped beignet into hot oil a few at a time, being careful not to crowd the pan. Fry, turning once, until browned on each side—should be about 2–3 minutes. (If your oil is too hot, the crust will burn before fish is cooked.)

Drain on paper towels and serve while hot. This makes enough for a big appetizer, or if you want to serve dinner for 4, add a pot of Creamy Eggplant Soup (page 109), Tomato and Cucumber Salad (page 201), and Hot Water Cornbread (page 237).

VACATION FISH

The topping for this fish is actually a hot artichoke dip that's been a southern party staple for the last decade or so. I was inspired to put it on a steak of fresh fish on the last night of a South Carolina beach vacation when its ingredients and the fish were the only things left to cook in our rented house. It turned out to be one of the best tasting fish dishes we'd ever had and has become a family favorite.

Any firm, thick fish suitable for baking is good, but swordfish is divine.

The flavor is so rich you'll want to serve nothing more than a simple salad and good bread with it.

2 half-pound swordfish steaks, about an inch thick

juice of 1 lime

2 tablespoons olive oil

4 drained, canned artichokes

1/2 cup mayonnaise

1/2 cup fresh grated Parmesan cheese

freshly ground black pepper

Put steaks in nonmetal baking dish, mix lime juice and olive oil and pour over the steaks. Turn them to coat each side, then refrigerate for about an hour.

When you're ready to bake, heat oven to 400 degrees. In a bowl, mash artichokes well with the back of a fork, then add mayonnaise, freshly grated Parmesan (not the canned kind), and a couple of grinds of black pepper. Mix well and then spread in an even layer across the tops of the fish steaks.

Pop into oven and bake for 20–25 minutes, until fish is firm and flaky and the artichoke topping has begun to brown. Serve immediately. *Enough for 2.*

LOW COUNTRY SHRIMP AND HOMINY

I have checked and there has never been a statute in the state of Kentucky making it illegal to cook shrimp another way besides breaded and deep fried. When I was growing up, though, there might as well have been because that was the only way I ever encountered these scrumptious crustaceans.

But once I made my way to the southern Atlantic coast and the Gulf of Mexico, I discovered folks eating bountiful shrimp all kinds of ways: steamed, barbecued, sautéed, pickled, and in pies. And I've adopted some of the best of these regional recipes for my own.

For instance, in the low country of South Carolina where we vacation from time to time, shrimp served with hominy grits is a breakfast staple. It's a great way to start a morning at the ocean, but at our house we also like to have it for supper with a fresh green salad on the side. Some South Carolinians fry up bacon to crumble over it and cook the shrimp in the drippings. But I think the browned butter gives it the best taste.

For more information on Good Grits, see page 167.

1 cup coarse grits
4 cups water
1 teaspoon salt
4 tablespoons butter
1/4 cup chopped green onion with stalks
1 pound peeled and deveined shrimp
salt
pepper

Put grits, water, and salt into top of double boiler and place directly on burner turned to high. Bring to a slow boil and cook, stirring constantly, for 10 minutes. (Be careful not to let the grits boil too rapidly, or the mixture will begin to bubble and pop and quite likely burn your hand.)

While grits are cooking, bring water in the bottom of the double boiler to a rolling boil and when the 10 minutes are up, put the top into the bottom, cover, and let the grits cook for another 30 minutes. When that time is up, let the grits continue cooking while you prepare the shrimp.

In a skillet (one with a lid), heat butter on high just until it browns. Toss in green onions and shrimp and stir and toss for a minute. Add a dash of salt and a couple of grinds of fresh black pepper, then cover and cook over medium heat stirring once or twice during the process.

For each serving, put a fist-sized mound of grits on a plate or in a bowl and top with shrimp and gravy. *Makes enough for 3–4.*

You may have grits left over. If so, you can chill them in a glass, then slide them out, slice, and fry them like mush for breakfast the next day.

"Just like fiddling, boat building, and folk tales, ways of preparing food are passed down from one generation to the next. And foodways is the most irrepressible tradition—one that continues on with families, even after they've stopped speaking the language or listening to the music."
—Richard Van Kleeck, director of folklore at the Kentucky Center for the Arts

BARBECUED SHRIMP

These Louisiana shrimp are not barbecued at all but baked in their shells in a pungent sauce—preferably in a cast-iron skillet. This skillet is then plunked down hot (on a trivet, of course) in the middle of a table covered in oil cloth or newspapers and surrounded by starving people who wait only until the top shrimp are cool enough to be gingerly handled before plunging in.

As soon as they can be grabbed (and there are those of us who cultivate asbestos fingers so we can be sure to get them while they're hot) shrimp are pulled from the pot, peeled to their tails, plunged back into the sauce, and then eaten. Shells can be dropped right on the table if you're dining on newspaper, but if you're going for something more formal, give each of your guests a paper plate for his discards.

Some folks also like to swipe the shrimp through a little custom-made cocktail sauce before consuming them, so when we serve these shrimp we put catsup, mayonnaise, horseradish, fresh lemon wedges, Worcestershire and—of course—Tabasco on the table. Everyone gets a spoon and little bowl of their own and in that bowl they get to blend any combination of the above to their taste bud's pleasure.

Barbecued Shrimp really must be served with Cajun Potatoes (page 184)—which are great dipped in either the shrimp's sauce or the cocktail sauce. You'll also want several loaves of hot, crusty French bread (three is just about enough for this amount of shrimp). You can put butter on the table for the bread if you want, but really what you want to do is dunk chunks of the bread in the shrimp sauce.

Eating these shrimp is a messy, communal business—a great feast for great friends. If you're a really good host or hostess you'll provide everyone with a big old T-shirt to wear while they work at it so no one has to worry about the mess. I have a bright pink smock my friends like to call my manicurist's shirt which I wear whenever we have shrimp Louisiana style.

In New Orleans the shrimp are cooked not only in the shell but with their heads still on—which makes eating them even more primal. But my fishmonger won't sell me shrimp with heads on this far inland because he says they deteriorate much faster than those that are decapitated. If you're close to the source, though, go for heads. I think it gives the sauce a richer flavor.

And if you can manage to get your hands on some Dixie Beer from New Orleans, that's what you want to drink with this. Otherwise go for any good beer in long-necked bottles that has been iced to the bone.

3 pounds medium shrimp, in shells

1/2 cup butter

1/2 cup olive oil

1 teaspoon salt

1 tablespoon cayenne

1 tablespoon black pepper

1 tablespoon paprika

1 tablespoon rosemary

1 cup flat beer

juice of 1 lemon

leaves from a bunch of celery

1 cup chopped green onion

Rinse shrimp well and let drain. Put the rest of the ingredients in a large pot (5-quart capacity, cast iron if you have it) that can be put in the oven, and cook on top of the stove on low heat for 20 minutes, stirring occasionally.

Heat oven to 375 degrees and when sauce is ready, dump shrimp into the pot and stir it so everything gets coated. The sauce won't cover the shrimp completely, but that's okay because you're going to stir it four or five more times as it bakes.

Put the pot in the oven and let it cook for 20–25 minutes, stirring the shrimp every 5 minutes or so, so they all get well sauced. When shrimp are firm and pink and savory, serve. Serve with Deviled Eggs (page 220), which can be eaten with messy fingers. *Makes enough for 6 fine, fearless folks.*

SHRIMP JOCELYN

Sweet yellow summer squash grows in abundance throughout the South in the summer and along the coastal areas cooks love to cook it up with fresh-caught shrimp. There are numerous recipes for summer squash and shrimp, many with numerous ingredients. But the best I've ever had is made simply by Jocelyn Mayfield, owner and head chef of Jocelyn's in Ocean Springs, Mississippi—a lovely and homey little restaurant where the food is delicious beyond saying.

Jocelyn was generous in explaining how she makes her shrimp and squash. The secret, she says, is slow, low cooking. But like most of the cooks who learned their art in a country kitchen, she wasn't sure in cups and spoonfuls just how much of what went into this.

"I'm a dump cook," she said, laughing. "I just dump until it looks and tastes right."

But with the memory of Jocelyn's fine shrimp dish still on my tongue and her directions at my side, I dumped also—but measured first to determine just how much I was dumping—and came up with this recipe.

On the menu for Jocelyn's there is this slogan: "Like this place, no other."

You can also be sure: "Like this shrimp, no other."

2 medium summer squash

4 tablespoons margarine or butter substitute

1 chopped whole green onion

salt

pepper

1 pound medium shrimp, peeled and deveined

pinch of basil

Parmesan cheese

Cut squash into small cubes. Melt margarine over medium low heat in a heavy skillet. Add squash, onion, and salt and pepper to taste. Keeping the heat low, cook for 20–25 minutes, stirring occasionally, until squash is tender and fragrant but not mushy.

Add the shrimp, turn heat up just a tiny bit, and cook for another 10 minutes, stirring occasionally until the shrimp are done and contents of the pot are juicy. Dot with butter, sprinkle on a pinch of basil, and top with grated Parmesan cheese. Let sit for just a moment until butter melts and cheese softens—then serve with thick, crusty bread. Succotash (page 173), also prepared Jocelyn-style, is excellent on the side. *Makes enough for 2.*

PICKLED SHRIMP

Every southern coastal hostess worth her soiree stripes has her own personal pickled shrimp recipe. This is one I developed after first tasting pickled shrimp in South Carolina and it transfers quite nicely to those landlocked parties we have around here at Derby time. The rice vinegar is a perfect companion for the shrimp. Serve it with a thinly sliced, good quality pumpernickel or with crisp melba toast rounds.

1 cup good olive oil

1 cup rice vinegar

juice of 3 fresh lemons

2 tablespoons white sugar

1 teaspoon coarsely crushed peppercorns

1 teaspoon dill seed

1 teaspoon celery salt

1 teaspoon dry mustard

1/2 teaspoon tarragon

3 pounds peeled and deveined medium shrimp

2 medium white onions, thinly sliced

In a medium saucepan combine all ingredients except the shrimp and onions. Heat until it's barely boiling. Add raw shrimp to the hot mixture in small batches—enough so the hot liquid covers shrimp completely but they're not crowded. Cook shrimp for 4–5 minutes, then remove with slotted spoon and continue the process until all shrimp are done.

In a large, nonmetal casserole with a lid, make a layer of onion slices and then top it with a layer of cooked shrimp. Keep making layers until all are used. Pour the hot marinade over. (Use a large wooden spoon to press gently on the shrimp and onions to submerge, if necessary.) Let the mixture cool a bit before covering well and refrigerating. If your casserole lid isn't really snug, you may want to wrap the whole shebang in plastic wrap to keep it from pickling your refrigerator.

Chill for at least 48 hours before serving. During this time, I usually open the casserole three or four times a day and stir the mixture to make sure the oil and vinegar are distributed evenly.

This makes a nice appetizer for a dozen or so—and you can keep any leftovers for a couple of days in the refrigerator.

MARYLAND CRAB CAKES

I married into Maryland Crab Cakes, a smarter match than one made for money. Although crab cakes are made all up and down the Atlantic coast and along the gulf, I'd never tasted one until I went home to Baltimore with Ken.

Now we have them whenever we can get good, fresh crabmeat—and they're easier than pie to make. Since Ken was brought up in Baltimore, he likes crab cakes that are spicy with a kiss of Old Bay Seasoning. If you can't find it in your store, try a pinch of whatever packaged crab or shrimp boil seasoning you can find.

In finer restaurants now, crab cakes are served all sorts of fancy ways (my favorite is sitting in a pool of homemade aioli). But around our house we eat these the way Ken grew up eating them, with a handful of Saltines, a splash of catsup—add horseradish if you want—and cold beer.

1 pound fresh crabmeat

1 egg

1/2 cup half and half

1 teaspoon Tabasco

2 teaspoons Worcestershire

2 tablespoons melted butter

1/4 teaspoon salt

1 teaspoon Old Bay Seasoning

4 green onions

1/2 cup bread crumbs

1 cup flour

1/2 teaspoon salt

1/4 teaspoon white pepper

canola oil for frying

Fishing for a Heartbreak

Singer Bobby Bare started fishing when he was about six years old "up in the cricks" around his family's house in Ironton, Ohio, an Ohio River town just north of Ashland, Kentucky.

Early on, Bare used a willow stalk with a line tied to the end and he and his sister Delma would make hooks out of safety pins. Then he discovered the wonders of a rod and reel.

"I was probably 13 or 14 and I painted this guy's fence for one of those old-timey rod and reels. I didn't know anything about 'em at all. But I could not wait to get to the crick and throw my line out to get it waaaaay out there.

"But when I got to the crick, it had been raining for four or five days and the water was way up. You couldn't get anywhere near it from the bank. But I got in the middle of a trestle—a railroad trestle. And I thought, 'Well, I can throw down through there.' Cause the water was flowing under it, real muddy. So I reared back and threw, and it backlashed. Jerked that rod right out of my hand and went right down in the water.

"I stood there, big tears rolling down my cheeks with a broken heart. Oh, it was sad. And that was the first time I ever had my heart broke.

"But the up side is, a week later I went back down and the water was down to normal. And I stood on the trestle telling this buddy of mine, saying:

'Right here's where I threw my rod away.'

"And we looked down there all sad and serious, you know, and saw it! It was laying down there and the water had cleared up and it wasn't that deep. So we went right down and got it.

"And most of my heartbreaks in life seem to have worked out about as good as that first one fishing."

Pick through crabmeat, discarding any shell or bits of cartilage, then set aside. Beat egg, then mix in half and half, Tabasco, Worcestershire, butter, salt, and Old Bay seasoning. Blend in bread crumbs and let sit while you wash and mince green onions.

In a shallow plate, mix flour, salt, and pepper to coat the crab cakes. Add crab and onions to bread crumb mixture and use your hands to mix it all together well. Form crab/crumb mix into patties about 3 inches in diameter. You should get 10–12. Turn each crab cake in the seasoned flour mix to coat, then put on a plate or cookie sheet. Cover with plastic wrap and refrigerate for at least a half an hour, up to 4 hours.

When you're ready to fry, heat a skillet on high, add canola oil 1/4 inch deep, and turn heat to medium high. When oil reaches 375 degrees, put crab

Towboat Kings

"We ate like kings on the towboats," John Hartford remembers about his early riverboat days.

"Most towboat cooks were country girls, and you know how they eat—steak, potatoes, meat loaf, hot breads.

"Working on a boat is hard physical labor. The army was a breeze after towboating. And the tradition on a boat is that your crew is only going to perform as good as your cook does—so you bet we'd eat good.

"And sometimes I'd wake up craving things. That's how I got to eating raw oysters. Somebody got me to eat an oyster one time, kind of on a dare. And I liked the sauce we put on them more than the oyster at the time. But two nights later I sat straight up out of a deep sleep and I had to have an oyster. I mean, I was craving them and I've been that way since.

"I usually take just a piece of a lemon and suck on it while I'm eating the oysters. If they're good and fresh, you won't want anything else."

cakes in it and fry about 2 minutes on each side—until they are a deep golden color and crisp. Remove and let drain on paper towels for a minute before serving.

Fry only a few crab cakes at a time; don't crowd them in the skillet. You can keep the early ones warm in the oven as you fry the rest.

Enough for 4.

GULF SHORES CRAB CLAWS

There seems to be a basic rule in southern cooking that says if anything tastes good boiled, broiled, or baked, it will be even better dipped in batter and deep fried. That's the premise behind this seafood specialty served as either appetizer or main course in the Gulf Shore regions of Mississippi, Alabama, and northwestern Florida.

I've found that the best crab fried claws are those with the lightest breading to enhance, but not overpower, the crab's sweet flavor. The claws have already been steamed or boiled and the ones I get here are usually then frozen. Thaw them before frying. You want small, bite-sized claws for this—but ones with a plump morsel of meat on them to make it worth your while. A dozen a person is not too many.

> 4 dozen boiled crab claws
> 2 cups buttermilk
> 2 eggs
> 1 teaspoon salt
> 1/2 teaspoon white pepper
> 1 teaspoon cayenne
> 1/2 cup flour
> canola oil for deep frying

Pat crab claws with paper towels to make sure they're dry before dipping in the batter. Whisk together milk, eggs, seasonings, and flour until well blended. In a deep fryer or other pot deep enough so that the oil won't boil over, pour canola oil 3 inches deep and heat to 375 degrees.

"Fish and whistle,

whistle and fish.

Eat everything that

they put on your dish

When we get through

we'll make a big

wish

That we never have to

do this again."

"Fish and Whistle" by

John Prine

When oil gets ready, dip 4–6 claws in batter, let excess drain for just a moment, then put one at a time into oil. They fry in a literal minute or less. When the crust is golden, pull them out with slotted spatula or deep fry basket and drain on paper towels while you fry more.

The crust on this is very thin—just enough to give the claws a crisping coat. Be sure to monitor the temperature of the oil with a deep fry thermometer, making sure it maintains a constant 375. And skim the oil frequently between fryings to get out any crust or shell particles that might burn and flavor the oil.

Serve with Cool Cucumber Sauce (page 340), tartar or cocktail sauce—or let guests make their own dipping sauces à la Barbecued Shrimp (page 92). If you're serving this for dinner, make Okra Succotash (page 172) and potato salad—either Mine and Mama's (page 213) or Polly's (page 211).

Serves 4.

OYSTER FRY

Although fresh seafood didn't often make its way as far inland as Kentucky when I was growing up, oysters were the exception. As the railroads moved into the region at the turn of the century, they brought big barrels of iced-down raw oysters with them. Raw oysters and fat oyster fritters became barroom staples. And an oyster fry at home was an excellent reason to gather family and friends together for a celebration.

My family was full of men who wore the blue-striped railroad cap to work each day, so it's appropriate that we were also big oyster eaters. The annual oyster fry at my aunts' in Corbin was a Christmas tradition.

Relatives would cram into the little living room and exchange silly gag presents. Then pretty soon the party would spill over into the big kitchen where my great-aunts, Rae and Minnie, and my cousin, Jessie, would trade shifts frying up quarts of oysters as fast as folks could eat them. When my sister Pat was a teenager, she and our cousins Reed Elliott and Bennie Terrell would race to see who could eat the most. The house record was 18.

There was plenty of crisp celery to eat with the oysters and potato salad or big pans of fried potatoes.

Although we don't have that annual Christmas party anymore, bits and pieces of the family still gather from time to time around a big electric skillet of frying oysters. Reed's wife Helen usually does the frying honors, having learned from Reed's mother, Minnie. Helen says you want big plump oysters, the biggest and freshest you can get. And since Reed's no longer a racing teenager, about eight per person is a good bet.

This is how she frys them and she cautions that: "If you do it right, people will be sitting there at your elbow with their fingers stretched out grabbing them before you can get 'em on paper towels to drain the oil off."

4 dozen oysters

4 cups cracker meal

5 eggs, beaten

salt

pepper

canola oil for frying

Drain oysters. Put cracker meal in one bowl, beaten eggs in another. You can buy cracker meal, or you can make your own by putting Saltines in a plastic bag and rolling them into crumbs with a rolling pin. Taste the cracker meal and add salt and pepper to suit.

Pour enough oil in a skillet to cover the oysters about halfway. Heat to 375 degrees F. While oil is heating, dip oysters one at a time in cracker meal, then in egg, then back in cracker meal.

When oil is ready, put the oysters in gently and fry until golden brown on each side, turning once carefully so as not to break the crust. It only takes a minute or two. Don't crowd oysters in the pan and skim the oil frequently to remove any crust that falls off and might burn. Add oil between batches when necessary, making sure temperature comes back up to 375 before you fry again.

Remove oysters with a slotted spoon or spatula and let drain on paper towels briefly, then serve while hot with plenty of crisp celery and Home Fries (page 182) or Mine and Mama's Potato Salad (page 213). *Makes enough for 6.*

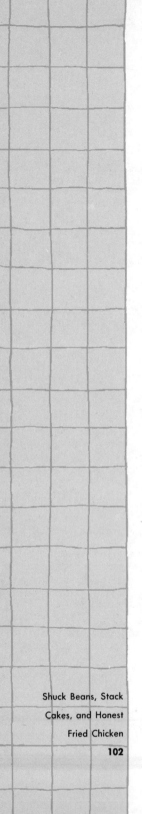

Mouse Dancing

Although it was the women in the family who did the cooking for the annual oyster fry, it was often my daddy and Uncle Charlie who went shopping for the supplies.

One year they had just come into the kitchen with arms full of brown paper sacks from the grocery when a couple of stalks of celery in the sack rubbed up against each other and let out an eerily lifelike squeak.

"I believe that's a mouse," Charlie said.

And at just that moment the celery squeaked again and my daddy got a quick muscle twitch in his right leg.

"I believe he's in my britches," Daddy hollered, grabbing his overall leg and getting a handful of something which he was sure was the mouse.

Charlie grabbed a broom nearby and started beating Daddy's leg to beat the band. All the women in the kitchen whooped and hollered as the two men hopped and danced and pounded their way into the adjacent bathroom. There Daddy dropped his pants but all they found was a wadded-up bandana, a big bruise, and a story that the two of them loved to tell again every Christmas for the rest of their lives.

COBBLER ROCKEFELLER

Oyster pies were a popular way of cooking up oysters with other leftover meat at the turn of the century. Chicken was often used, as was ham.

Oysters Rockefeller, of course, is the succulent oyster appetizer invented at Antoine's in New Orleans and so rich it was named in honor of John D. Rockefeller. This humble but scrumptious cobbler uses country ham with oysters to pay homage to both traditions.

By the way, it's no mistake that the only salt in this dish is in the cobbler crust. In the filling, both the ham and oyster liquor make salt enough.

1 cup flour

1/2 teaspoon salt

1/3 cup buttermilk

2 tablespoons canola oil

10-ounce package frozen spinach

1/4 cup water

1 dozen large oysters and liquor

1 tablespoon dijon mustard

half and half

1 celery stalk

2 green onions

3 tablespoons butter or substitute

2 tablespoons flour

1 cup shredded country ham

Sift flour and salt together. Mix buttermilk and oil. Make a well in middle of flour, pour in buttermilk and oil, mix until it holds together, then knead ten times. Roll out on floured board then trim to fit the top of a small casserole or deep-dish pie pan.

Heat oven to 375 degrees.

While oven is heating, bring frozen spinach and 1/4 cup water to boil in a saucepan, break spinach apart, turn heat to simmer, cover, and let cook for 2 minutes. Drain spinach well, discarding juice.

Drain oysters, reserving all liquor. If liquor is gritty, strain through a colander lined with paper towel or muslin cloth. Whisk dijon mustard into oyster liquor, then add half and half to make 1 1/2 cups of liquid.

Chop onion and celery finely. Melt butter in heavy saucepan and add onion and celery, cooking until just softened. Remove vegetables from pan with slotted spoon to leave as much butter in the pan as possible, then add flour to butter and juices in pan and stir over low heat until well blended. Slowly add oyster/dijon/cream liquid and stir and simmer until it just begins to thicken. Add oysters, spinach, ham, celery, and green onions and stir just enough to mix and warm everything nicely.

Pour the mixture into the very lightly greased casserole or pie pan and cover with crust. Make several slits in the top of the crust and brush with melted butter so it will brown.

Pop in the oven and bake for 25–30 minutes, until crust is firm and browned. Serve warm. *Enough for 4.*

Most fishermen come home and clean their catch, but when my grandfather Bill Fore landed this whopper at a lake near Corbin, Kentucky, he came home and cleaned himself. Then he put on his best suit and went downtown to have this portrait made.

SOUPS AND STEWS

BEEF STEW

BEEF AND CORNMEAL DUMPLING STEW

JAMBALAYA

CHICKEN AND SAUSAGE GUMBO

KENTUCKY BURGOO

NEW YEAR'S STEW

SLUMGULLION

MYSTERY RAGOUT

TEXAS CHILI

CINCINNATI CHILI

GREEN CHILI PORK STEW

CHILI BUNS

STOCK

When kinfolks were sighted around the bend or even on the doorstep, the first thing a country cook was likely to think of was her stew pot. Soups, stews, and chilis don't need to be sliced or meted out meticulously. They have no drumsticks to quarrel over; no "best cuts" to feel rewarded or slighted by. They make the most (and a whole lot of it) out of bits and pieces of other good stuff. They're inexpensive to prepare, but they can be ever so luxurious in the consuming.

The secret to the rich flavor of many one-pot meals is most often a homemade stock. Nothing was ever wasted in a country kitchen and so it was that meat scraps, bones, and scorned pieces of the chicken like the scrawny neck and back were turned into rich brown or golden broth by simmering in a pot on the back of the stove. Chicken feet were even scrubbed and boiled to make a rich, jelly-like consommé prized out in the country.

I'm not suggesting you try to find some chicken feet of your own, but it's simple enough to make a basic stock from scraps—both before and after dinner.

For instance, at Thanksgiving I start a first stock in the morning just after I put the turkey in the oven. This one takes about two quarts of water, if it's a big bird. Into that I put the rinsed turkey neck, heart, liver, and gizzards, about four ribs of celery, a whole peeled onion, and a couple of carrots. I let it simmer while the turkey roasts and season it with salt and pepper according to my taste. When it's time to make dressing or gravy, I have plenty of fresh stock available. Whatever's left I strain and refrigerate.

After dinner I make a second batch of turkey stock. I pull all the usable meat from the turkey carcass and refrigerate it for Hot Browns (page 22) or Turkey and Sausage Gumbo (page 133) the next day. If we've eaten in the early afternoon, I dump the skin and bones and all the pan drippings into my big stock pot, cover with water, add more celery, onion, and carrots and let it simmer for several hours before straining and refrigerating. If Thanksgiving dinner has ended in the evening, though, I just refrigerate all my stock ingredients and put them in the pot and cook them up the next day. This after-dinner stock is roastier, browner stock than the early one.

You can use the same technique with chicken, beef, or lamb—and I

"Kinfolks a-comin',
they're comin' by the
dozen
Eatin' everything from
soup to hay.
And right after dinner,
they ain't lookin' any
thinner
And here's what you
can hear them say:
Y'all come! Y'all come!
Y'all come and see us
now and then.
Y'all come! Y'all come!
Y'all come to see us
when you can.
"Y'all Come" by Arleigh
Duff

almost always add garlic to these stocks, although I don't care for it with turkey. But while you can add herbs and spices to any stock-in-the-making, I usually don't. I've found it's much more useful to have plain stock on hand and then add appropriate seasonings when I get ready to add stock to a dish.

Strain the stock and chill well so the solidified fat can be easily skimmed off the top. Stock keeps about two days in the refrigerator without spoiling. You can extend that for an additional 24 hours if you take it out after two days, bring it to a boil to kill bacteria, then refrigerate for one more day.

But the best way of keeping stock is to freeze it since it keeps well from 4–6 months that way. And one of the best things I've found for freezing it in are those little one-cup plastic yogurt containers with their own lids. The one-cup size makes it easy to add the right measure of stock to any given recipe. When ready to use, run warm water over the bottom and sides of the cup and the frozen stock will pop right out like an ice cube.

Or you can freeze stock in ice cube trays, then turn the cubes out into plastic bags and tie them tight for storage. You can pull out one, two, or as many cubes as you need.

PEPPERCORN BROCCOLI SOUP

A light cream of broccoli soup topped with grated cheese has become a staple in southern lunch spots in the last few years. But the best broccoli soup I've ever eaten was a heartier, spicier brew concocted by Jocelyn Mayfield at her restaurant, Jocelyn's, in Ocean Springs, Mississippi. It had a rich brown broth and a kick of black pepper that imprinted itself firmly on my memory. When I returned home from that trip I went to work in the kitchen to come up with my own version. Here it is and it's perfect anytime broccoli is plentiful.

> 2 full heads of broccoli
>
> 2 cups 2 percent milk
>
> 3 tablespoons butter or margarine
>
> 2 tablespoons flour
>
> 1 teaspoon coarse ground black pepper
>
> 1 quart chicken stock
>
> 1 teaspoon salt

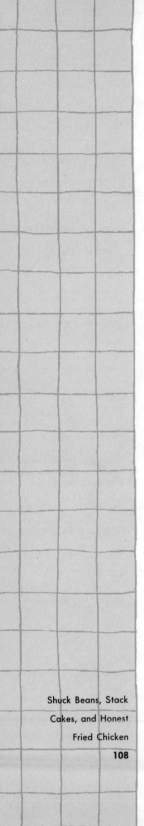

Wash broccoli well and cut off florets. Trim off tough ends, then chop the rest of the stem into small pieces to make about 4 cups. Steam for 15–20 minutes until tender, then puree with milk in blender.

Steam florets for 15 minutes. While they're steaming, melt butter or margarine in a large saucepan and sprinkle in flour mixed with black pepper. Stir over low heat for 10 minutes until it makes a medium-brown roux. Slowly add 4 cups of stock, stirring all the time so flour doesn't lump. Raise heat until liquid is steaming, but not boiling. Add pureed broccoli and when that's hot, add broccoli florets. *Serves 6–8.*

CREAMY EGGPLANT SOUP

This traditional Louisiana soup is like an exotic variation on that good old standby, cream of potato soup. Like most great Creole dishes, its flavor is both subtle and spicy, strange but familiar, and totally delicious.

4 tablespoons butter

1 1/2 cups celery, minced

1 large onion, chopped finely

1 1/2 teaspoons curry powder

1/2 teaspoon dried basil

1 large eggplant

1 large potato

1 quart chicken stock

1/4 teaspoon white pepper

1/2 teaspoon salt

1 cup half and half

Melt butter in a heavy soup pan, then add celery, onion, curry, and basil. Stir, then cover and let simmer over low heat for about 10 minutes. Peel eggplant and potato and dice both. Add to the soup pot, stir and cover again, this time cooking for about 20 minutes. You'll need to stir the mixture several times during this period to keep it from sticking. Add stock, salt, and pepper and bring to a quick bubble, then turn heat down to low, cover, and let simmer for

20 more minutes. When done, remove pot from heat and carefully use a potato masher to puree the vegetables coarsely. Return to low heat and stir in half and half. Let it warm up just a bit, but be careful not to boil. Serve immediately and pass Tabasco for those who want a bit of zip. *Serves about 8.*

COUNTRY VEGETABLE SOUP

"Now where can you go to see the country music stars

Sitting drinking coffee until 4?

Shoney's closed at 9 o'clock

And there's no place else to go.

Nobody eats at Linebaugh's anymore."

"Nobody Eats at Linebaugh's Anymore" by John Hartford

"Nobody Eats at Linebaugh's Anymore," John Hartford's musical lament for a closed restaurant, chronicles the changing of an era in Nashville. In the early 1970s, when the Grand Ole Opry moved from the downtown Ryman Auditorium to a brand new hall in the Opryland theme park out in the city's suburbs, many of the venerable old businesses and performer haunts around the Ryman folded. That included one of Hartford's favorites, Linebaugh's, a late night and early morning gathering place for the old guard.

The move came just as the country music industry began one of its most impressive boom periods, the Urban Cowboy–countrypolitan phase. The subsequent growth of the industry changed not only the area around the Ryman, but the folksy scene that had existed on Music Row.

The Music Row area of some dozen blocks from 15th to 18th streets just south of downtown is where the majority of recording studios and music industry offices have been in Nashville. These days the neighborhood is almost all a business area. But up until the late 1970s, many of the comfortable old bungalows that have now been converted to office space then housed performers, songwriters, and music business folks. And after work was done, the mood in the neighborhood was often that of one big party.

Marie Barrett, who was to later become John's wife, was a single mother living in one of those houses on Music Row and working for Tompall Glaser, the creative executive behind the "Outlaw" scene starring Willie Nelson, Waylon Jennings, Kris Kristofferson, Bobby Bare, David Alan Coe, etc.

"My house was two doors down from Glaser's office—a big old two story. And when everyone found out I could cook, then the doors were open all the time," Marie said. Outside those doors, to the side of the house, was a large vacant lot where a perpetual badminton game seemed to be in progress. Inside the kitchen bubbled a perpetual pot of soup.

"There ain't nobody in the world who can fix vegetable soup better than Marie Hartford," Bobby Bare recalls. "There was a time when Marie's soup is what a bunch of us lived on. And I still think it's about the best soup I've ever had."

Like most country cooks, Marie doesn't use a recipe for her vegetable soup, and no two pots are ever the same since she incorporates whatever ingredients she has on hand when the soup-making spirit strikes.

"There comes a point in making this soup where I just open the refrigerator door and start pulling out whatever leftover vegetables I have in there, or look in the cupboard or the freezer and I start going 'Yeah, that would be good.' And then I just throw in the kitchen sink."

Before she gets to the sink, though, Marie does have a fundamental formula that creates a meaty base that serves as the soup's foundation. Her method of cooking the meat low and slow without first browning it gives a rich broth without depriving the beef itself of flavor. And it yields surprisingly tender meat. Follow the formula, and then follow your own instincts and resources to create a pot of classic country vegetable soup.

1 1/2 pounds of stew beef in small chunks

1 large onion, chopped

water

1 teaspoon Worcestershire sauce

1 large can of tomatoes

1 small can of tomato sauce

1 can of corn

1 can of peas

1/2 cup celery, cut up

2 tablespoons butter substitute

various vegetables

salt and pepper to taste

Put the stew meat and onion in a large, heavy soup pot and cover with water about an inch higher than the meat. Add Worcestershire sauce, bring to a boil, and then immediately turn heat down to a low simmer. Cover and let simmer for one hour.

Add the tomatoes and sauce, crushing the whole tomatoes with your hands. Add corn, peas, celery, and butter substitute, then whatever vegetables your heart desires or you have on hand in about one-cup increments. You can use fresh, canned, frozen, or leftover. Marie says a particularly tasty addition is butter beans—and any kind of cooked, dried bean will give the soup extra resonance. After you've added the vegetables, let the whole thing simmer for another 30 minutes or so while you make Real Cornbread (page 235) to serve with it. Marie says, "You have just got to make cornbread, because to do all that to make the soup and then eat it with crackers would be a sin." *Makes enough to serve a houseful.*

SUMMER VEGETABLE SOUP

Actually, I often make this soup in winter, too, since it's so easy and so tasty. But it's especially good in the summer when zucchini and yellow squash are overabundant (the recipe can be tripled and any extra frozen). It's equally good served hot or chilled.

The recipe is adapted from one I used to make as a cook at the Jefferson

The Longer It Sits, the Better It Gets

"When I was little, I remember eating our big meal early in the day," Brenda Lee recalls.

"We'd have dinner not long after we came home from school, and then Mother would cover everything over with a cloth on the back of the stove and we'd eat on it the rest of the evening. I guess that would scare some of these food experts to death now. They say you're supposed to refrigerate everything so bacteria won't grow. But we didn't have a refrigerator, just an ice box that the ice man brought big cakes of ice for. And mother never did put any food up in it until we were done and ready to go to bed. I don't remember any of us ever getting sick from it, though. And it even seemed like some stuff—the fried chicken for instance—got better the longer it set."

Street Soup Company, now gone from Santa Fe. Pat Greathouse, who originated the recipe there, told me that the secret to its full flavor is in letting the tomatoes and onions simmer together for a while before adding the other ingredients. I've added green peppers to the original recipe, though, and I put them in with the onions and tomatoes so their distinctive taste is also infused in the broth.

3 tablespoons olive oil

1 medium onion

1 clove of garlic

1 bell pepper

2 14 1/2-ounce cans of tomatoes, with juice

1 teaspoon dried basil

1 medium zucchini

1 medium yellow squash

1 can kidney beans

(1 can black-eyed peas, optional)

salt

pepper

cooked macaroni

Parmesan cheese

Put the olive oil in a heavy soup pan and heat on medium low. Peel onion, quarter and slice; crush garlic and add both onion and garlic to the oil, cooking over low heat until the onions soften. Remove stems and seeds from bell pepper (I use yellow ones when I can get them for their color and mild flavor), and quarter and slice. Add to the oil and stir until well coated. Let cook for a few minutes until pepper begins to soften, then add tomatoes, crushing them between your fingers and adding all the juice. Add basil and stir, then cover snugly with a lid and let simmer on very low for about 20 minutes.

Cut off stems and blossom ends, but don't peel the squash. Cut squash in half and slice into crescents about 1/4 inch thick. Add squash and beans to the tomato broth and stir well. (I always use the kidney beans and add the black-eyed peas in the wintertime for a sturdier soup.) Add salt and pepper to taste, cover and let simmer for 30 minutes. If you want it hot, serve now. If you want it chilled, transfer to a glass or ceramic container, cover, and chill in refrigerator for about two hours.

When you're ready to serve, put about 1/4 cup of cooked macaroni (either small shells or elbows) in the bottom of each bowl and cover with the soup. (Don't put the macaroni in the soup until you're ready to serve it, or it will get mushy and make the soup taste starchy the longer it keeps.)

Pass freshly grated Parmesan on the side and serve with crusty bread. *Makes about a dozen servings.*

WINTER VEGETABLE SOUP

Several old Louisiana cookbooks I came across had recipes for meatless Lenten soups with cabbage as their base and a cream broth. While the concept sounded appealing to me, the product never quite lived up to my expectations until it occurred to me to substitute buttermilk for its less tangy cousin. That and grating the carrots and onions are the secret to this soup's wonderful harmony of flavors. The taste is a bit like borscht with sour cream—but more complex and, I think, a bit better.

4 tablespoons butter substitute

1 medium onion

2 stalks celery

4 cups shredded cabbage

1 medium Idaho potato

4 large carrots

1 ten-ounce package frozen chopped spinach

4 cups vegetable or chicken stock

salt and pepper

buttermilk

Melt the butter substitute in a heavy soup pan over medium low heat. Peel onion and dice and chop celery, including leaves. Add to the butter substitute and cook until soft.

Using a knife (not a grater), cut cabbage into thin shreds until you have 4 cups full—about half of a small head. Add to the pot and stir until coated with the butter, then turn heat very low, cover, and simmer while you prepare the rest of the vegetables.

Wash the potato and grate it, skin and all. Peel the carrots and grate them. Add them with the frozen spinach to the pot, mix, cover, and simmer for about 20 minutes, stirring from time to time to keep vegetables from sticking. Add stock, bring to a boil, and then turn heat to low again and simmer for 30 minutes more. Season to taste with salt and freshly ground pepper.

When you're ready to serve, ladle into bowls but not to the brim. Add about 3 tablespoons of buttermilk to each bowl and stir in. (You may want more buttermilk. I usually do—but not everyone will.) *Makes about 10 servings and is especially good with Light Bread (page 248) or Real Cornbread (page 235).*

Soupe a l'Oignon King Louis De Ville

My French cookbook tells me that the original onion soup was invented when King Louis XIV and his entourage found themselves ravenous and stranded in a castle with nothing but onions, butter, and Champagne. Voilà! Out of necessity, a classic soup was born.

Although the story isn't American, it certainly is country, since the art of most down-home cooking is the ability to make the most of what's available. Perhaps that's why onion soup became such a popular dish in kitchens so far removed from France. Almost all cooks have a stash of onions on hand at any given time, and with some butter, a good stock, and a dash of this and dollop of that, a magnificent winter meal can be had.

My own version of onion soup is one created once out of necessity, but kept around and repeated for years out of love for its golden, soothing flavor—a taste I've never encountered in a restaurant version, since those onion soups are too often made from boullion cubes or oversalted canned beef stock. And because it's an Americanized version of something classically French, I've named it after the town I grew up in, which was, after all, named after one of the royal Louises to begin with.

My French cookbook told me proper onion soup must have Champagne or dry white wine, cognac, gobs of butter, meat glaze, and potato flour—all of which I was out of when I set out to make my first pot. Instead, plain flour sat in for the potato flour just fine and apple cider (in the first version, replaced from time to time by sweet vermouth in subsequent renderings) added its own ruby glow to the broth. Good homemade beef and chicken Stock (page 107) are the soul of this soup and, of course, the onions, browned slowly until golden, are its heart.

Serve this on a crisp fall day with a plate of apples, homemade bread, and good cheese.

6 medium onions

4 tablespoons butter

2 cups beef stock

1 tablespoon flour

1 teaspoon dried mustard

1 quart chicken stock

3/4 cup apple cider or sweet vermouth

salt

pepper

6 thick slices of French bread, dried

1 cup grated Gruyère cheese

Peel onions, cut in half lengthwise, and slice 1/2 inch thick. Melt butter in a large, heavy pan and add the onions. Cook them slowly until golden brown over low heat. The process takes approximately 30 minutes and you will need to occasionally stir the onions (gently, don't mush them up) to keep them from sticking and burning.

Toward the end of the onion cooking time, in a separate pan, warm the beef and chicken stock. (If you want a beefier broth for your soup, you can increase the beef stock and decrease the chicken proportionately.)

When the onions are rich and golden, take the pan off the heat. Gradually mix 2 cups of stock with the flour and mustard—I use a whisk to keep the mixture from lumping. Pour over the onions and return to heat, bring to bubbling, and then add the rest of the stock. Bring this to a boil and then turn down and let simmer for 20 minutes, covered. Add vermouth and salt and pepper to taste.

You can serve immediately, but I like to put the whole thing in the refrigerator and let the flavors get cozy with one another overnight before serving. Reheat the soup very gently the next day, being careful not to boil, but to get it good and hot through and through.

If you're using the overnight method, slice pieces of French bread 1/2 inch thick and leave out overnight to dry. If you are eating on the spot (or you forgot to put the bread out), you can simply toast the bread in a 400 degree oven with a little butter on each side until browned.

For each serving, place a piece of bread in the bottom of an ovenproof soup bowl, ladle soup over the top, and sprinkle the grated cheese over that. Pop under a hot broiler until the cheese browns. Serve immediately.

Serves 6.

SEAFOOD CHOWDER O'BRIEN

Curry-seasoned seafood or chicken dishes are a southern tradition. But family food traditions don't just spread from mothers to daughters in a straight line. Fathers, sons, aunts, uncles, grandparents, and cousins all get into the act. Best of all is when a recipe crosses in-law lines.

"I started making this chowder on New Year's Eve, I don't really remember quite when," said Amy O'Brien, mother of country singer-songwriter Tim.

"It's complicated and expensive, but everyone always seemed to like it. I knew it was a success, though, the year Tim's wife Kit called me right before New Year's from Colorado and had me tell her exactly how I made it. Now that's the highest compliment your daughter-in-law is ever going to pay you, to get one of your recipes and duplicate it."

And there's good reason for it as you'll see when you make this sumptuous seafood chowder.

5 cups water

1 small peeled whole onion

1/8 teaspoon salt

2 thick slices lemon

1 small lobster

1 pound small shrimp in shell

1 pound bay scallops or sea scallops, quartered

1 pound firm whitefish

2 cups peeled and diced potatoes

1 pound fresh crabmeat

1/4 pound bacon, diced
2 medium onions, chopped
1 tablespoon curry powder

1 teaspoon salt
2 cups half and half
3 cups milk
1 teaspoon paprika
dash of white pepper

Put water in a large saucepan, add onion, salt, and lemon and bring to a boil. Toss lobster into pot, then add shrimp and turn down, cover and simmer for 15 minutes. Remove seafood and let cool a bit until it can be handled. Remove lobster meat and shrimp, returning shells to the pot and letting them simmer for 30 minutes. Devein shrimp, and cut it and lobster into bite-sized pieces and refrigerate.

Strain stock and discard shells, onion, and lemon. Return stock to the pot on medium heat and add scallops, sole, and potatoes. Cook for 15 minutes. Flake the fish filets with a fork if necessary. Add the crab meat and let simmer.

In a large skillet, brown bacon and then sauté the onion in the grease. Stir in curry powder. Add bacon and curried onions to the chowder, being sure to get all the dregs out of the frying pan and into the soup pot. Toss in the lobster and shrimp. Add cream, milk, paprika, and pepper. Bring almost, but not quite, to a boil, then turn heat to warm until ready to serve. *Serves 8–10 very happy people.*

STONE SOUP

"I dip my cup of soup back from the gurglin', cracklin' cauldron in some train yard," John Hartford sings in his classic "Gentle on My Mind." The words don't just call up the image of a man finding food on the hobo rails. They also tell about the comfort to be found when a community of friends or even

When Tim O'Brien and his sister, Mollie, completed "Take Me Back," their 1988 album of traditional country duets, they decided the cover should have a picture from their childhood—Mollie kissing a pint-sized Tim all decked out in cowboy duds. Their mother, Amy O'Brien, went to her cookbooks to find it. That album-cover shot and this picture of Tim and Mollie helping Amy in their Wheeling, West Virginia, kitchen in 1958 are just two of the many photographs that Amy has squirreled away in her cookbooks.

"I also have lots of little drawings that Tim did when he was a little kid. One I really like is of the clothesline with all the wash hanging on it. It makes me think about that backyard long ago," Amy says.

"I have a lot of things—photos, drawings, little notes the kids wrote—tucked in my cookbooks. It makes such a great surprise. I never know when I open a page if I'm going to run across a picture and have a nice memory."

strangers share in a communal pot and in the process create a "whole" more satisfying than any of its parts.

One of the finest stories in folklore concerns a wandering minstrel who comes to a strange town with nothing but an empty belly, empty cauldron, and a clean and well-worn stone. He fills his pot with water at the town well, builds a tidy fire under it, and as a woman who has come there to get her water watches, he lovingly lays his stone inside it.

"What's that?" she asks.

"Stone Soup," he replies and begins to recount in mouth-watering detail the concoction he plans to dip up from the pot in only a few hours. "All it

needs to make it just right is a couple of potatoes, and I just don't have a one."

Immediately the woman offers to bring him the necessary potatoes if he will share his soup with her later, and he, of course, agrees. And so it goes all through the day as the townspeople come and he tells this one he needs a few carrots, that one a marrow bone, and yet another a bag of onions.

By evening everyone in town has committed something from her or his larder to the pot, and the fragrances of the mingled foods dance in the air merrily, mixing with the sounds of convivial voices.

The musician and burghers eat until they can't take another bite more, noting how much finer this community stew is than any ever made at home alone. And then the minstrel pulls out his fiddle, someone else a mandolin, and yet another a banjo, and the whole town dances until nearly dawn.

When it's over, the town goes to bed satisfied and the minstrel washes his pot, wraps up his stone, and heads down the road for the next meal of Stone Soup.

This recipe is not one for a specific dish, but is instead one for a fine experience. It works best on a chilly fall weekend.

Start with 6–8 cups of good homemade stock. Check your cupboards and refrigerator for further inspiration. Add onions and garlic. Look for a starch—potatoes, rice, barley, macaroni. Add bits of leftover meat or vegetables. How about a can of beans? Think of what else would be good, then start calling friends and see who can come and bring what. When you've got about half a dozen assembled, put everyone's ingredient in the pot, turn it down to simmer, and settle down for an hour or more of playing cards, telling tales, or picking some homemade music.

When the soup in the pot starts to smell so good you can't stand it, make a big skillet of Real Cornbread (page 235), pull out some jars of pickles, or slice some apples. Grate cheese, chop green onions, spoon out some sour cream, and open a bottle of Tabasco so it can be added to the soup as your guests wish. Fill everyone's bowl and settle in to savor the experience of real Stone Soup. Seconds are available.

SOUP BEANS

Navy beans, black beans, red beans, and big dried butter beans can all be made into delicious and delectable soups. But if you say "Soup Beans" to a mountain-raised man or woman, you can mean only one kind—pinto beans cooked soft and tender in a thick, brown, bacon-seasoned broth.

The first autumn pot of beans in my mother's kitchen was the harbinger of winter to me. I'd come home from school and see the little window by the porch steamed opaque from the day-long cooking. Opening the door, I'd be surrounded by the finest smell ever—savory bacon mixed with the beans' own

Renfro Valley Bean Soup

Homer and Jethro had a 40-year career that brought them international fame as country comedians and the respect of their musical peers for their instrumental brilliance.

Guitarist Henry D. "Homer" Haynes died in 1971, and mandolin maestro Kenneth "Jethro" Burns in 1988. Jethro sat for an interview the year before he died and had especially sweet memories of the early days of that career when all it took to make an evening was a good hand of poker and a pot of soup beans.

It was 1939 and the two had just been signed to the Renfro Valley Barn Dance outside of Mount Vernon, Kentucky.

"We lived in Mount Vernon in what was like a boarding house over there. Most everybody else in the cast lived there, too, and it was great—like living in a party.

"Mount Vernon only had a population of about 1,200 or so and after me and Homer had been there for a while, it got so everybody knew us. We'd go downtown to a restaurant there and just walk right on back in the kitchen and take off the lids and look and see what was cooking in the pot.

sweet earthy scent. Add a skillet of hot cornbread and a slab of sweet (or stalk of green) onion on the side, and I'm not the only hillbilly whose eyes mist over with the memory.

> 1 pound dried pinto beans
> water
> 1/2 pound salt pork (also called white bacon)
> 1 small onion
> 1 clove garlic
> salt and pepper to taste

The night before you want to serve them, rinse the dried beans well and pick out any stones or dirt that may have gotten mixed in with them. Put them

Shuck Beans, Stack Cakes, and Honest Fried Chicken

122

"And one time we went up to the bank to see about a loan. We'd seen a car we wanted real bad, but they weren't about to give a couple of performers a loan, you know. But after we'd fooled around with the guy at the bank and carried on and messed with his ink stand and made too many jokes, well, they gave us that loan—I think maybe just to get rid of us.

"And every night up at the boarding house, where we stayed, it was just like a party. Seemed like there was always a big potful of soup beans on the back of the stove in the kitchen, and a big plate of cornbread on the table. And we'd play poker there around the kitchen table—all the guys and some of the girls in the show, too. I tell you, some of those girls were mean poker players.

"And when you'd get hungry, you'd just go over and dip you up a big bowl of beans from that pot. And for old Tennessee mountain boys like Homer and me there wasn't anything we liked better than to have soup beans and cornbread. Seemed like that pot never stopped cooking, day or night. And there was no reason for anybody to throw a party, because the party went on around the clock."

in a big bowl and cover with water about an inch above the beans. Let soak at room temperature overnight.

When you're ready to cook, drain the soaking water off the beans and rinse them lightly again. Put them in a big heavy pot with a lid and cover with water again to about an inch above the beans. Rinse the salt pork and add to the pot along with the whole onion and whole garlic clove, both peeled.

Some folks like to use a ham hock instead of salt pork, and if you've got one from a real country ham, the soup beans will taste mighty good. But my mother always says there's nothing quite like the marriage of flavors between beans and salt pork. The taste is a little sweeter, with a little fuller pinto flavor than it is when you use a ham hock, which tends to dominate the broth. So I save my ham hocks for cooking up navy beans, which don't have as much flavor themselves as pintos.

Bring to a boil and then turn heat down to simmer and cover the pot. Cook at a simmer for about two hours—or until the beans are very soft and breaking open. (Taste one to figure out if they're there yet. Don't just trust your eyes.)

When beans are soft enough, remove the salt pork and onion from the pot. Squeeze the onion to get out all the juice and then throw it out. Set the salt pork aside until it's cooled enough to handle. While you're waiting, put about half a cup of the beans with a little soup in a bowl and mash with the back of a fork until smooth and pasty. Put this back in the pot and stir it around. It will thicken the soup.

When the pork is cool enough to handle, pull all the bits of edible meat from the fat and put them back in the pot. Discard the fat. Taste the beans and soup and add salt and pepper to your satisfaction.

Now pay attention here because this is important. Don't put any salt in the pot until the beans are just as soft as you want them to be when you serve them. If you add the salt sooner, the beans will stop softening and their skins stay just as firm and tough as they were when you put the salt in no matter how many hours you may continue to cook them. So only add the salt when the beans are tender enough.

Turn the heat up just a smidgen—enough so you can see the soup is cooking, but not enough so it's boiling—and cook the beans for at least another half an hour, uncovered.

The absolutely best way to eat beans is with a piece of hot cornbread crumbled up in the bottom of the bowl and lots and lots of bean soup poured on top. Serve raw onion and Deane's Brown Sugar Bread 'n' Butter Pickles (page 340) on the side. *Serves 8–12.*

Pork Shoulder and Beans

Bring up the subject of good cooking with anyone raised in the country and you're sure to stumble on to a great recipe. That's what happened when I told Jackie Sturgeon, who cuts my hair, about this book. He told me about his mother from Meade County and her quintessential country dinner—a meal he says is the best he ever had.

Jo Ann Sturgeon told me that it was her mother who taught her how to make the dish. "It's a kind of hand-me-down," is how she described it.

This is fortifying winter food and although it requires a pressure cooker and takes the better part of a day to cook, its rich and savory taste is well worth it. It must be served with a skillet of Real Cornbread (page 235).

1 pound Great Northern beans

7 cups water

7–8 pound smoked pork shoulder

3 cups water

5 potatoes

2 cups water

1/2 head cabbage

pepper

Have the butcher remove the bone and chop the pork shoulder into fist-sized chunks—but make sure he gives you the bone.

In a large Dutch oven or other big covered cooker, put beans and water and bring to a hearty boil. Remove from heat and let stand for 1 hour.

While beans are standing, put the chopped pork shoulder—fat, bone and all—in a pressure cooker. Add 3 cups water, seal the cooker with gauge set for 15 pounds of pressure, and put on high heat. When gauge begins to rattle incessantly, turn heat down to medium (or until gauge only rattles occasionally) and cook for 40–45 minutes. Remove from heat and cool until cooker can be opened. Meat should fall apart when touched with a fork.

Add 2 cups of the shoulder broth to the bean pot and bring to a boil, then turn to simmer for 90 minutes, until beans are good and tender.

While the beans cook, remove the meat from the broth in the pressure cooker, removing any fat you'd like from the meat and discard bone. Refrigerate both meat and broth.

When beans are tender, add 3 cups of the meat, season with pepper to taste, and let cook a little longer. You won't need any salt. The shoulder will provide enough.

About 30 minutes before the beans are ready, peel the potatoes, cut them in half, and lay them in the bottom of the empty pressure cooker. Add 2 cups of water and 1 cup of the shoulder broth. If your pressure cooker has a basket insert, fill it with half the head of cabbage, coarsely chopped. (Mine doesn't have a basket, so I used a round layer cake pan for the cabbage and let it sit on top of the potatoes.)

Seal the pressure cooker, set gauge to 15 pounds, and cook potatoes and cabbage on medium heat for 15 minutes after gauge begins to rattle.

Put potatoes in one bowl to serve. Put cabbage in another and add 1/2 cup of shoulder broth, 1/2 cup of meat, and a dash of pepper. Serve with big bowls of beans and plenty of cornbread. *Makes enough for 6–8 very hungry people.*

BEEF STEW

When I was little, my favorite play was imagining I was taking a wagon train across Texas. In between attacks by surly Indians I cultivated a budding romance with a trail boss who looked remarkably like Roy Rogers, my favorite singing cowboy.

In those girlhood fantasies I always won my cowboy's heart with my quick wit and cool countenance (even under Indian attack) and by my ability to whip up one good Beef Stew.

I stirred these vats of stew in a black cast-iron cauldron and I imagined the finished product to be sturdy, steaming and fragrant, its fantasized flavors complex yet fundamental—just the thing to charm the most heroically preoccupied cowboy.

But when I grew up and tried to whip up some real beef stew, for a long time none I made lived up to those expectations. None seemed to reach that state where each of its elements is distinct and flavorful, yet all are blissfully married to one another. If the meat was rich and tasty, then the broth and vegetables most likely were not full-bodied enough. Or if the whole was thick and satisfying, its individual ingredients were likely to have lost their distinctive characteristics in the process.

I experimented for a while, adding wines and herbs and tomatoes and strange vegetables to my pot, looking for a dramatic solution. The results were often tasty, always interesting. But I could not shake the vision of my imaginary cowboy taking the spoon from his mouth with a quizzical eyebrow raised, wondering if such Frenchified style as was evidenced by wine-drenched tastes would not be a fatal flaw in a prairie wife.

Nope, what I was after was a stew that was purely American: straightforward on the surface, but with strengths hidden beneath.

I finally hit on the perfect equation, by paring back the stew's ingredients to the basics, but leaving a few tricks in the preparation. The meat in this stew is marinated overnight so that even after long, slow cooking, it retains a lovely, full taste. And the broth is homemade Beef Stock (page 107), giving the stew a hearty body that doesn't require overcooking to build it.

There is nothing fancy in this stew's flavor—but it is full-bodied and fully satisfying. I serve it with a peppermill, Tabasco bottle, and other condiments on the table for anyone who wants to spice it up a bit more. And when my real-life pardner now raises his spoon to his mouth, his eyes crinkle with pleasure as he pronounces this stew, "mighty fine."

MARINADE

1 cup red wine

1 crushed garlic clove

1 teaspoon celery salt

1 bay leaf

1 tablespoon dijon mustard

1 1/2 pounds chuck with fat trimmed, cut in 1-inch cubes

3 tablespoons olive oil

1 onion, chopped

freshly ground pepper

1/4 cup all-purpose flour

1 quart of beef stock

6 medium potatoes with skins, cut in 1-inch cubes

1 pound carrots, peeled and chopped in 3/4-inch-long rounds

The night before, trim fat from chuck and cut into 1-inch cubes. In a glass or crockery dish, mix the wine, garlic clove, celery salt, bay leaf, and mustard. If you don't want to use wine, apple cider is a nice alternative. Add the meat,

"Oh, you'll be soup for

Uncle Sam's Injuns

'It's beef, heap beef,' I

hear them cry.

Git along, git along,

git along little dogies

You're going to be

beef stew by and by.

Whoopee ti yi yo, git

along little dogies,

It's your misfortune

and none of my own;

Whoopee ti yi yo, git

along little dogies

For you know

Wyoming will be

your new home."

Traditional cowboy song

Soups and Stews

pressing down a bit so it is just covered by the liquid. Cover and refrigerate overnight.

(If you don't have beef stock already made, buy a chuck roast with the bone. Use it, with scraps of meat attached, and trimmings to make beef stock according to the recipe on page 107.)

A cowboy on the Texas range in 1946 cooks up a cast-iron kettle of hearty Beef Stew (page 126), just as I dreamed of doing as a child.

When you are ready to make the stew, heat 3 tablespoons of olive oil in a large, heavy pot with a lid. Drain the meat, reserving all the liquid in the refrigerator. Add meat to the hot oil, browning it on all sides. Don't crowd the meat. If your stew pot isn't large enough to accommodate it all at once, brown in batches then return all the meat to the pot.

Add the chopped onion and several grinds of fresh black pepper. Turn heat down and cook until onions are translucent, stirring occasionally to keep from burning. Sprinkle 1/4 cup of flour over meat and onions, and stir to flavor the flour and keep it from sticking. Add 1 quart of stock quickly, cover, and let simmer for 1 hour.

Wash and cut 6 medium potatoes into 1-inch pieces (leave skins on) and add to pot, stirring to distribute throughout. Cover and simmer for an additional hour.

Peel and cut 1 pound of carrots into 3/4-inch-long rounds. Add to pot along with reserved marinade liquid. Simmer one more hour. Taste and add salt and pepper as desired. Serve with Freedom Bread (page 254) and Cobbler (page 291) for dessert. *Makes enough for 6.*

Country's Queen and the King of the Cowboys

The first time I interviewed Loretta Lynn I discovered we had something in common beyond our eastern Kentucky roots. She, too, had harbored a girlhood crush on the King of the Cowboys, Roy Rogers. And the year she was nominated for induction into the Country Music Hall of Fame—1988—Rogers was also a nominee. Before the awards show Loretta confessed that she would prefer her hero to win instead of her.

"Oh, Lord, I just love him," she said breathlessly. "I've always thought he was so handsome, even when I was a little girl. And I think that's partly why I fell in love with my husband. I've always thought Doo and Roy look just alike."

Loretta's dream came true when both she and Rogers were chosen for the honor that year.

BEEF AND CORNMEAL DUMPLING STEW

Dumplings are a clever way to get more eating out of the stew pot. Most are made of bland little balls or pinches of flour dough that take on the flavor of the stew as they simmer in its broth. But Cornmeal Dumplings, a mountain delicacy, bring their own special flavor to the dance. Golden and grainy, their taste is unforgettable when paired with savory shredded beef.

BEEF

3-pound shoulder roast with marrow bone

salt

pepper

1 medium onion

2 stalks celery

1 carrot

water

DUMPLINGS

1/2 cup cornmeal

1/4 teaspoon salt

1/8 teaspoon baking powder

1/8 teaspoon baking soda

1/4 cup boiling beef broth

1 egg

flour

To accommodate the roast and to make the dumplings right, you'll need a wide-topped cooking pot with a lid—a Dutch oven will do fine.

Trim fat from meat and reserve. Set pot on high heat and when it's good and hot, put in the fat and render it until you have about 2 tablespoonfuls in the pan. Discard the fat.

Rub all sides of the meat with salt and pepper and place in hot fat, then turn down to medium and brown well on all sides. As it browns, use a teaspoon to scoop marrow from the center of the bone and drop that in the pan to "brown" also.

Peel and cut onion in half and when the roast is well browned, lay the onion, cut sides down, on top of the roast. Wash and trim celery and lay on top of the roast along with peeled carrot. Pour water into the pot to cover the roast and vegetables; turn the heat to low and simmer for 2 hours.

When meat is tender, remove and set aside to cool. Put cooked onion, celery, and carrot into a strainer and press with the back of a spoon to get all the juices out and back into the pot. Discard the pressed vegetables.

Now it's time to make the dumplings.

Bring broth in pot to a boil. While you're doing that, mix meal, salt, baking powder, and soda in a bowl. Extract 1/4 cup boiling broth from the stewpan and turn the heat down to low so the liquid will now start to simmer. Pour the 1/4 cup of broth into the cornmeal and mix it up well. Add 1 egg and mix it in, then add enough flour to make a dough that you can just handle.

Pat dough together lightly and pinch off pieces to roll lightly into balls about 1 inch in diameter. This should make 1 dozen dumplings.

Handle the dough very lightly and don't press together too hard. Drop the dumpling balls into the liquid which is now just simmering, cover, and let cook for 12 minutes. Don't take the top off the pot while the dumplings are cooking.

While they do, though, you should pull the meat from the roast with a fork, "shredding" it. Either divide the meat evenly into 6 serving bowls or place in a large tureen for serving at the table.

As soon as dumplings are ready, lay on top of the beef in serving bowls or tureen, two to a customer. Ladle lots of hot broth over the top. *Serves 6 and tastes great with Jerry's Slaw (page 216).*

JAMBALAYA

Hank Williams's wife, Miss Audrey, has said "Jambalaya" was inspired by a trip of nonstop eating through Louisiana in the late '40s. This paean to life and cooking on the bayou is surely justified, for the country cooking of Louisiana's Acadian and Creole cultures is worth singing about.

The haute cuisine of New Orleans is one thing, but the hefty, hearty cooking of Cajun country as it's practiced up in the bayous and prairies that surround Lafayette, Louisiana, is something else. Rough and rich and made from the elements at hand, it's as different from its big city cousin as the fleet-fiddle, chanky-chank dance music of Cajun country is from the Crescent City's jazz. Both Cajun music and Cajun cooking are linked to American country traditions—although with a distinctive swamp-French flavor all their own.

Jambalaya is an inspired tribute to the frontier art of "making do"—and of making something delicious with whatever is at hand. This version is made from leftover Country Ham (page 27), but if you don't have any ham remnants substitute andouille or another hot, smoky sausage. In fact, just about any meat will do in jambalaya as long as you like it.

With the pride typical of the defenders of most regional cuisines, Cajuns argue interminably over what constitutes real jambalaya and how it is to be put together. About the only thing everyone agrees on is that his or her mother makes absolutely the best. This version makes no claims to be "authentic," "the best," or better than any Thibodeaux's mama's. It's just mine, and it's good.

3 cups water

1 1/2 cups brown rice

dash of salt

1 tablespoon olive oil

1 onion, chopped

2 bell peppers, chopped

3 stalks celery, chopped

1 teaspoon ground cayenne

1 teaspoon black pepper

2 cups broth

14 1/2-ounce can chopped tomatoes

1 pound country ham or other flavorful meat, shredded

1 tablespoon thyme vinegar

Bring water to boil in heavy saucepan, add rice and salt, stir once, then cover with a close-fitting lid and let simmer for 45 minutes until rice is done. When it is, heat the olive oil in a large pan and toss in the onion, bell peppers, and celery—cooking them lightly, just to coat with oil. Add the cooked rice, spices, broth, and tomatoes and bring the mix quickly to a boil, then turn the heat down to simmer. Mix in the country ham and thyme vinegar and let the flavors cohabitate on low heat for about 20 minutes, stirring occasionally to keep it from sticking. Add water if it's needed, but the finished product should be thick and viscous, not soupy. *Serves 6 as main course and tastes mighty good with a green onion, sweet pickle, and dash of Tabasco in accompaniment.*

CHICKEN AND SAUSAGE GUMBO

If jambalaya is the art of making much with little, gumbo is a celebration of abundance. During Mardi Gras in Cajun country, the "Courir du Mardi Gras"—bands of costumed men on horses—ride through the countryside demanding booty from every household.

The costumes range from elaborate silk outfits bought in the store to rough homemade masks of dyed feathers, or made from window screen pieces molded and painted to resemble a face.

Women in the households visited by the riders hand up live chickens, hot sausages, vegetables, and rice to be used to make a huge community gumbo. And that night everyone—courir and housewife, grandmas and tiny tots—gather together to feast and dance.

There are as many variations on the gumbo themes as there are versions of the Cajun national anthem, "Jolie Blonde." Many use filé—sassafras root—to thicken and flavor, but this one gets its thickness just from the roux.

2 tablespoons olive oil

12 ounces andouille, chorizo, or other hot sausage

1/4 cup flour

2 quarts stock

14 1/2-ounce can chopped tomatoes

2 cups chopped onions

1 cup chopped bell peppers

1 cup chopped celery

2 cups fresh or frozen okra, sliced in 1/4-inch rounds

1 tablespoon salt

2 cloves garlic, mashed

2 tablespoons cayenne pepper

2 tablespoons black pepper

3 cups cooked chicken or turkey meat, skins and bones removed

1 pint shucked oysters

4 cups cooked white rice

Heat olive oil in a large soup kettle and brown the sausage. If you are using andouille, or a "solid" sausage, you can cut it into bite-sized chunks and brown. But if you are using a crumbly sausage like chorizo, you'll want to brown it whole, then cut it into chunks later. When the sausage is browned, remove from the oil and set aside while you make roux.

Turn the heat very low, add the flour to the oil and sausage drippings in the pan, then stir it slowly over very low heat for a long time, about 20 minutes, until the paste is a dark chocolate color. When the paste is browned, gradually add the stock, still stirring.

Add the rest of the ingredients to the stock, including the cut-up sausage —but not the oysters or rice. Bring the whole mixture to a boil while stirring, then turn the heat low and let it simmer for at least an hour. The vegetables should be well cooked and the broth nice and thick. Like most stews, this one is best if you can let it sit in the refrigerator overnight before serving.

When you are ready to serve, heat the gumbo thoroughly (if it's been refrigerated), add the oysters and cover the pot to let them simmer for 10 minutes, or until the edges of the oysters curl in appetizing doneness. Ladle the gumbo over about 1/2 cup of cooked rice for each person and serve with Tabasco sauce on the table for those who like it hot. *Serves 8–10 and is wonderful accompanied by crusty French bread.*

KENTUCKY BURGOO

If gumbo is the national stew of Cajun country, burgoo is the stew of Kentucky. And like gumbo and jambalaya, burgoo sparks plenty of arguments among its fans—not only about who makes the best, but also over where the stew and its name originally came from.

One theory holds that the word was used for a porridge eaten by British sailors in the 1700s and eventually made its way inland to become the name for this meat and vegetable stew. Others say that "burgoo" is the mispronunciation of either "bird stew" or "barbecue" (often made and served with burgoo). One charming story suggests that the mispronunciation was coined when an early, too-enthusiastic eater burned his tongue on a steaming spoonful of the stew.

Burgoo's origin is equally vague. Some credit the French with originating the basic concept (and theorize that "burgoo" is an Americanization of the French "ragout").

Scottish and Irish cooks also made a similar stew as did American Indians. Brunswick Stew from North Carolina is similar and surely an antecedent. But burgoo is so ubiquitous around the bluegrass state at county fairs, political picnics, church socials, and music festivals that it has come to be known as Kentucky Burgoo.

It was Gus Jaubert, a Frenchman famed as a cook around Lexington, Kentucky, who was first dubbed the Burgoo King. Legend has it that he cooked thousands of gallons of the stew for the Confederacy's General John Hunt Morgan and his raiders. More legend says that when he died, J. T. Looney, another Lexington cook, inherited both Jaubert's pot and his title. Colonel E. R. Bradley named a colt after Looney (who was a popular chef on the bluegrass horsey circuit) and in 1932 Burgoo King won the Kentucky Derby.

Traditionally burgoo was made with squirrel meat as an ingredient, but woodland squirrels are pretty hard to come by these days so this recipe just uses chicken, beef, and pork. In the barbecue-mutton realms of western Kentucky, burgoo often has lamb in it and a deep, thick barbecue sauce like broth. Here I use lamb bone or oxtail for just a hint of the musty flavor and the broth is lighter.

vegetable oil

1 pound beef, cut in stew-sized chunks

1 pound pork, cut in stew-sized chunks

1 2-pound chicken

1 medium onion, peeled

6 sticks of celery

1 lamb bone (left over from roast lamb is fine) or oxtail

2 28-ounce cans of tomatoes, chopped

1 10-ounce box frozen lima beans

1 10-ounce box frozen green beans

1 10-ounce box frozen okra

1 16-ounce bag of frozen shoepeg corn

16 ounces canned green chilies (not jalapeños) or 2 green bell peppers, chopped

1 very large onion, diced

1 bay leaf

1 tablespoon Worcestershire sauce

salt

pepper

Old Bay Seasoning

Burgoo, like most stews, is best after a day or so of cogitation and foment. Consequently, the first thing I do when I decide to make a vat is to clear a big place in the refrigerator for a 3-gallon stew pot to sit overnight.

The day before you are going to serve the burgoo, heat the pot, then put enough vegetable oil in the bottom to keep meat from sticking. Brown the beef and pork in the oil, then remove the meat from the pot and set aside in the refrigerator.

Add 3 quarts of water to the pot and drop in the whole chicken (including neck and giblets), onion, and 6 celery stalks (washed). Bring water to a boil, then lower heat and simmer for 1 hour.

Remove chicken from the pot and, after it's slightly cooled, remove all the usable meat from the carcass and set aside with the pork and beef. Return the skin, bones, and remaining parts of chicken to the stew pot along with the lamb bone or oxtail. Simmer for at least another hour, skimming residue from the top of the pot occasionally. Then remove bones, skin, onions, and celery from the broth and return chicken, beef, and pork to the pot.

Add the vegetables, bay leaf, Worcestershire and then add salt, pepper, and Old Bay Seasoning to taste. Be inventive if you feel like it—adding other vegetables, meats, and spices that you like. Let the whole thing simmer for at least another hour, then remove from heat, let cool a bit, and put in the refrigerator overnight. Reheat thoroughly the next day and serve with crusty French rolls or Hot Water Cornbread (page 237). Makes enough for a small army or a houseful of relatives *(about 2 dozen servings)*.

New Year's Stew

"I don't know where that old superstition started, or why. But it's a southern belief that every New Year's Eve you have to have black-eyed peas. And my mother, being a great southern cook, cooked up a big pot of black-eyed peas every New Year's Day I knew," Brenda Lee recalls.

We abide by that tradition in our house also. But over the years it's seemed to me to be at cross purpose to spend the day vowing to good resolutions such as "Lose ten pounds for sure" and "Cut down on saturated fat" while all the while I keep dipping out of a big pot of black-eyed peas simmering along with a fat, salty ham hock. So a few years ago I came up with a leaner alternative with chicken. It's become a favorite among family and friends and is now our traditional New Year's meal.

2 cups dried black-eyed peas

3 cups water

1 garlic clove

2 cups chicken stock

2 tablespoons olive oil

1 pound skinless, boneless chicken

1 onion, chopped

1 red bell pepper, chopped

1 cup red wine

1 teaspoon salt

1/4 teaspoon black pepper

1/4 teaspoon crushed rosemary

3 cups cooked rice

Rinse and sort black-eyed peas. Put them in a heavy saucepan with lid, add water and the peeled clove of garlic. Bring to a boil, then turn heat to simmer, cover and cook until peas are tender—about 30 minutes. Add the chicken broth and simmer for 20 minutes more while you prepare the following.

Heat a heavy Dutch oven on medium-high flame, add olive oil and brown the chicken, which has been cut into bite-sized pieces. When browned, remove from the pot and set aside. Put chopped onion and bell pepper into the oil and drippings and sauté until well coated with it.

Remove from heat and pour in the cup of wine. Return chicken to the pan and dump the black-eyed peas in. Sprinkle with salt, pepper, and rosemary and stir to mix well. Pop into 350 degree oven and bake covered for 1 hour. Serve over rice. *Makes enough for 6 to greet the New Year.*

SLUMGULLION

Ground beef was an inexpensive way to get a little meat to go a long way. Just as most mamas created their own distinctive meat loaf recipe, most also cooked their own variation of a hamburger stew. Augmented by rice, potatoes, or macaroni, flavored with other vegetables (some of which a picky-eating child would disdain otherwise) and served hot from a great big pot, these inventive dishes were not only inexpensive, they were often delicious. Perhaps that's why when I interviewed performers they often cited a simple hamburger stew as one of their favorite family dishes.

Grace Rainwater, Brenda Lee's mother, called her stew Spanish Rice. Hamburger Chowder is what Polly Rideout, Naomi Judd's mother and Wynonna's grandmother, calls hers. And both Ruth Ann Rankey and her mother, Earlene Tibbs, made a hamburger and bean concoction that Dwight Yoakam remembers fondly as "West Virginia Chili."

My mother called her humble hamburger dish Slumgullion, although she's not exactly sure why.

"I must have heard it somewhere and it seemed like a good description."

The American Heritage Dictionary says "slumgullion" has old German roots and now is a slang term for "a watery meat stew." But those would have been fighting words around our house if anyone had described Mother's slumgullion as such—especially if my cousin Armand Hamelin (better known as Ham) had been there. Ham, an Army sergeant who'd grown up in Massachusetts, married into our family in the mid-1950s and had eaten in some of the nicest restaurants in the world.

But just as it had been love at first sight when he met my cousin Billy, so it was love at first bite when he dipped into my mother's Slumgullion. They'd come by our house after having dinner out somewhere, but my mother—who's never let a visitor pass through her doorway without feeding them something—insisted Ham have just a bite of the Slumgullion she was putting on the table. Three helpings and a couple of servings of mashed potatoes later, my mother was saying she was awful glad he hadn't been hungry to begin with because she didn't think she'd have had enough to feed him.

Ham still requests this dish every time he gets near my mother's kitchen. And although it shares many of the same ingredients with that ubiquitous cafeteria dish, Johnny Marzetti (don't ask me where that name comes from), I guarantee you that my mother's is a sure sight finer.

The secret is not in any special ingredient, but in the way she cooks the macaroni: coating it first with onion-and-pepper-flavored oil, then letting it cook in the juices of the stew, not boiling it separately in water and adding it later as many similar recipes call for.

2 tablespoons olive oil
1 medium onion, diced
1 medium bell pepper, diced
1 cup elbow macaroni
1 pound ground beef
1   14 1/2-ounce can whole tomatoes
water
salt and pepper to taste

In a large, heavy pot with lid, heat olive oil over medium high heat, then add onions, green pepper, and uncooked macaroni. Sauté, stirring, until all ingredients are coated with the oil, and the onions and green pepper are just beginning to get soft.

Crumble the ground beef into the vegetables and cook it over medium high heat until it's no longer red. Add the can of tomatoes, crushing the tomatoes first between your fingers. Add a can of water, stir, and turn the heat to simmer. Cover and cook until the macaroni is soft—usually 30–45 minutes. Keep an eye on the pot while cooking, stirring occasionally to keep from sticking. Add a little water if necessary. When macaroni is nice and tender, but not disintegrating, season with salt and pepper to taste. Serve with Mashed Potatoes (page 179). *This makes enough to feed 6, unless one of them is my cousin Ham, in which case you'd better double the recipe.*

MYSTERY RAGOUT

Amy O'Brien's signature hamburger dish was something of a literary invention.

"It was one summer when Tim and Mollie were home and we all read this mystery novel. I don't remember much about the book except that it involved a bunch of students living in a house and the clue to the murder was a ragout that all the suspects made, but everybody made it a little bit differently. They figured out that whoever had made the ragout on the night of the murder was the perpetrator and then they figured out who it was because of the ingredients. I think the murderer favored lots of onion.

"So we finished reading this book together one afternoon and then the three of us drove out to see the Gem of Egypt. It was a big coal stripping machine they'd just brought into Wheeling and could strip more coal than anything you'd ever seen. We were just wiling away the time in the summer and having fun. When we were driving back, I said, 'You know, I think I'll try to make that Mystery Ragout for dinner tonight.' And the kids were all excited and everybody has been pretty crazy about it since.

"You can make it in the proportions you want, you know. A little more of this or a little less of that depending on what you like. I like to put lots of onion in it," she said, with only a slightly wicked gleam in her eye.

This ragout tastes better than you'd deduce just from reading the ingredients. The bacon melds with the burger to make a tasty "mystery meat." But be sure to keep an eye on the pot while it cooks because it can burn easily.

6 strips bacon

3/4–1 pound of ground chuck

2 cups thin-sliced red potatoes

2 cups grated carrots

1 cup thin-sliced onion

salt and pepper to taste

Use a heavy, wide pot with a lid, and line the bottom and about 1 inch up the sides of the pot with bacon strips. Crumble the ground chuck over that (use 80 per cent lean chuck instead of regular to cut down on the amount of saturated fat). Wash potatoes, but don't peel them. Cut them in half and then cut each half in very thin slices. Layer these over the chuck. Sprinkle grated carrots over potatoes and lay very thin-sliced onion rings over the carrots. Sprinkle salt and several grinds of black pepper over the whole thing. Put on the lid, set on a burner turned to medium low and cook for 30–45 minutes until done. Begin checking to make sure it doesn't burn after 25 minutes or so. *Serves 4.*

Willie's Chili

To Willie Nelson, born in Abbott, Texas, in 1933, chili has but one definition:

" . . . Great Depression chili, the greasy red ambrosia that used to cost a dime a bowl with all the soda crackers you wanted. Dish of pinto beans on the side. Jar of jalapeño peppers on the table next to a bowl of chopped white onions. Not a trace of tomatoes or celery or other foreign objects that over the years have drifted into what people who don't know better call chili. Chili was invented in South Texas as a dish to make tough, stringy beef taste good, and sold by vendors on the streets of San Antonio before the Battle of the Alamo in 1836. Chili is a serious matter to any native-born Texan old enough to remember when a ten-cent bowl of red would keep you feeling feisty all day." (from *Willie: An Autobiography,* by Willie Nelson, Simon & Schuster, 1988)

TEXAS CHILI

This recipe fits Willie Nelson's definition of real chili (page 141) to a T for Texas.

By the way, the ground red chili powder called for in this and the following chili recipes is not a commercial chili powder blend with other spices like you often see in groceries. It's instead pure, ground red chili—preferably from northern New Mexico—with nothing else added. Some of these recipes call for pinto beans and you can use canned ones or—much better—make your own according to the recipe for Soup Beans (page 121). Others use kidney beans, which you can buy canned.

> 2 pounds chuck, cut in 1-inch cubes
>
> 1 1/2 teaspoons olive oil
>
> 1/4 cup ground red chili
>
> 3 cloves garlic, chopped
>
> 1 teaspoon dried coriander leaves
>
> 1 1/2 teaspoons cumin
>
> 1/2 teaspoon salt
>
> 1 cup water
>
> 2 cups beef broth (or substitute 1/2 cup flat beer for part of broth)
>
> 4 cups cooked pinto beans
>
> 1 jar sliced jalapeños
>
> 1 white onion, chopped finely

In a heavy pan with a lid, heat oil over medium, then add beef and brown, stirring occasionally to keep from sticking. While it's browning put chili, garlic, coriander, cumin, and salt in a blender with water and blend well.

When the meat is browned, add the chili sauce and cook, stirring and scraping the bottom of the pan for about 5 minutes more. Add the broth (or broth and beer) and bring to a boil. Turn the heat down and simmer for an hour. Sauce should thicken to the consistency of heavy cream. If it starts to get thicker, add water.

When you're ready to serve, heat pinto beans and serve them on the side along with dishes of jalapeño and onion. Have all the soda crackers you want—unless, of course, you would really rather have flour tortillas. Even Willie wouldn't fault you for that. *Serves 12–15.*

Hell-Fire and Chili

One man's chili can be another man's culture shock.

Dwight Yoakam left his home in Columbus, Ohio, and set out to make his fortune in country music in 1977. His first stop was Nashville, where the recording industry executives told him his hillbilly twang was too country for commercial country music. His next stop was the Southwest. He landed in southern California tired and homesick.

"I went into a restaurant and sat down to order, and I looked at that menu and I thought, 'Boy, chili'd be good!' You know, that was something we had up at home a lot. It was hot and comforting—a soup my mother made. And that's what I thought I was asking for.

"But then they brought out this stuff looked like some kind of beef paste and it was hotter than *fire.* And all of a sudden I was hollering: 'My Lord, have mercy!'

"My lips burned, my tongue burned, my throat burned. Everything burned. Everything thereafter connected to it burned. I had two bites and I ordered something else. That wasn't chili. Not like the chili mother and my granny made."

"Money was scarce
  and times was bad
The groceries mighty
  plain.
Was it to do over
  boys,
I'd live them times
  again."
"Uncle" by Norman
Blake

Soups and Stews

143

CINCINNATI CHILI

As Dwight Yoakam's chili tale (page 143) proves, there can be more than one definition of the word. And different regions of the country have developed some distinctive chili styles.

In the southern Ohio town of Cincinnati and surrounding northern Kentucky, the basic chili building block is the "three-way": an exotically spiced chili meat mixture heaped on cooked spaghetti and topped with cheese. Order a "four-way" and you get the "three-way" with chopped onions on top; "five-way" means they add kidney beans to a "four-way."

If you want the beans, but not the onions, you say, "Gimme a five-way, hold the onions."

If you don't care about beans, want the onions and think spaghetti has got no business in a bowl of chili, you say, "Gimme a four-way, hold the spaghetti." You can get it any way you want, but you can get mighty confused in the process. Better to make this recipe in the safety of your own home. It serves 6 many ways, including amply.

2 28-ounce cans of tomatoes

1 pound ground beef

1 pound ground pork

2 onions, chopped

1 1/2 teaspoons white vinegar

1 teaspoon Worcestershire sauce

2 tablespoons ground red chili

1 tablespoon ground cayenne

2 teaspoons ground cumin

2 cloves garlic, crushed

1 teaspoon ground cardamom

1 teaspoon ground coriander seed

1 teaspoon ground cinnamon

1 tablespoon cocoa powder

1 1/2 teaspoons salt

cooked thin spaghetti (8 ounces dry)

1 1/2 cups grated cheddar cheese

1 white onion, finely chopped

3 cups cooked kidney beans

Puree the tomatoes and their juice in a blender. Place the meat, onions, and tomato puree in a deep pan with a lid and mix together lightly. Cook over low heat until the meat turns brown, then add vinegar, Worcestershire, seasonings, and spices. Cover pot and simmer for 3 hours—stirring occasionally to keep from sticking. If you prepare this the day before and refrigerate, you can skim the chilled fat off the top the next day before re-heating and serving.

To serve, cook and drain thin spaghetti, figuring half as much per person than you would make for a spaghetti dinner. Chop onion and heat kidney beans. In big bowls, put a serving of spaghetti, then heap chili on top. Let each person add cheese, onions, and beans as they choose. Have Tabasco ready for die-hards. It's traditional to eat this with oyster crackers. *Serves 6.*

GREEN CHILI PORK STEW

In New Mexico, where I lived for half a dozen very good years, there are many interpretations of chili. This one uses chunks of pork and is more like a hearty meat and vegetable stew than the ground beef mélange that is often called chili.

This recipe calls for canned green chili peppers because that is how they are most easily found east of the Mississippi. But if you can get fresh New Mexican green chilies (the best!) or California Anaheims, do. You will need half a dozen and you will need to roast and peel them.

During the peeling process, be careful not to touch your face or eyes, since the juices of the chili are very caustic. Wash your hands carefully when you are finished.

Roast chilies by placing them on a cookie sheet underneath the broiler. When the skin begins to brown, blister, and pop, turn them to an unexposed side and broil again until skin is charred or blistered all over. It takes 1–2 minutes per side, and you should be careful not to burn the flesh of the chilies.

Place chilies in a brown paper bag, close, and let them steam for about 5 minutes. Remove and rub chilies lightly between the hands to loosen the skins. They should peel easily. Some people prefer to hold them under cool running water to aid the process.

Remove stems and seeds, dice the chilies, and add to stew as directed for canned chilies. Remember to wash the cutting board well after using.

1 tablespoon oil

2 1/2 pounds pork, cut in bite-sized chunks

2 yellow onions, coarsely chopped

3 large cloves garlic, crushed

3 teaspoons ground red chili

1 teaspoon ground cumin

1 teaspoon crushed dried coriander leaves

2 28-ounce cans of tomatoes

5 medium potatoes (with skins), cubed

1/2 teaspoon salt

5 4-ounce cans chopped green chilies

2 cups water

2 corn tortillas

Brown meat in the oil over medium heat. Add onions and garlic and cook until onions are soft. Sprinkle ground chili, cumin, and coriander over the meat and heat for 5 minutes, stirring so it doesn't stick.

Add tomatoes and their juice, breaking up the tomatoes into small pieces. Add potatoes, salt, and green chilies with any juices from the can (or cutting board, if using fresh). Tear tortillas in small pieces into blender with water and blend until tortillas are pulverized. Add to stew, mix well, bring to a boil, then turn heat down and simmer for an hour. Stir occasionally to keep from sticking. Serve with thick flour tortillas. *Enough for 8.*

CHILI BUNS

Down in Corbin, Kentucky, where I was born, there's an altogether different kind of chili that they make and serve up as Chili Buns.

These are not to be confused with either bowl chili or chili dogs, two treats usually associated with healthy outdoor events like firehouse chili cook-offs, church suppers, baseball games, or amusement parks.

Chili buns were born in sin, in the pool halls of southeastern Kentucky. They have little redeeming social or nutritional value to commend them—except that they are one of the best-tasting things you'll ever put in your mouth.

The ultimate chili bun—says my mother, the ultimate chili-bun connoisseur—was made at Nevels Pool Hall in Corbin, Kentucky, in the 1930s. She suspects they maybe added a little pool chalk to the mix as a secret ingredient. She's always sworn there were none better—nor hotter.

"Those chili buns were so hot they could make the sweat pop out on your upper lip," she says. But she also says this version, made with hot, homemade chili powder "is pretty darn near as good" as the legendary Nevels'.

1 quart cheap beer

7 pounds ground chuck

1 pound ground pork

3 teaspoons salt

2 cloves minced garlic

3 onions, chopped finely

5 tablespoons ground red chili

3 tablespoons ground cumin

1 tablespoon dried coriander leaves

3 cloves garlic, minced

16 soft hot dog buns

yellow mustard

1 white onion, chopped finely

A few hours before you are ready to make the chili (or the night before) open the beer and let it go flat. When you are ready to cook, put the meat into a large, unheated kettle and mix the burger and pork together lightly. Take care not to compress the meat with your fingers. Chili bun chili shouldn't have lumps like bowl chili, but should cook down to a fine, mealy grain.

Sprinkle the salt, garlic, and onions over the meat and pour flat beer over all. Again, mix lightly, taking care not to compress. (It's easiest if you use your hands.)

Turn the burner up to high and stir the mixture until it begins to boil, taking care none sticks to the bottom of the pan. Then turn the heat to medium low and cook for 90 minutes, stirring occasionally to prevent from sticking.

After that time, mix the spices well together (I put them in a small blender cup and whir until the garlic is pulverized); then sprinkle them over the chili. Turn the heat down very low and let them seep in for about 10 minutes.

Chowl of Billy

Sam Bush broke just about every bluegrass musical tradition as a hard-picking, electrified, rock-and-roll-influenced teen prodigy in the early 1970s. Brilliant on both mandolin and fiddle, this western Kentucky boy became the driving force of the progressive bluegrass movement that reshaped the bluegrass sound for a new generation.

But there was one tradition of bluegrass Bush always held to—that's the time-honored rite of nurturing the next generation of musicians. One bitter winter night in 1979 he drove about 25 miles through a furious snowstorm to Westport, Kentucky, because he'd promised to show a few licks to a hot-picking kid he'd heard about.

Phil Wakeman Jr. was only ten years old the night Bush showed up at his house, nose frozen and mandolin case in hand.

"I was shocked," he said. "I mean, there was my idol, my musical God standing in the living room. So I did the only logical thing. I shook his hand, excused myself and ran

While they're seeping, you can wrap 8 buns in aluminum foil and heat them briefly in the oven. They should be just a bit crisp on the outside, but very soft inside. You want inexpensive hot dog buns for this chili, not something with a classy French crust chew.

Turn the heat up high under the chili and cook for 10 minutes, stirring constantly to mix the spices in well. The result should be moist and juicy, but not at all soupy.

Sprinkle onion down the center of each bun and paint a thin swatch of yellow mustard (not dijon, but "ballpark") down one side. Pack the chili into the bun tightly (these are not sloppy joes) by placing a heaping spoonful in the center of the bun and then packing and smoothing it firmly with the back of the spoon. Build up and out to the ends from there, packing well.

Top with chopped onion.

Heat the rest of the buns while you eat the first round, and repeat the process. *Makes enough for two buns each for 8.*

upstairs and cleaned my whole room top to bottom."

Eventually Phil and Sam settled down for a mandolin lesson. But Phil wasn't the only one in the house flustered by Bush's presence.

Phil Senior and his wife, Deane Patton, were also knocked out that Bush was there.

"I kept thinking, 'Oh, wow, here's this star right in our living room playing mandolin with our kid,' " Deane said.

"But I thought I was being pretty cool about the whole thing. And I'd made this big pot of chili that day and I was real proud of it and I thought that I'd be very gracious and offer Sam some. So I walk over and say, 'Sam, are you hungry? How about a nice hot chowl of billy?'

"And, of course, don't you know, chowl of billy is what everybody's called it in our family since."

VEGETABLES AND SIDE DISHES

COUNTRY COOKED GREEN BEANS WITH NEW POTATOES

BEANS IN BROWN SAUCE

SHUCK BEANS

CREAMED CORN

SUMMER CORN PUDDING

WINTER CORN PUDDING

ROAST CORN WITH BACON

GOOD GRITS

CHEESE GRITS

CORNMEAL MUSH

GRILLED ASPARAGUS

OKRA SUCCOTASH

SUCCOTASH

SPECKLED BUTTER BEANS

LONE OAK SQUASH CASSEROLE

RATATOUILLE

MASHED POTATOES

COLD TATER CAKES

HOME FRIES

CORNMEAL HOME FRIES

CAJUN POTATOES

YAMMY PUDDING

FRIED GREEN TOMATOES

GREEN TOMATO CASSEROLE

TOMATO PIE

GREENS WITH POT LIKKER

HEALTHY, HEARTY GREENS

SKILLET SPINACH

FRIED APPLES

NATURALLY CARAMEL CARROTS

GRILLED CABBAGE

COUNTRY COOKED GREEN BEANS WITH NEW POTATOES

Sometimes on summer afternoons at my aunts' house in Corbin, Kentucky, the haul from the garden would be piles of white half-runner beans and all the women in the house would gather on the back porch to string them. As the ladies did, they drank from tumblers of iced tea with plenty of sugar and lemon and they talked. The clink of the ice and the rhythmic snap of the beans would counterpoint the low, melodious east Kentucky cadencies to make summer music. I got my own little lapful of beans on these occasions and felt quite the grown-up when they, too, went in the pot for dinner later on that evening.

I still get a glow of pride when I look at the first pot of summer beans, neatly broken and strung. The job isn't tedious to me, but is instead sweetly calming with a natural rhythm best underscored by the creak of a porch swing or rocking chair. First I gently snap one end—just enough to break the flesh of the bean but leave the thin green thread that runs down its side intact. Then I use the snapped end to pull that thread down the bean, snap the other end and pull the other side's thread off too. Toss that away, then—pop, pop, pop, pop—break the bean into five pieces and toss them into the pan.

If I find a bean with its flesh already turning dry and woody, or with blemishes or rust marks on the outside, I just slit its length with my thumbnail and pop out the white seed beans inside to go in the pot and cook up all mealy and sweet.

Mountain folk generally hold the white half-runner (sometimes called the mountain half-runner) in highest regard for its tender green flesh and full-flavored beans. But any small-to-medium-sized green bean with plenty of white beans inside will make a tasty potful.

Country cooked green beans, of course, make health food folks roll their eyes in despair. If done right, they simmer for nearly two hours. But country eaters lick their lips in pleasure at the thought of beans cooked to such a perfect state of tenderness and flavor.

When fresh white corn and really ripe tomatoes are available, ask a bunch of friends over to help you string the beans and keep you company while they cook. When they're nearly ready, make up a skillet of Creamed Corn

"Y'all come! Y'all come!

Y'all come and see us now and then.

Y'all come! Y'all come! Y'all come to see us when you can.

"Y'all Come" by Arleigh Duff

(page 158), Tomato and Cucumber Salad (page 201), Jerry's Slaw (page 216), and Hot Water Cornbread (page 237). Brew fresh iced tea to be served sweetened, with wedges of lemon. That's the makings of a genuine Kentucky summer feast.

8 cups of strung and broken green beans

water

1/4 pound salt pork

1–2 tablespoons salt

8 medium new potatoes

Rinse beans well and put in a large, heavy pot with a lid. Cover with water and add the piece of salt pork (also called white bacon). Bring to a boil, then cover, turn down heat, and let simmer rapidly for one hour. Check pot occasionally and add water if beans start to boil dry.

After an hour taste the bean broth and add salt accordingly. Beans will take 1–2 tablespoons of salt depending on how salty the meat is. Stir to mix salt in well, then put the new potatoes (rinsed well, but with their skins still on) on top of the beans. Cover and let simmer again for another hour. *Serves 8.*

BEANS IN BROWN SAUCE

If you're looking for a lower cholesterol variation on Country Cooked Green Beans, this recipe offers a similar full, tawny flavor without using saturated fats.

4 cups broken green beans

1 tablespoon dark sesame oil

1 tablespoon canola oil

1/2 onion, chopped

1 heaping teaspoon flour

2 cups water

1/2 teaspoon brown sugar

1/2 teaspoon salt

freshly ground pepper

Wash, string, and break green beans into inch-long pieces. In a heavy pan with a lid, heat the two oils over moderate flame and add chopped onion, cooking until softened. Sprinkle with flour, stirring to keep from sticking, and add the water very slowly, stirring constantly to keep the flour from lumping. When all the water has been added, add sugar, salt, and a few grinds of black pepper. Cook until the mixture is barely thickened, then stir in the beans. Cover, turn the heat very low, and simmer for 1 1/2 hours until beans are very tender. Add water if necessary, but if you have the heat low enough, it shouldn't be necessary. These beans are quite tasty with Mother's Roast and Brown Gravy (page 55) or Polly's Meat Loaf (page 62). *Makes enough for a dinner side dish for 6.*

SHUCK BEANS

Shuck beans—also called shucky beans or leather britches—are khaki brown, wrinkled, ugly little things. To have a pot of them in the winter, you have to start preparing them in the summer. And when it's finally time to cook them, it's a two-day event.

Shuck beans were invented in pioneer times as a means of drying and storing green beans through the winter in the days before canning. And there's only one earthly reason why someone would go to the trouble to make them in this day of canned and frozen food. That's because they taste so good—full-bodied, salty, and with a deep, tawny flavor unlike any other.

Vegetables and
Side Dishes

155

And that flavor is why I and plenty of my cousins will still take the time in the busiest of summers to buy lots of white half-runner beans, string them, then sew them onto long threads to dry. For people like me with mountain roots, a pot of shuck beans and a skillet of cornbread is the best part of winter eating. And as for strangers, well my suburban-Baltimore-reared husband to this day swears that the reason he married me is because I introduced him to his favorite food, shuck beans.

Shuck beans have to be made in two stages. First you dry them in the summer. For this you will need:

5 pounds white half-runner beans

The traditional way to dry shuck beans is to remove the ends and strings from white half-runners or any other firm, small-to-medium-sized green bean with lots of beans in the pod. (See Country Cooked Green Beans on page 153 for directions on removing strings—but don't break the beans into pieces once you've strung them.) If the beans are damp, pat them dry and discard any with lots of blemishes. (If the bean just has a small blemish at one end or the other, though, you can break that off and use the rest.)

Then thread a large needle with strong thread about a foot long when doubled. Tie a knot in the end. Push the needle through the bean about midway along its length, then pull the thread through the bean, leaving a little thread at the end. Use that thread end to tie a loop around this first bean so it, and all the others to come behind it, won't fall off the string.

Then proceed to thread more beans on the strand, leaving about two inches of thread at the top. Snip the needle off and tie a knot at the end of the top thread, leaving a loop so you can hang the string of beans to dry.

String up all the beans this way. You should have about a dozen strings when you are done.

Dry the beans by hanging the threads in a sunny, dry place. We have an enclosed porch with a coat rack that doesn't get used in the summer that works well. But the year we had a puppy living on that porch, I used the plant hangers in the house to dry my beans. All the plants were on the back porch to catch the summer sun, and the beans hung nicely in their places in the sunny windows—and were an interesting conversation piece as well.

Beans take about three weeks to dry. They should be crisp—not a little pliant—and sound raspy when you lightly shake the string. After they are dried, you can store them in a covered jar or coffee can to keep them out of the dust and light. Or you can put them in airtight plastic bags and freeze them. You can also cook them right away, if you want. But what is best is to wait until the dead of winter. When it's good and cold and you know you are going to be good and hungry the next day, you will need:

4 cups of the dried shuck beans

water

1/4 pound white bacon

salt

pepper

Rinse the beans well and drain several times. If you see any strings on the beans, pull them off. Put beans in a deep bowl and cover with water about two inches higher than the beans. Leave overnight. Beans need to soak about 12 hours before cooking.

When you're ready to cook them, drain the beans and rinse once again. Put them in a large pot and again cover them with water about two inches deeper than the beans. Put a 1/4-pound piece of white bacon (ham hock will do) in the pot and bring it to a boil. Turn the heat down to a very slow boil and cover the pot. Cook for 6–8 hours, adding boiling water to the pot if it starts to cook dry. Beans will be tender when they are ready to eat—although not as soft as cooked green beans.

When the beans are tender—but not before—add salt to taste and a little pepper. If you add the salt before the beans are ready, they never will cook up tender but their skins will stay just as tough as they were when you put in the salt. The beans should have a slightly salty flavor—but be careful not to add so much as to make them briny. You'll have to taste to determine how much salt, since the saltiness of the bacon or ham hock will also have an effect. Pepper should be just an accent.

You can serve the beans in a bowl with lots of broth like soup beans, or you can cook uncovered for a while longer to cook the broth down like green beans. I like them like soup beans so I can soak my cornbread in the pot likker once my beans are gone. *This will serve 6–8 and should be accompanied by a big skillet of Real Cornbread (page 235) and fresh raw onion slices.*

Picking and Sinning

Bertha Monroe, older sister of Bill Monroe, the legendary father of bluegrass music, says that when she and her brother were growing up in Rosine, Kentucky, it was their lot as the two youngest of eight children, to pick the green beans for drying and canning.

"And, oh my, honey, there could surely be a lot of them. One time we picked and picked and picked until we thought we'd picked enough, William and me. But there was still plenty on the vines. So we took our sacks and tried to cover them up, and moved the leaves around like so you wouldn't see how many. And boy we thought we'd done something clever then.

"But Mama caught us, don't you know. And whoooo, did she ever take after us for trying to shirk our work."

CREAMED CORN

Corn cut fresh from the cob and then creamed is a genuine country delicacy whose good name has been sullied by the sweetened, gelatinous product sold in cans as "creamed corn." Made fresh, the dish is both crisp and creamy and bursting with the buttery, sunny flavor of corn right off the cob. Served with Country Cooked Green Beans (page 153) and Tomato and Cucumber Salad (page 201) or fresh sliced tomatoes and Wib's Favorite Cucumbers (page 210) it makes a satisfying summer meal.

Like many country recipes, this one has a simple list of ingredients. The real secret to its unforgettable taste is in the way the corn is cut from the cob.

There are places that sell corn cutters or reamers designed to make this job easier. They consist of a long, narrow board with a hole in it for the corn to fall through, a blade above the hole to shear the corn, and a small metal grate to scrape the milk from the remaining cob. There are people who swear by these contraptions, but my mother isn't one of them.

She says there's not been one made that doesn't cut too deep into the kernel. And too big a kernel results in a skillet of corn that is too tough and not creamy enough.

To cream corn correctly, she maintains, you have to use a small, sharp knife. With it you cut down the length of the shucked and silked corncob, taking just the tops off the fresh, raw kernels. After you've cut the corn all around like that, you take a small kitchen spoon, turn its back toward your face, and scrape down and around the cob again, this time scraping out all the rest of the corn and its milk, too. If the corn is really milky, you can use your hand to squeeze the rest of the juice out if you like.

Once you get the hang of it, this is easy to do. Even city folks seem to get the hang of it after a cob or two. You can use yellow corn for this, but the best creamed corn is made with white corn as fresh off the stalk as you can get it.

6 ears of corn

4 tablespoons butter

4 tablespoons half and half

salt

pepper

Leather Britches

Shuck beans are also called "leather britches" in the mountains. And "Leather Britches" is also the title of one of the most popular traditional fiddle tunes. In fact, legend has it that "Leather Britches" was the first country song to be played on radio station WLS out of Chicago in the 1920s. Fiddler Tommy Dandurand played the song during a broadcast from the mezzanine of the Sherman Hotel, and the story goes that the audience mail-in response was so overwhelming that the management of the station decided to program lots more country. Pretty soon the Chicago station was home to one of the most influential country radio shows of the era, the WLS Barn Dance.

When you are ready to cook the corn, remove shucks and silk from it, rinse, and dry. Hold the cob pointing down into a wide-mouthed bowl. Using a small, sharp knife, cut down the length of the corn shearing off the tops of the kernels, cutting no more than half the kernel deep. When all the tops have been sheared, use a teaspoon to scrape the rest of the corn and its milk from the cob.

Six ears make about four cups of cut corn. For each cup of corn, put a tablespoon of butter or butter substitute in a skillet on medium high and melt. As soon as it's melted, add the corn to the skillet. Then add a tablespoon of half and half for each cup of corn. (In the country, folks often use bacon grease instead of butter and this gives the corn a wonderful, slightly different flavor.) If the corn begins to dry up too quickly, you may want to add more half and half—but the dish isn't supposed to be soupy.

Cook, stirring frequently, over medium high heat for 8–10 minutes. The mixture will bubble like lava toward the end of the process, but you must be careful not to let it burn or stick. Turn down the heat if necessary. Corn varies in freshness so you'll want to taste to see when it's done. When it's ready, the kernels will still be a little crisp and fresh tasting, but the dish will taste buttery and "cooked," not raw. Add salt and pepper to taste and serve it immediately.

This makes enough for 4 as a side dish for dinner, but it also makes a tasty breakfast dish.

Silver Threads and Golden Shuck Beans

"My mother would take a needle and thread up green beans to hang them up to dry to make shuck beans," Ruth Ann Rankey, Dwight Yoakam's mother, recalls.

"And I think that must have been a pretty mystifying thing for a child to watch when we'd go down there to Kentucky to visit her. One time I remember one of the boys—I don't know if it was Dwight or his younger brother, Ronnie—but one of them came running out of my mother's house with his eyes all big and hollered: 'Mama, you'd better get in there quick! Granny's sewing up her green beans again!' "

Metal graters made shucking corn in quantity for canning much easier. That's what this mountain cook is doing. But my mother says to forget the grater if you're making Creamed Corn (page 158). To do it right, you'd best use a sharp knife and a teaspoon.

Summer Corn Pudding

"Well, hot corn, cold
corn, bring along a
demijohn.

Hot corn, cold corn,
bring along a
demijohn.

Hot corn, cold corn,
bring along a
demijohn.

Fare thee well pretty
girl, see you in the
morning, yes sir."

"Hot Corn, Cold Corn,"
Old Kentucky moonshine
song

When I was little and heard someone sing "Hot Corn, Cold Corn," I thought the corn was meant for eating and imagined the "demijohn" mentioned was one of those little fellows with an unbelievably big appetite who was being invited along to do such a bounty of hot and cold corn justice.

Of course, I grew up to learn that a demijohn is a long-necked, earthenware jug and the corn in the song is the drinking kind which would require such a vessel. But even so, when I hear the song it still puts me in mind of eating, and of Amy O'Brien's corn puddings in particular.

That's because she's a pudding maker for all seasons. Corn pudding was such a favorite around the O'Brien household when country crooner Tim was growing up that his mother devised two recipes for it—one for fresh summer corn and one for canned corn in the winter. Hot corn, cold corn, if you will—and I bet you will often after tasting Mrs. O'Brien's puddings.

4 cups yellow corn, cut fresh from the cob (6 big ears)

2 eggs, well beaten

1/2 cup half and half

6 tablespoons melted butter

2 tablespoons sugar

Planting the Seeds

Most historians date the start of commercial country music on August 1 and 2, 1927, when the Carter Family and Jimmie Rodgers went to Bristol, Tennessee, to make their first recordings for Victor Records. Not knowing if those recordings would be issued or whether they'd be asked back to do more, the Carters went back to their home in the Clinch Mountains of Virginia.

Asked what they did while they waited to discover the fate of their music, Sara said: "Why, we went home and planted the corn."

3 tablespoons flour

1/4 teaspoon nutmeg

1/4 teaspoon salt

1/8 teaspoon cayenne pepper

1/2 teaspoon Worcestershire sauce

1/4 cup fresh grated Parmesan

Cut corn from cob according to directions with Creamed Corn (page 158) making sure to catch all the juice to go in the pudding.

In a big bowl, beat eggs, then add half and half, and melted butter. Mix in sugar, flour, nutmeg, salt, cayenne, and Worcestershire and when all are well blended, fold in the cut corn. Pour into a greased 2 1/2-quart casserole, sprinkle Parmesan on top and bake at 375 degrees for 45 minutes until pudding is firm and has a nice brown crust. *This corn pudding has a savory, tangy taste, not a sweet one, and will serve 8—unless one is a hungry "Demijohn."*

WINTER CORN PUDDING

2 one-pound cans cream-style corn

4 beaten eggs

1 tablespoon sugar

1/2 teaspoon salt

1/2 cup milk

Mix all ingredients together well, then pour into a greased 2-quart casserole. Place the casserole in a shallow pan of water and the pan with casserole into a 350 degree oven. Bake for 1 hour—or until the center is firm and a knife inserted in the middle comes out clean. Serve warm. *Enough for 12.*

Roast Corn with Bacon

Ah summer! Time for sweet slabs of watermelon on the back porch; grilled burgers and chicken; fresh-picked, boiled or roasted ears of sweet corn and our annual family dispute over the proper way to devour the latter.

I have the weight of culture on my side. As any fellow American raised on Saturday morning cartoons knows, the proper way to eat corn off the cob is from left to right, typewriter-style, with an occasional "Ding!" at the end for flair.

But just like a man, my husband brings logic to the argument. He points out that if you eat the corn in vertical strips around the cob instead of lateral ones, your upper lip won't wipe the salt and butter off the next row before your taste buds get there.

Actually, I've tried it his way and he does have a point. But in my book, tradition usually outweighs reason, and so every time we savor fresh corn, we also savor our annual spat.

Fortunately, we do agree on one thing: that this recipe for preparing corn on the cob is one of the most delicious invented. Corn roasted on coals and seasoned with strips of bacon works excellently for a modern day cookout. You want to roast the corn for about 25 minutes over hot coals in a covered grill. If you don't like the flavor of bacon, you can just rub the corn with olive oil or butter and roast.

6 ears of fresh white kernel corn, unshucked

6 strips of bacon

Gently pull shucks back from the ear so you can remove the silk. When silk is off, rinse the corn well and shake to drain. Then wrap a strip of bacon around the corn in a spiral from top to bottom. Pull shucks back up to cover the corn and tie the top with twine or wrap with a cap of aluminum foil to hold shucks in place.

When coals are glowing hot, place rack about four inches from them and lay corn across the rack. Cover and let grill for 25 minutes, turning corn every 5 minutes. Keep a spray bottle of water handy while you do this since shucks sometimes catch on fire and have to be doused.

Corn should be done in the allotted time, but the bacon won't be. That's okay because you're not going to eat it. You only use it for seasoning while you cook and when you get ready to serve the corn, you pull off the shucks and pitch both them and the bacon. Serve with plenty of salt and pepper and eat your corn any which way you want. *Enough to serve 6.*

Corn and the Death of a President

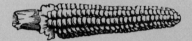

Peyton Hoge of Anchorage, Kentucky, is a sterling regional cook from a long line of such. Hoge is a man fascinated by food traditions and none captured him more than the way his grandfather ate corn on the cob.

His grandpa's technique?

He would score the kernels with his fork first to break them open and then slice the corn off with his knife to eat it.

"My grandmother was appalled every time he did this and made it plain," Hoge remembers. "But my grandfather was convinced that if you ate the corn with the kernels whole, you could get sick and perhaps even die."

And his grandfather ate on with the stubborn conviction of a man who had history on his side. You see, he'd learned the technique from his father who in turn had learned it from his father who had been a great friend of President Zachary Taylor. And when the twelfth president of the United States died, Thomas Floyd Smith was sure he knew exactly why.

"Zachary Taylor died of cholera morbis because he didn't know how to eat his corn," he said, firmly believing it was whole kernels that had killed him. So every time he was served corn on the cob for dinner, Smith scored and cut it off the cob, just as generations of Smith and Hoge children did after him.

Bacon Popcorn

My old traveling buddy, Cindy Clark, introduced me to the ultimate snack food, corn popped in bacon grease. Back in 1971, Cindy and I set out from Kentucky for Colorado in her old blue Valiant station wagon. We settled for a while next to the Poudre River, north of Fort Collins, in a little log cabin that had dimity curtains on the windows and a periwinkle blue teapot in the cupboard. In the mornings we'd make bacon and eggs for breakfast and eat them on the little porch, watching the river dance by.

At night, Cindy would use the bacon grease she'd saved to make a big pot of popcorn. Then we'd sit on the iron bedstead in the front room and, in the glow of kerosene lamps, discuss adventures, both past and potential. No wonder the smell of this dish fills me with nostalgia as well as appetite.

To make this popcorn, you need a heavy pan with a lid. Melt enough bacon grease to cover the bottom of the pan a kernel deep. Just as the grease gets almost hot enough to smoke (but not yet smoking), pour the popcorn in, one layer deep. Put the top on and shake the pan over high heat until the kernels stop popping. Pour into large bowl and sprinkle lightly with salt.

If you're making enough for a crowd, it's better to make this in several small batches than in one big one to keep the grease from burning. Back when Cindy was growing up in Owensboro, Kentucky, her mom used to pour the batches into a big brown paper sack until there was enough for five kids. Then she'd pour in the salt, roll up the top of the sack and shake before serving.

GOOD GRITS

"I'd never even heard of grits until I moved down to Georgia to live with my dad for a while," said Chet Atkins, who spent his earliest childhood eating mountain-style food cooked by his mother in east Tennessee.

"Then when I first moved to Georgia, I hated grits. But I finally found out, grits don't have a taste really. You have to add the taste. So you add salt and butter and gravy or whatever and hell, they're great."

Like Atkins, I didn't grow up eating grits. And my first encounters with this cotton-belt favorite—in chain restaurants that cooked them fast and served them runny—couldn't convince me of their rumored charm.

But over the years I've learned that there are grits and there are good grits. And the secret to good grits is in the grind and the cooking.

Grits are ground from hominy—dried corn kernels that have been soaked in lye water to remove the outer husk. Some folks like to call them by their full name, hominy grits, or little hominy. And in the low country of South Carolina, grits are often called just hominy, although if you ask for hominy in other parts of the South what you'll likely get is a side dish of the dried whole kernel corn heated up with a small piece of meat for seasoning. To be sure, just ask for grits, and to be assured of the best taste, try to find coarse ground ones.

Eugenia Harris, Emmylou's mother, and a grits connoisseur from her girlhood in Alabama, says that if they're cooked right, the commercially packaged grits you find in grocery stores are better than no grits at all: "But what I really want is a good, fresh, coarse ground grit, so I have Emmy send me care packages from Tennessee, or my sister send them from down south."

Those care packages usually contain grits that are ground at the few small stone mills that still operate primarily as historic tourist attractions. Mostly they grind and sell cornmeal and grits as souvenirs.

For several years Emmylou sent her mother grits from such a mill every time she passed through the Nashville airport where they were sold in a gift shop. You don't have to fly to Nashville to get the same grits, however. They can be ordered by mail from the Falls Mill and Country Store, Route 1, Box 44, Belvidere, Tennessee 37306. Write and they will send prices and information.

"Wake up, Jacon,

day's a-breakin'

Fryin' pan's on an'

hoecake bakin.'

Bacon in the pan,

coffee in the pot.

Git up now and git it

while it's hot."

Traditional cowboy song

I ordered a sack myself and thought they were the most full-flavored grits I'd found. But Arrowhead Mills, a whole foods company in Hereford, Texas, also grinds a good, coarse white corn grit and it's available in many health food stores.

After you find a good, coarse ground grit, the next step is cooking it right. Most package directions on grits tell you to toss them into boiling water, simmer for about five minutes and then serve. The grits you get are a runny gruel which might be pleasing if you're starved as Oliver Twist, but they are not the pride of the South. Good grits need to simmer longer and cook up firmer, albeit still creamily. I've found the best recipe for making good grits is this one.

4 cups cold water

1 teaspoon salt

1 cup coarse ground grits

Half fill the bottom of a double boiler with water and set on stove until you're ready to heat it.

Next bring 4 cups of salted water to a boil in the top of the double boiler

Good Grits

"There are foods that are just close to my heart, like grits," says Alabama-born-and-bred Emmylou Harris. "I never knew what a hash brown potato was. We always had grits. And grits with butter was good, but best in the morning was cutting up your eggs and bacon in the grits—making a nice mess of it. I liked to do that when I was a kid."

But you can't just do anything you want with grits, says Emmylou's dad, Bucky: "We were talking grits up around Washington one time and somebody said, 'Can you eat them with sugar and cream?'

"And I said, 'You know, the last lynching we had in Alabama was a Yankee who put sugar and cream on his grits and we strung him up right there in the middle of town.' "

set directly on the burner. Stir in the grits slowly to prevent lumping. Turn heat down to simmer and cook, stirring constantly, for 10 minutes.

While grits are cooking, bring the water in the bottom half of the double boiler to a rolling boil. When 10 minutes are up, place top half of boiler in the bottom half and cover. Turn heat to medium and let cook for at least 30 minutes, stirring occasionally to keep grits from sticking. *Makes a side dish for 4.*

Grits are great served with gravy or butter, and this is how you make grits for Low Country Shrimp and Hominy (page 90) or Cheese Grits (page 169).

CHEESE GRITS

Emmylou Harris's family was hard pressed to find good grits when her father's marine career stationed them out of the Deep South.

"It seemed so strange to me that something we grew up eating all the time, you couldn't even find in the grocery stores some places," said her mother, Eugenia.

But when Georgian Jimmy Carter was president and Eugenia and Bucky were living outside Washington, D.C., it was as if their grits train had finally come in.

"All of a sudden grits became gourmet food," Eugenia said. "That's where Safeway suddenly had them—in their gourmet section."

And suddenly grits—especially cheese grits—were served at the toniest parties around town.

Eugenia said, "I told Bucky that I couldn't believe something we had every morning for breakfast is now the party food of the town. It seemed kind of silly to me, but it sure tasted good."

Cheese grits went out of fashion in Washington when the Carters left town, but this recipe from Eugenia will never lose favor at our house. It's good for both parties and breakfast.

6 cups water

1 1/2 teaspoons salt

1 1/2 cups uncooked coarse ground grits

1/2 cup butter

4 cups (1 pound) shredded sharp cheddar cheese

3 eggs, beaten

Heat salted water in a heavy saucepan and bring to a boil. Stir in grits, turn to a simmer and cook for 10 minutes, stirring constantly. Remove from heat and add butter and 3 3/4 cups of the cheese, stirring until both are melted. Slowly add several tablespoonfuls of hot grits to the beaten eggs, stirring constantly. Then when eggs are warmed up, pour them back into the remaining grits and mix well. Turn everything out into a lightly greased 2 1/2-quart baking dish. Sprinkle the remaining cheese on top and bake for 1 hour in a 350 degree oven. *Makes 6–8 servings.*

Cornmeal Mush

I'm not one for eating mush as a hot cereal for breakfast, but it's worth the trouble of making it to chill it into a loaf, then slice it and serve it fried—either in butter or meat drippings for breakfast, or in fried chicken drippings for Chicken Extenders (page 246).

1 cup white cornmeal

1 teaspoon salt

4 cups water

Mix cornmeal and salt together well. In the top of a double boiler, bring water to a boil. (While you're doing this, have water heating up in the bottom of the double boiler on another burner.)

There are two tricks to making mush without lumps. The first is to pour the cornmeal into the boiling water in a very thin trickle. I put the meal in my hand so I can control the flow. The second is to stir it into the water with a whisk. Add the meal slowly to the water, whisking all the time. When it's all been added, stir until the mixture comes to a boil. Then remove pan from burner and place over simmering water in bottom of double boiler. Cover and let cook for 20 minutes, stirring occasionally to keep the mush from sticking.

Pour mush into lightly oiled loaf pan, smooth the top with the back of a spoon, and refrigerate overnight. When you're ready to cook, turn the mush out of the pan and slice. Fry until each side is a golden brown. *Enough to serve 8.*

GRILLED ASPARAGUS

The best way to eat asparagus is sitting right in the garden, breaking off new tender shoots, and chewing slowly to savor their deep spring flavor. The next best way is this: marinated lightly in garlic and olive oil, then grilled outside over charcoal until the skin gets lightly scorched and papery crisp. The asparagus only takes a few minutes on the grill, so cook your meat or fish first, then pop the asparagus over the still-hot coals.

2 dozen medium stalks of fresh asparagus

1/2 lemon

1 tablespoon of olive oil

3 cloves garlic, crushed

1/4 teaspoon freshly ground black pepper

1/4 teaspoon salt

Wash asparagus and trim thick or woody ends. Put in steamer with water and drizzle juice of half a lemon over the stalks. Steam for about 12 minutes until just tender, but not too soft.

Lay the asparagus in a large, shallow glass dish. Mix olive oil, garlic, salt, and pepper and drizzle over the asparagus, rubbing with your fingers and turning the asparagus so it's coated all over. Let sit for about an hour.

When coals are red hot, lay asparagus across a grill about 4 inches above the coals. Turn once when they begin to brown on the coal side; then remove when the other side is brown. (I use small tongs to turn them spear by spear, but if you have a fish or vegetable holder for the grill, that will work even better.) *Serves 4.*

OKRA SUCCOTASH

This dish is best made in the heart of summer when tomatoes are bursting with juice, corn is full flavored, and little tender pods of okra are tucked into the corners of the produce stand. Sure, you can make it in the winter with frozen corn and okra and canned tomatoes and it will taste pretty good, but in the summer, it's divine.

2 tablespoons olive oil

1/2 cup (3 stalks) chopped green onion

1/4 cup minced celery

2 ears small kernel yellow corn

1 1/2 cups chopped okra

1 large or 2 medium peeled tomatoes

1–2 tablespoons water

1 teaspoon salt

black pepper

Heat the oil on a medium-low flame in a large skillet with a lid. Add the green onion and celery. Cut the corn from the stalk according to directions for Creamed Corn (page 158) and when the onion and celery are softened, add corn to the skillet and stir. Then add okra that has had its stems removed and been cut into rounds about 1/4 inch thick. Chop tomatoes and add to the skillet with all their juice, then if the mixture looks very dry, add a tablespoon or 2 of water (the dryness will depend on how milky the corn and juicy the

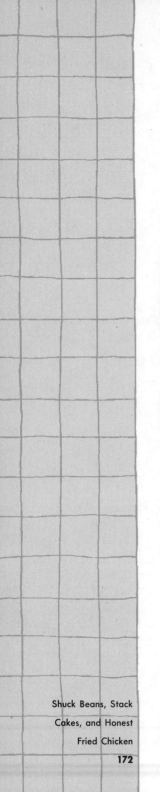

tomatoes are). Add salt and pepper to taste, stir everything well, turn heat to low, cover and let simmer for 20 minutes, stirring occasionally to keep it from sticking to the pan. The corn and okra juices will make a very thick natural sauce. Served hot, it's especially fine with Hot Water Cornbread (page 237). *Enough for 4.*

SUCCOTASH

Jocelyn Mayfield said that when she was a child, succotash usually had corn and limas, okra and tomatoes, onions, and even some sweet bell peppers in it. But at her restaurant, Jocelyn's, in Ocean Springs, Mississippi, she simplifies the dish and in the process creates perfection.

This succotash seems deceptively simple, but cooking over low heat lets the vegetable juices marry to make a rich tasting sauce. Fresh limas and corn would probably be sublime, but Jocelyn uses frozen vegetables and gets great

Okraphobia

My Uncle Jack wouldn't touch okra—swore its viscous juices made him sick, and refused to have a bite no matter how hard his okra-eating relatives tried to persuade him.

One day Jack showed up at our house at dinnertime, though, when my mother had just cooked up a big pot of okra succotash and hot water cornbread. Distracted no doubt by the fresh corn and tomatoes, Jack didn't realize the plump green chunks of vegetable in the stew he was shoveling in was the dreaded okra.

Smacking his lips, he downed two big bowls before he turned to my mother and said, "Sis, what was that?"

When she told him, he slapped down his fork and said, "Dammit! You know I can't eat okra!"

results. Baby limas and white shoepeg corn cook up the very best. The latter is a small, white-kernel corn marketed by Green Giant and a few other frozen vegetable purveyors—and its flavor and tenderness are noteworthy enough to make it worth your while to look for it. Because this succotash is made with frozen vegetables, it can add both summery flavor and color to your winter table.

4 tablespoons butter substitute

1 small onion, minced

20-ounce package baby lima beans

16-ounce package shoepeg white corn

salt

pepper

Melt the butter substitute in a large saucepan with a lid. Add the onion and sauté on low until tender. Add the frozen beans, corn, and salt and pepper to taste. Break apart any big chunks of the frozen vegetables, mix well, cover, and let cook on low heat for 15–20 minutes. The water on the frozen vegetables and their juices should provide enough liquid, but check after 10 minutes and, if needed, add just a splash of milk. *Serves 6 and is even better warmed up the next day.*

SPECKLED BUTTER BEANS

Speckled butter beans are a kissing cousin to lima beans. They look like baby limas, but with brown and purplish skin. But when they cook up, the similarity ends. Limas are sharp, green-flavored vegetables, while speckled butter beans have a rich, full-bodied, buttery taste. They are prized on southern tables and can be found fresh at produce stands there in the spring and the fall. But they are also packaged and sold frozen—and they're one vegetable that tastes as fine after freezing as they do fresh.

> 16-ounce package of frozen speckled butter beans
> 2 cups water
> 2 tablespoons butter
> 2 tablespoons half and half
> salt

In a saucepan with a lid, bring water to a boil and then add butter beans. Cover and bring water to a boil, then reduce heat and simmer for 20–25 minutes until tender. Stir the beans occasionally to keep from sticking and add small amounts of water to keep them from burning, if necessary. But you want most of the water to cook out of the beans by the time the 20–25 minutes are up. Add butter to the beans and let melt, then add half and half. Stir and then cover and simmer on low for another 5 minutes until butter and milk form sauce. Salt to taste and serve with Real Cornbread (page 235). *Serves 4.*

LONE OAK SQUASH CASSEROLE

The Lone Oak Restaurant is up the winding Old Scottsville Road outside of Bowling Green, Kentucky, about 45 minutes north of Nashville. It's not easy to find—even when you see it. The building looks like an old-time country gas station; it has rusting pumps out front, and the big sign in the parking lot has "Ashland Oil" in huge letters across the middle with "The Lone Oak" painted in small script at the top.

But more than a few people know that the Lone Oak is worth seeking out for its all-you-can-eat country dinners trundled out to the tables on groaning three-shelf carts. This is where former Oak Ridge Boy William Golden brings his wife to celebrate her birthdays and where film director John Carpenter and his starlet wife Adrienne Barbeau had their wedding dinner.

Simple dishes cooked just right are the attraction, and this squash casserole from Mrs. Forest Stice, owner of the Lone Oak, is about the best way I've ever found for cooking yellow crooknecks.

"My father has the King of Gardens up at his house in Clarksville, Maryland," Emmylou Harris brags. "He grows just about anything you can think of—the best corn and potatoes with wonderful skins like nothing you've ever found in a supermarket. If you can grow it, Daddy does—everything except he can't have a rice paddy because Mother won't let him flood the front yard."

4 cups fresh sliced, yellow summer squash

1/4 teaspoon salt

4 tablespoons butter

4 tablespoons sugar

1/4 cup minced white onion

While the oven is preheating to 350 degrees, steam squash for about 12 minutes—until very tender. (If you use a steamer that keeps the juices with the vegetable, your squash casserole will taste better but take longer to bake

A Patch of Shrubby Beans

Brenda Lee grew up outside the little town of Lathonia, Georgia. And although she was a child of the '50s and a pre-teen rockabilly queen, her earliest years were spent living a rural life.

"I want to say Mama cooked on a wood stove when I was real little because I remember bringing in the wood. But it might have been for the fireplace because that's how we heated.

"But it didn't matter what she cooked on because my mother was an excellent southern cook. And we didn't have much store-bought meat but we always had a garden, so we always had fresh vegetables—corn, squash, potatoes, okra, turnips, and all kinds of collards. My mother's the only person ever cooked a rutabaga I'd eat.

"They used to give us kids each a little patch of something to grow, so we were in the garden too. We'd have to mark it out and plant our own stuff. We got to pick what we wanted to grow and then we'd have to take care of it, make sure it was nourished and grew and produced. So it was a learning process for us and it was fun.

"And I grew mostly beans—plain old green beans. They were easy. And they were pretty growing, a kind of shrubby type look. My brothers and sisters chose other stuff. I don't know why I always chose beans. Must be some Freudian thing there."

than if you use the kind of steamer that lets the juices run out. This recipe is for squash with juice.)

Mash the cooked squash with butter and sugar then add onion and "get them worked up real good together," Mrs. Stice says.

The mixture will be soupy. Pour into a buttered casserole dish and bake in a 350 degree oven "until it's a little dried up and browned," Mrs. Stice says.

Serve it right away "and try not to make a pig of yourself," I say. *Makes enough for 4.*

RATATOUILLE

Ratatouille is just one big garden party in a pot. This is not quite the traditional dish from Provence (no eggplant), but a personal variation that makes use of abundant squash and tomatoes in midsummer. It makes a fine side dish to any meal, but we also eat it as our main dish with cornbread on the side, or over a cupful of macaroni.

1 medium onion

1 red bell pepper

1 green bell pepper

2 medium zucchini

2 medium yellow squash

3 tablespoons of olive oil

1 crushed garlic clove

3 medium peeled tomatoes

1/2 teaspoon salt

a few grinds of black pepper

1/2 teaspoon fresh chopped basil

freshly grated Parmesan or Romano cheese

Chop onion coarsely. Remove stem and seeds from bell peppers and cut them into bite-sized chunks. Slice squash in half and then cut into 1/4-inch-thick slices. In a large saucepan with lid, heat the olive oil on medium low, then add crushed garlic and onion. Cook until onion is softened. Add peppers and stir until the pieces are coated with oil. Add squash and stir, then chop peeled tomatoes into eighths and add to pot. Add salt, pepper, and basil, stirring once more, then cover and let simmer for 25 minutes. Serve with grated cheese on top. *Enough for 6.*

MASHED POTATOES

My mother's mashed potatoes are the finest mashed potatoes in the world. Do you doubt me? Then consider this: I have put my mother's gravy—smooth cream chicken, rich roast brown, or golden turkey giblet—on nearly every food known to man including biscuits, cornbread, home fries, and tomatoes (both fried green or red ripe), but never on her mashed potatoes.

That's because my mother's potatoes are heavenly on their own. The secret is in the mashing, the whipping, and the butter—all done to excess and then some.

> 6 medium potatoes
> boiling water
> 8 tablespoons butter
> milk
> 3/4 tablespoon salt

Peel the potatoes and cut in quarters into a heavy pot with a good handle and a lid. Add boiling water to cover and cook for 20–30 minutes until a fork penetrates easily into a quarter, breaking it apart. Put the lid on and slide it back just a smidgen to pour the water off, being careful not to burn yourself.

Using a good potato masher (see Things Your Mama Didn't Tell You, but Mine Told Me on page 180), mash through all the potatoes in the pot 4 or 5 times. Drop butter in clumps into the potatoes and mash it until it's all well blended and the potatoes are smooth, with no lumps.

Now you're going to add the milk, and how much depends on the potatoes. Some potatoes absorb more milk than others, so you'll need to use your judgment. A cup of milk is about right in most cases—and what you are looking for is a full, fluffy consistency that isn't runny, but also isn't stiff. To get it, you add the milk gradually; and while you add it, you whip the dickens out of the potatoes with a big spoon.

"The more you beat 'em, the better they are," is my mother's rule about her potatoes.

When they're beaten full and airy and delicious, sprinkle the salt on them and whip that in. Taste and add butter, milk, or salt if needed. If you don't have a nearly uncontrollable urge to eat all the mashed potatoes out of the pan right then and there, you haven't done them right.

Serve them right away to 6.

If for any reason you have potatoes left over, see Cold Tater Cakes (page 181) to find out what to do next.

Things Your Mama Didn't Tell You, But Mine Told Me

"You can't make decent mashed potatoes with an electric beater," my mama told me. "If you're beating them like that you're making whipped potatoes and they just won't taste right."

To make mashed potatoes, you've got to mash. And to mash well, you've got to have a first-rate masher.

You're likely to encounter two kinds of potato mashers in most kitchen stores. The first has a masher that is a firm, zigzagged metal rod across the bottom. My mama told me not to fool with that kind because no matter how long you mash it's going to leave your potatoes with lumps.

The masher that you want has a round, open waffle grid across its bottom that the potatoes are pressed through. My mama prefers that one "because it mashes the potatoes faster and that way they won't get cold. But you've got to be careful when you buy one, because they make a lot out of flimsy metal that are just not worth a hoot."

To make sure the masher isn't one of those hootless flimsy kinds, pick it up by its handle in one hand then press real hard against its masher with the other. If you feel any give, it's not worth your money. But if it stands firm and looks well made and sturdy, buy it, because, like my mama told me, a good masher is hard to find.

"When I was a little boy around the table at home
I remember very well when company would come
I would have to be right still until the whole crowd ate
My mama always said to me, 'Just take a tater and wait.' "

"Take an Old Cold Tater (and Wait)" by E. M. Bartlett

COLD TATER CAKES

Little Jimmy Dickens sang "Take an Old Cold Tater and Wait" for so many years on the Grand Ole Opry it became his trademark song. But someone should have told him that an old cold tater is the first step to some of the best food in a country cook's kitchen.

You can take an old cold tater and wait until the morning after to slice and sizzle it into yummy Home Fries (page 182).

And leftover mashed potatoes are the secret to Mystery Morning Cake (page 269). But my favorite old cold tater recipe is this one for leftover potato

Luckily, by the time I came around children didn't have to bide their time with a cold tater, but sat down to eat with the grown folks. Here I am at age five, sampling gourmet burgers at the Little Tavern in Louisville with (left to right) Uncle Carper Lundy, Mother, Father, Aunt Lib, cousin Larry, and Uncle Jack Fore.

cakes just like my mother used to make. In fact, we liked these so much that she would usually mash extra potatoes for dinner one night so she'd have plenty left over to make potato cakes the next.

For every cup or so of mashed potatoes she had left, she mixed in about 1/4 cup of finely minced onion—either white or green. She added salt to taste if necessary, although often it wasn't since her potatoes were already seasoned. But she always added black pepper. Then she cracked an egg, beat it a little, and mixed it in with the potatoes.

She'd heat the skillet until it was very hot, and put in just enough oil or grease to make the bottom of the pan slick. The oil flavors the potatoes as well as cooking them, so if you want to use something like bacon grease, or put a few drops of sesame oil in safflower oil to flavor it, you can.

Then she'd turn the heat down to medium and plop potato cakes into the pan a big spoonful at a time, flattening the tops a bit with the back of her spoon. A cup of potatoes makes about 4 cakes, about 3 inches in diameter.

Cook them until they're brown on one side, then turn them over with a spatula, being very careful so you lift up all the crust and don't leave any stuck on the pan. You cook them on the second side until that's brown, too, then serve them while they're hot.

When I was little, I always ate mine with store-bought catsup, but now I prefer Mama Nell's Catsup (page 336). They're also yummy with sour cream.

HOME FRIES

Whenever we have baked potatoes we make an extra one to be used for Home Fries the morning after. Or you can use a potato that's been boiled just to tenderness with its skin still on.

> 1 baked or boiled potato with skin
>
> 1 very small onion, finely chopped
>
> 2 tablespoons sausage or bacon grease, or butter
>
> salt
>
> pepper
>
> paprika

Fry bacon or sausage for breakfast, then leave about 2 tablespoons of grease in the skillet. Or melt 2 tablespoons of butter in a skillet on medium heat. Cut potato into quarters lengthwise, then slice about 1/2 inch thick. Put into skillet one layer deep and let fry until a golden brown crust is formed on one side. Turn potatoes and add onions to the skillet. Salt and pepper to taste and add paprika for a little color. Cook until potatoes are golden on the second side. *Makes a side dish to a big breakfast for 4, or is a great big serving for 2.*

CORNMEAL HOME FRIES

If you didn't bake or boil a potato the night before, but you still want something fine and homey for breakfast, these tasty taters are just the ticket. My cousin, June Terrell, gave me this recipe and warns that you should only make it for family, never for a big crowd "or you'll be in there frying potatoes all day long since nobody will stop eating them."

1 large potato

3 tablespoons cornmeal

3 tablespoons butter or butter substitute

Slice the raw potato (with its skin left on) very thinly.

Melt butter or butter substitute in skillet on medium-low heat.

Dip the slices of potato in cornmeal just enough so they're well dusted. Then fry the potatoes, a few at a time and turning only once, in the butter. You may need to add more butter; if too much cornmeal flakes off into the skillet and starts to turn brown, you'll want to wipe it clean with a paper towel after each batch, too. Let folks add salt and pepper to taste. *This makes enough for 2.*

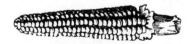

Cajun Potatoes

Way down in Louisiana they boil up crawfish in big vats of pepper-spiced water and then serve them to you by the dishpan-full. Into those vats they also often throw little new potatoes that soak up the spices and make the perfect side dish—for crawfish or just about anything.

Deanie's, one of the least pretentious restaurants in New Orleans, serves these spicy potatoes chilled as an appetizer with every meal. They bring them to your table before you even order and then you eat them with butter or Cajun sauce of your own making (see Barbecued Shrimp, page 92) while waiting for your crawfish or shrimp to come.

> **2 dozen golf-ball-sized new potatoes**
>
> **3 quarts water**
>
> **1 tablespoon cayenne**
>
> **1 tablespoon white pepper**
>
> **1 tablespoon black pepper**
>
> **1 teaspoon salt**

Wash potatoes and remove any eyes or blemishes. Bring 3 quarts of water to a boil in a big pot, add potatoes and spices (and I do mean *tablespoons* of pepper—this dish is supposed to burn your lips with bliss). Bring back to a boil, then cover and turn down to simmer for 20–25 minutes, until potatoes are fork-tender. Remove and drain. Can be served immediately or refrigerated. *Enough for 4–6.* If you have any left over, they are wonderful sliced and fried in a little oil with green onion the next morning.

Yammy Pudding

"I love a yam," says Bucky Harris, father of Emmylou.

"I have no use for a Yankee sweet potato, all stringy and yellow. Give me a fat, firm, orange-y yam any day."

Technically speaking, of course, Bucky Harris isn't speaking technically. Yams (Dioscorea genus) are produced and primarily eaten in the tropics and subtropics. They do bear a resemblance to the sweet potato (Ipomoea batatus), grown and consumed in the United States, although in fact they are not even of the same species. But slaves called sweet potatoes "yams" after the food they had loved in Africa. The name spread and these days "yam" and "sweet potato" are often used interchangeably for the North American vegetable.

The distinction that Harris makes is an interesting one, though. In *Uncommon Fruits and Vegetables: A Commonsense Guide* (Harper & Row, 1986), author Elizabeth Schneider tells us that in the 1930s a very sweet, very orange sweet potato was introduced to the market and called a Louisiana "yam" to distinguish it from its paler, less sweet cousins grown in New Jersey, Maryland, and Virginia.

Most Southerners would be inclined to agree with Harris that the sweeter, more orange-y a sweet potato is, the better. And since the Louisiana "yam" was noticeably distinguished on both counts, that may well explain how "yam" came to distinguish the first rate from an ordinary sweet potato. And it may also explain why Bucky Harris and many Southerners believe that the "yammiest" of sweet potatoes are likely to come from the deep South.

When Harris does get his hands on some of these Confederate "yams," he's likely to turn them over to his wife, Eugenia, who shreds them and whips them up into one of the most delicious sweet-potato dishes ever invented—and there's no argument about that.

The recipe she uses came from the Purefoy Hotel which used to be the finest spot for eating and sleeping in Talladega, Alabama. She and Bucky drove there in a '49 Nash sometime before the Korean War. Eugenia began making the pudding from the hotel's recipe soon after.

"I really can't take credit for this recipe since I didn't think it up," she said. "But I've made this potato pudding for so many years it's become a family dish. It's delicious for Thanksgiving or Christmas dinner."

To make it, you want to get the sweetest, deepest orange sweet potatoes you can find.

> 2 cups raw grated sweet potatoes
> 1 cup sugar
> 2 beaten eggs
> 4 tablespoons butter, melted
> 1 1/2 cups milk
> 1 teaspoon nutmeg

It takes about one long, fat sweet potato to produce 2 cups grated. Wash the outside well, trim off any blemishes, and grate, skin and all. Mix sugar, beaten eggs, melted butter, milk, and nutmeg, then fold in sweet potatoes and mix well. Pour in a shallow, greased baking dish and bake at 350 degrees for about 45 minutes—until pudding is set and browned. *Serves 6.*

FRIED GREEN TOMATOES

Some stores sell green tomatoes and some folks buy them to put on the window sill at home and ripen. But while they may turn red, they'll never get that vine-ripened taste. And what a waste it is to treat them that way anyway when fried green tomatoes are just about the finest food known to man.

Fried green tomatoes were not a side dish in my family, they were the pièce de résistance of any meal at which they appeared. My mother would serve them with her famous Coleslaw (page 216), Mashed Potatoes (page 179),

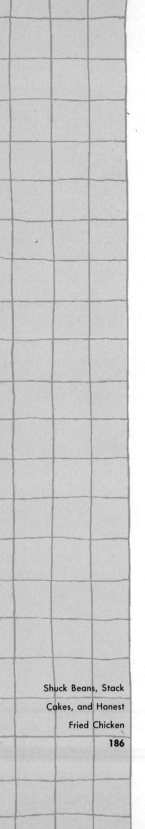

Shuck Beans, Stack Cakes, and Honest Fried Chicken

186

and Speckled Butter Beans (page 174). They're also a wonderful breakfast dish with eggs over easy and hot biscuits. You make a tangy, tart gravy with the tomato drippings, using the Cream Gravy recipe on page 8.

The best tomatoes to use are those that are full sized and moist feeling, but still green. You can also use firm tomatoes that have just started to turn pink in places.

> 3 green tomatoes
> 1 cup of cornmeal
> 1 teaspoon salt
> 1/4 teaspoon freshly ground black pepper
> 1/2 cup buttermilk
> oil or bacon grease

Wash and dry tomatoes and cut out the hard stem area at the top. Slice about 1/4 inch thick. In a shallow bowl, mix cornmeal, salt, and pepper. Pour buttermilk in a second bowl. Put skillet on a burner, and when hot add oil or bacon grease to coat the bottom of the pan.

Dip each tomato slice in buttermilk until coated, then in cornmeal to coat again. Handle the slices gingerly so your fingers don't take off too much of the coating. Lay each slice in the hot skillet and turn heat down immediately to medium. Fry until golden brown on both sides, turning over once. Drain on paper towels and make Cream Gravy (page 8) with the drippings. *Serves 4.*

GREEN TOMATO CASSEROLE

For years I fried every green tomato that came my way, in love with their tangy, fine, and puckery flavor. I was faithful. Fried mushrooms and zucchini never won my affections the way fried green tomatoes had. Fried okra was mighty fine eating, but still not my heart's desire.

Then a recipe came my way for green tomatoes baked in a cracker-crumb casserole, and for the first time my stalwart devotion swayed. This recipe has the same flavorful whang, but none of the drawbacks of frying. Not only is it gentler to the heart and digestive system, but it's fairly muss free.

"Eat 'em with eggs,
    eat 'em with gravy.
Eat 'em with beans,
    pinto or navy.
Put 'em on the side,
    put 'em in the
    middle.
Put homegrown
    tomatoes on a
    hotcake griddle."
"Homegrown Tomatoes"
by Guy Clark

All the work is in the preparation and it's not much: chopping tomatoes and onion, crushing cracker crumbs. Pop the whole thing in the oven and 45 minutes later you have a side dish that is earthy and unusual, with a subtly seductive flavor. It goes well with Soup Beans (page 121) and Real Cornbread (page 235) or a mess of Grace Rainwater's Buttermilk Chicken (page 7).

You can use solid green tomatoes for this casserole but it looks just lovely made with those that are just starting to turn pinkish-red.

5 medium green tomatoes, some just starting to ripen

1 medium onion

2 dozen soda crackers

1 tablespoon melted butter

1/8 teaspoon salt

ground black pepper

1/2 cup buttermilk

Chop tomatoes into pieces about 1/4 inch square and put in a large bowl. Chop onion very fine and toss to mix well with tomatoes. With a rolling pin, crush crackers and add to tomatoes. Pour butter, salt, and as much pepper as you want (we like a lot) over the tomatoes and mix. Then add buttermilk and mix well. Pour into a 2-quart buttered casserole and bake at 325 degrees for 45 minutes. If top isn't brown, run under broiler for a few minutes. Serve warm.

This makes enough for a side dish for 6 and reheats well the next day.

TOMATO PIE

This old mountain way of cooking either canned or fresh tomatoes must be the precursor to the southern restaurant dish, stewed tomatoes. But while the restaurant version—with cubes of white bread turned to mush in sugary tomato glop—has never appealed to me, this is a variation on the same principle with integrity and a delicate, scrumptious taste.

1 cup flour

1/2 teaspoon salt

2 tablespoons softened butter substitute

1/3 cup milk

1 tablespoon vinegar

1 tablespoon butter

1/2 cup chopped onion

1 large (28 1/2-ounce) can tomatoes or 3 1/2 cups fresh tomatoes and juice, peeled and chopped

1 cup milk

1 tablespoon brown sugar

1 tablespoon cornstarch

1/2 teaspoon black pepper

1/2 teaspoon basil

1/2 teaspoon salt

Sift flour and salt together, then use fingers to lightly work softened butter substitute into it. Mix milk and vinegar then pour into flour and stir until well blended. It will be a damp dough. Turn out onto well-floured board and roll out to about the size and shape of a large cast-iron skillet. Cut it into strips about an inch wide.

Melt the tablespoon of butter in a skillet, add onions, and cook until softened. Drain juice from the tomatoes into a large bowl and add milk. Whisk sugar, cornstarch, and spices into the tomato juice and milk, making sure all is well blended. Pour into the skillet and turn heat up to medium. Add the tomatoes, cut into bite-sized pieces, and bring to a boil, stirring constantly.

Let mixture boil for 1 minute, stirring all the while, then remove from heat. Lay strips of dough over the top of the tomato mixture, overlapping if necessary to get them all in. (The tomato mixture is supposed to bubble up through the strips of dough to flavor them.)

Put the skillet in a 375 degree oven and bake for 25 minutes until dough is nicely browned. *Serves 4–6 as a side dish.*

If you don't have a big skillet that can go from the burner to the oven, you can heat the tomato mixture first in a heavy saucepan, then pour it into a wide, shallow 2 1/2-quart casserole for baking. But the deep pink of the tomato filling and the browned crust looks especially nice in cast iron.

GREENS WITH POT LIKKER

John Hartford admits he's a fool for greens: "I'm a lover of good fresh turnip greens. Now I love asparagus and soup beans and sweet potatoes cooked with the skins still on them and plenty of melting butter. But turnip greens are my one true favorite.

"And several years ago, I was in a health food store and they had a chart of the best foods you could eat and I was real pleased to see that greens were right on top.

"Of course, the way I like to eat 'em, I'm not sure how healthy they are. My greens are usually cooked with bacon and I have a big piece of raw onion on the side."

And that's about the best way to have greens, served with a slice of Real

Cornbread (page 235) to sop up all the pot likker.

Pot likker is the juice that cooks up in the pot when you make the greens. In my family, you got the pot likker served up right along with your greens in a big bowl, and when you finished the greens, you crumbled your cornbread into the likker and ate it last. Greens were also always served with Mama's Mashed Potatoes (page 179) on the side.

But there are folks who like to dress pot likker up and serve it as an appetizer. To do that, you drain the greens before serving, reserving the pot likker. Mix it with equal parts chicken broth, bring it to a boil, and serve it hot with a thin slice of lemon floating on top.

Make this recipe with turnip or kale greens, as young and fresh as you can get it. Older greens, especially kale, sometimes have a bitter backbite.

> 6 cups water
>
> 1/4 pound salt pork
>
> 1 pound greens
>
> 2 teaspoons salt
>
> 1/2 teaspoon white pepper

Put water and salt pork in a big, heavy pot with a lid and bring to a boil. Turn down, cover, and simmer for 30 minutes.

While it's simmering, clean greens of any dirt, rinsing several times until the water is clear. Remove any thick stems and tear greens into bite-sized pieces.

Add salt and pepper to the water and stir, then add greens, pushing them down into the simmering water with a wooden spoon. You may have to wait for one bunch to cook down a bit to make room for the next one. When all the greens are in the pot, cover and simmer for an hour. Serve hot with cornbread and (this is essential!) plenty of slices of raw onion on the side. The best way to eat greens is with a little bit of greens, a little bit of cornbread, and a little bit of raw onion in every bite. Mashed Potatoes (page 179) are the appropriate accompaniment. *Serves 4–6.*

HEALTHY, HEARTY GREENS

For those who don't want to cook their greens to perdition, this dish offers both freshness and robust flavor. It can only be made with very young, very tender greens, though, so search for them when they first come into the produce stand in the spring. Gomasio, used in this recipe, is a sesame seed and salt seasoning. Directions for making it are in Killed Lettuce That Won't Kill You (page 206).

Detroit City Dandelion Greens

My mother remembers her grandmother, Ma Fore, picking wild greens every spring from the fields around their house in Kentucky.

"She'd pick poke and dandelion and maybe foxglove and bring them all home and boil them first, then sauté them in a little bacon grease and those are about the tastiest greens you can have," she said.

But Mother was afraid to pick them for herself when she grew up "because I never learned which ones were okay and which ones weren't, and if you didn't know what you were doing, you could end up poisoned.

"When your daddy and I moved to Detroit, though, in the early '40s, he worked with a fellow up there in the plants whose wife and I became good friends. And she was from down in the country and she loved fresh spring dandelion greens. So one day she drove us both out to some big highway that had a median right down the middle of it. And we parked the car and got out and spent the day picking the little green leaves off of dandelions. And we cooked them up that night and it tasted just like being home."

1 pound young greens

juice of 1/2 lemon

1/2 tablespoon sesame oil

1 tablespoon gomasio

Wash greens very well and remove any thick stems. Steam them for 15–20 minutes until just softened. Put them in a wide, shallow bowl and drizzle lemon juice and then oil over them. Toss so all are coated. Then sprinkle gomasio over them and toss again. Serve immediately. *Enough for 4.*

SKILLET SPINACH

This is a quick, delicious way of preparing fresh spinach and it works equally well with a mess of young, tender dandelion greens. Serve it as a side dish with supper or as a hot salad for lunch.

1 pound fresh raw spinach

1 tablespoon bacon grease

1 cup cooked pork or ham, chopped

1 teaspoon vinegar

1 egg, beaten

1/2 cup half and half

1 green onion, chopped

salt

pepper

Rinse spinach thoroughly and trim stems. If leaves are very large, tear in half. Shake to dry.

This takes no time at all to cook and you have to add ingredients quickly, so before you start heating the bacon grease, chop green onion and beat the egg, then mix it well with the half and half.

In the biggest skillet you have, heat bacon grease on medium-high flame, then add pork or ham and just brown a bit. Turn heat to low and add vinegar, then stir in egg and cream mix. Stir for just a second and then begin to add spinach, a skilletful at a time. Stir and let cook down until more spinach can be added. Continue until all the spinach is in the pan. Sprinkle green onions over top and stir and heat until the last batch of spinach is wilted. Salt and pepper to taste and serve immediately.

The cream and egg mixture will curdle and actually becomes a garnish, not a sauce. But the water on the spinach creates a tasty pot likker, so serve this in bowls. Real Cornbread (page 235) is the perfect accompaniment. *Serves 4.*

FRIED APPLES

I'm sure God made little green apples just so my mother could cut them into slices, cover them with butter and brown sugar, and make the most delicious side dish for pork, ham, or breakfast that a child ever tasted.

If you've ever had something called "fried" apples in a restaurant, don't base your opinion of them on that experience. Most restaurant "fried" apples are skinned, stewed, and tricked out with cinnamon to disguise the fact that all the flavor has been cooked out of them.

Real fried apples are first of all made from firm, tart apples—the best being the hard-to-find, sour-as-pickles June apple of green apple fame. But any apple, red or green, with crisp, solid flesh and a tart, fragrant flavor makes a good cooking apple. And the best way to cook them is to soften them in butter and then top them with just enough brown sugar to glaze them with caramel.

I like to eat fried apples with any pork dish for dinner, or at breakfast put them on top of Kentucky Cakes (page 277) or between the layers of Stack Pie (page 270). And once in a spirit of real decadence, my sister Pat and I put dollops of sour cream on ours. If you're feeling in a wicked mood, I recommend you try it. It's a taste worth sinning for.

6 medium apples

2 tablespoons butter

1/4–1/2 cup brown sugar

While butter is melting over low heat in a skillet, cut apples into fourths, core them, and then cut each fourth into three slices longways. (Taste a slice here and if the apple is really sweet use the lesser amount of sugar when it comes time to add it. Use more if the apples are really tart.)

Toss the apples in the butter, cover, and cook on medium-low heat for about 5 minutes, turning a couple of times. Sprinkle sugar over the apples and let it melt just a bit, then gently turn the apples so all the slices get coated with the sugar. Some of the apples will mush up a bit while others will stay in slices—and that's just what you want. Cook over medium-low heat for another 10 minutes until the sugar begins to thicken just a bit into syrup, then serve hot. *This makes a side dish for 6.*

Ruth Ann's Natural Apples

"Fried apples," Dwight Yoakam says before the question is even completely asked. "That's what you wanted to know, right? If there was some food that I longed for when I left home? That I wanted whenever I would come back? That would be my favorite food I remember? Fried apples is it.

"And the great thing is, I don't eat refined sugar anymore, but neither does my mother and she's now gotten where she can do fried apples real well without any sugar at all."

Dwight's mother, Ruth Ann Rankey, cooks either winesap or jonathan apples whenever her country crooning son leaves Los Angeles to visit her in Columbus. She fries them in a tablespoon of margarine in a covered skillet on real low heat to bring out the natural sugar. Then when they're softened, she takes the lid off to set the sugar glaze. If the apples are especially tart, she dribbles just a couple of tablespoons of maple syrup over them.

"They taste wonderful," her son says. "Just like I remember them from when I was a little kid, playing and eating at my granny's."

"And if that's not loving you, Then God didn't make little green apples And it don't rain in Indianapolis In the summertime." "Little Green Apples" by Roger Miller

Vegetables and Side Dishes

195

NATURALLY CARAMEL CARROTS

My mother used to cook carrots with butter and lots of brown sugar—delicious but a downright wicked thing to do to such a healthful vegetable. Then a friend in Albuquerque, Dennis Dunnum, taught me how to get a sweet, natural glaze from the carrot itself. The trick is in the pre-steaming—a step you can't omit to get these just right. It's also important to slice the carrots into very thin strips.

1 pound carrots

1 tablespoon butter

Peel and cut carrots into julienne strips about 1 1/2 inches long. Put in vegetable steamer and steam for about 10 minutes. Carrots should still be crispy, but quite moist. Drain.

In a heavy skillet, melt butter. Add carrots and cook over low heat, turning occasionally, until the carrots are tender and glazed a caramel brown. *Serve immediately to 4.*

GRILLED CABBAGE

Boiling cabbage down with a little butter or bacon seasoning and a lot of salt and pepper makes a pungent, savory side dish much beloved in country kitchens. But boiling cabbage down can fill your house up fast with a not-too-pleasant aroma that seems to linger forever.

That's why this recipe for "grilled" cabbage is such a delight. You get the same wonderfully flavored vegetable dish but without a whiff of cabbage odor in the house because it's cooked outside on a charcoal grill. We like it so much that I'd be willing to fire up the grill to make the cabbage alone. But wrapped in single-portion aluminum foil packages, it's also easy to scatter the cabbage on the grill around spicy sausages or Grilled Blue Tenderloin (page 51)—two meats it's delicious with.

For each serving:

1 cup slivered cabbage

1/8 teaspoon salt

1/16 teaspoon white pepper

1 tablespoon half and half

pat of butter

For each serving you'll need a piece of aluminum foil about a foot square. Lightly grease the non-shiny side with a little bit of butter.

Chop the cabbage in thin slivers, about an inch long and 1/8 inch thick—1 cup for each person. Put in a bowl and sprinkle with salt and pepper, then toss to mix seasonings with the cabbage. Put a cup of cabbage in the center of each piece of buttered foil, and drizzle a tablespoon of half and half over each cup of cabbage. Then top each cabbage mound with a butter pat about 1/8 inch thick. Fold the foil up to make a snugly closed pouch.

Put the cabbage on a grill 4 inches above a bed of hot charcoal. Let cook 12–15 minutes. If you're having a picnic, you can eat right from the foil pack; or you can turn out into an individual serving dish, making sure to get all the creamy juices. The cabbage doesn't pick up any smoke flavor in its foil pack, but it does have a surprisingly peppery bite.

"Boil 'em cabbage down and down

Turn them hoecakes round and round

The onliest song I ever did sing

Was 'Boil 'em cabbage down.'"

Traditional dance tune

Vegetables and Side Dishes

197

SALADS

Lemon Slaw

Deviled Eggs

Christmas Fruit Salad

Christmas Fruit Salad Dressing

Ambrosia

Ham or Smoked Turkey Salad

Mama's Chicken Salad

Tuna Waldorf

Mandarin Cream Cheese

Benedictine Cheese

TOMATO AND CUCUMBER SALAD

We had no garden in Louisville where I grew up, but that didn't mean there wasn't a garden in my life. My great-aunts in Corbin had a huge one out in the back of their house—the house where I spent many summers and some of the best days of my childhood. The garden was a warm, prickly place—always sunny when I was there and always a little scary with big, green, leafy plants growing well above my head.

Aunt Johnnie was the main gardener in the family—a large, warm woman with a grin almost as broad as her ample hips. She would put on a "house-dress" (looser, older, and more comforting for a child to grasp onto than a "town dress") and a floppy sunbonnet and wander in among the rows with a hoe and a basket or a "warsh" pan. ("Warsh" pans were something you "warshed" and "wrenched" your clothes in most times.) When she came out later, her basket or pan and her apron, too, would be full of bounty.

Most prized of all the garden's yield were the tomatoes. Aunt Johnnie would line them up on the window ledges of the screened back porch, arranged according to ripeness. We ate out on this porch in the summer around a big round pedestal table covered with an oilcloth. The green, acrid scent of the tomatoes mixing with the sweet and savory fragrances pouring out of the kitchen made every meal smell and taste like a feast of summer itself.

"Tommy toes" is what Aunt Johnnie called the little round red and yellow cherry tomatoes she collected in her pockets. I was allowed to eat as many as I could countenance and I popped them into my mouth as fast as Christmas candies. They were sun-warm and so full of juice it squirted right out between my lips and dribbled down my chin when I'd bite. The red ones were tart and made my eyes sting, but the yellow ones were sweet, almost buttery.

I could eat the big tomatoes off the porch, too, provided they were ripe. Sometimes I would carry my prize around to the front porch where the big white and yellow metal swing waited. Aunt Johnnie would join me after her chores were done, now wearing a better dress, her hair damp and combed and her fleshy arms sweet smelling from her afternoon bath.

She would bring a newspaper to spread across her lap, a salt shaker, and a handful of sour green June apples from the tree over in the side yard. I would pour a little salt in the nest of my left palm, take a bite from my tomato, then

"Ain't nothin' in the world that I like better Than bacon and lettuce and homegrown tomatoes."

"Homegrown Tomatoes" by Guy Clark

commence dipping the tomato in the salt and eating, one salted bite at a time.

Johnnie cut her apples into eighths, pared the core away, then salted them lightly before she ate them. She was always generous and offered to share with me, but these apples were a sorry experience for a little girl who expected sweetness at every bite. They were sour as green cherries, Florida lemons, first love gone wrong—and no amount of my Aunt Johnnie rolling her eyes and swearing they were "right tasty if you eat 'em with just a little salt" could make me venture one again after my first disastrous try.

Besides, bursting ripe summer tomatoes were fine treat enough for me.

And bursting ripe summer tomatoes are what you'll need for this simple salad, which has a complex and delicious flavor if all the ingredients are fresh. I like to use sweet Georgia Vidalia onions when they're in season, and if you can do the same, it will make this salad all the more delicious.

> 2 big, ripe tomatoes
>
> 2 medium cucumbers
>
> 1 medium sweet onion
>
> salt and freshly ground pepper

Peel tomatoes and chop into bite-sized chunks in a bowl. Peel cucumbers and chop into bite-sized chunks. Peel and chop the onion into smaller pieces. Sprinkle with salt and pepper to taste, toss together, and chill covered for 1–4 hours. *Serves 4.*

TOMATO ASPIC

Most contemporary recipes for tomato aspic call for canned tomato juice mixed with boxed and flavored gelatin. That's a shame since tomato aspic made country style, with ripe tomatoes and real lemon, is one of the freshest delights of summer.

> 2 1/2 cups of tomatoes, peeled, chopped and packed tight
>
> 4 whole cloves

5 black peppercorns

1/8 teaspoon coriander seed

1/2 teaspoon salt

1 teaspoon sugar

1/4 cup fresh celery leaves

1/2 cup fresh lemon juice (about 4 lemons)

1 packet gelatin

Put tomatoes, spices, and celery in a saucepan with a lid. Mash tomatoes with a wooden spoon while they heat up. When steam is rising from the pan, cover, turn heat to low, and let simmer for 15 minutes.

While tomatoes are cooking, juice lemons, remove seeds, and sprinkle gelatin over the juice to dissolve it. When tomatoes are cooked, use a wooden spoon to strain them through a small mesh wire sieve. Some tomato pulp will come through with the juice and you want that.

Mix tomato with lemon and gelatin and stir well. Pour into a lightly oiled mold, or individual molds. Refrigerate overnight to set. Serve with a dollop of good mayonnaise on top. *Serves 6.*

Root Salad

This is one of the simplest salads in the world, and also one of the prettiest. If the beets, turnips, and carrots are fresh and sweet from the garden, it's also one of the most refreshing you'll ever taste. You can add salt or pepper if you must, but that actually detracts from the delicate flavors of the raw vegetables.

1 medium beet

1 medium turnip

2 large carrots

1 lemon

2 large, attractive leaves of lettuce

Wash and peel the beet, turnip, and carrot, then grate each separately. Be sure to rinse the knife and the grater after each vegetable so the flavor (and, in the case of the beet, the color) of one doesn't interfere with the other. Squeeze lemon juice over each and toss to make sure the juice coats them well. Place washed and dried lettuce leaves on two salad plates and arrange the vegetables prettily on it in three separate scoops. This is a striking, crisp accompaniment for the Butter Beans and Sausage (page 44). *Serves 2.*

KILLED LETTUCE

Chet Atkins, dean of country music guitar and one of Nashville's most respected producers, was born in east Tennessee in the gorgeous-to-the-eye, but hard-on-the-pocket Clinch Mountain region just beyond Knoxville. Though his early years were marked by poverty, the favorite food from his boyhood is a rich one.

"We can start back home, where I was raised," said Atkins when asked to recall his most beloved dish.

"My mother was just a country girl and the foods she cooked were country foods, but good. I remember in the springtime she fixed killed lettuce, she called it. And it was lettuce with onions cut up in it and she put hot grease on it. Have you ever heard of that? I always loved that just about best of anything."

Atkins is not alone. Nearly everyone I know who grew up next to a country kitchen cites killed lettuce as a favorite food.

"You get a bowl full of that and a hot piece of cornbread and a glass of cold milk and you've got you a dinner," Brenda Lee said.

To the uninitiated, Killed Lettuce may sound strange, perhaps unappetizing. But to those of us who grew up eating it, Killed Lettuce stirs deep, dark cravings in the heart.

Best made with tender lettuce picked fresh from the garden in the spring, Killed Lettuce goes well with any number of dishes from a down-home bowl of beans to an uptown grilled swordfish steak.

> 1/4 pound sturdy leaf lettuce—romaine is good
> 2 green onions, chopped finely
> 6 slices bacon
> 1/4 cup vinegar
> salt and freshly ground pepper to taste

Killed Lettuce must be made right when it's ready to serve. It will not keep.

Pour warm water in a bowl and set aside. Wash lettuce, towel dry well, and tear into small pieces. Chop the onion finely.

In a skillet, fry the bacon crisp. Turn off skillet, put bacon on paper towels to drain, and reserve bacon grease in the skillet.

Empty warm water from bowl and dry it carefully. Put the lettuce and onion in it and toss lightly to mix. Heat the bacon grease in the skillet until it's very hot, but not smoking. While it's heating, pour vinegar over lettuce and toss to coat it evenly. Pour hot bacon grease over the mixture, tossing again. Crumble bacon over it; taste and add salt and pepper as desired, then serve immediately. *Serves 4.*

"Well, hot corn, cold corn, bring along a demijohn. Hot corn, cold corn, bring along a demijohn. Hot corn, cold corn, bring along a demijohn. Fare thee well pretty girl, see you in the morning, yes sir."

"Hot Corn, Cold Corn," Old Kentucky moonshine song

Salads

205

KILLED LETTUCE THAT WON'T KILL YOU

While all of us who grew up eating country food may rank Killed Lettuce among our favorite foods, its splash of bacon grease doesn't make it especially healthful.

My friend Lenore Crenshaw grew up in Monticello, Kentucky, eating the same good country foods I thrived on as a girl. But when she became a vegetarian in the early 1970s, there were some tastes she just didn't want to give up. So she's done some research into meatless versions of traditional country foods, and one of her finest creations is this recipe for "Killed Lettuce That Won't Kill You."

To approximate that rich bacon taste, Lenore uses Tamari soy sauce. Naturally fermented, it is full-bodied and saltier than most other soy sauces. You can find it at most health food stores or at markets specializing in oriental foods. And that's where you can find the other unusual ingredient in this recipe, the tart, salty umeboshi plum vinegar.

1 large head romaine lettuce

1 green onion

juice of half a lemon

1 tablespoon tamari soy sauce

1 tablespoon umeboshi plum vinegar

1/4 cup cold-pressed sesame oil

1 tablespoon dark sesame oil

Wash lettuce carefully, cut in thin shreds, and place in big bowl. Split green onion down the middle lengthwise, then chop very, very finely and sprinkle over the lettuce. Mix lemon juice and soy sauce and pour over the lettuce, tossing so it is well distributed. Sprinkle vinegar over the lettuce.

In a skillet, heat the oils until almost smoking. Pour over the lettuce, tossing it at the same time, being careful not to burn yourself in the process. Serve immediately. The tamari is salty enough that additional salt is unnecessary. *Serves 4.*

Variation: Inspired by Lenore, I came up with my own variation, this one with more onion and a slightly more robust flavor from gomasio, an oriental seasoning made from roasted sesame seeds ground with salt. Its toasty flavor is similar to that of bacon and gomasio is also delicious sprinkled on top of plain baked potatoes and Healthy, Hearty Greens (page 192).

To make gomasio, you need:

8 tablespoons sesame seeds

1 tablespoon salt

Heat a heavy cast-iron skillet on high, pour the sesame seeds in, turn immediately to medium-low and toast stirring constantly with a metal spatula. The toasting takes about 2 to 3 minutes. Some of the seeds will turn golden, others a dark mahogany brown. They don't have to be uniform in color. When most of the seeds are brown, sprinkle the tablespoon of salt over them and heat for one more minute, still stirring. Remove from heat.

Using a mortar and pestle, crush the seeds and salt a few spoonfuls at a time. Crush them just enough to crack the seeds open and release more flavor, but don't pulverize them into dust. Some people use a blender to crush the seeds, but I think it grinds the gomasio too fine.

Put the crushed gomasio in a jar or other container with a tight-fitting lid. Let it cool completely before covering, or moisture will form inside the jar. Keeps for two or three weeks covered in the refrigerator, but tastes best when it's fresh.

To make my Killed Lettuce with gomasio, you need:

1 large head romaine lettuce

3 green onions

1 tablespoon balsamic vinegar

1/8 cup dark sesame oil

1/4 cup gomasio

Wash lettuce carefully, cut in thin shreds, and place in big bowl. Split green onions down the middle lengthwise, then chop very, very finely and sprinkle over the lettuce.

Heat the sesame oil in a skillet until almost smoking. Pour over the lettuce and onion, tossing at the same time, being careful not to get burned in the process. Sprinkle the gomasio over the lettuce and toss that quickly also. Serve immediately. *Should be enough for 4.*

Long before any restaurateur set up the first salad bar, country cooks were laying out bounteous spreads from the garden, such as this table full of salads and other homemade goodies at a 1945 Humble Oil Company picnic in Banderas, Texas.

Wib's Favorite Cucumbers

The year Polly Judd Rideout, Naomi's mother, turned 50, she took a job as cook on one of the many barges plying its way from the upper Ohio River down the Mississippi to New Orleans.

"I thought it was an adventure. When you step off land onto that boat, you're in another world altogether."

In that world, ordinary diversions are at a premium: "A newspaper on a boat is a treasure. If people are smart and want your business, they'll bring you a newspaper, a magazine, or a book down when you dock. That's how to win over the people on the boats. And when you get one, you dare not lay it down. You can leave a $10 bill out and nobody will touch it on a boat, but a book is gone in a minute."

The three daily meals she cooked were also diversion for the crew as well as nourishment. Lots of men on the boats fell in love with her cooking. One of them also fell in love with the cook. Pretty soon Polly and pilot Wib Rideout were married and in 1984 she gave up her barge job and came back to the Judd house in Ashland to cook for Wib full time.

"Wilbert took one look at what a little thing I was back then and married me to save me from all that work," she says.

He says his favorite dish is Polly's Cucumber and Onions—a deceptively simple-looking salad with a cooked dressing that makes all the difference.

3 large cucumbers

3 medium white onions

1/3 cup sugar

1 cup water

1/4 cup cider vinegar

3/4 teaspoon salt

1/4 teaspoon white pepper

3/4 cup light vegetable oil

Peel and slice the onions and cucumbers 1/4 inch thick. Arrange in layers in a big crockery or glass bowl, preferably one with a cover, although you can also cover with plastic wrap.

In a small saucepan over medium heat, dissolve sugar in water. Add vinegar, salt, and pepper and bring to a boil. Add the oil and boil for about 30 seconds longer, stirring to mix well. Pour the hot mixture over the cucumbers and onions and let the whole thing sit covered in the refrigerator overnight. (You may want to spoon the dressing over the top cucumbers a few times while it's marinating, although it's not necessary.) *Serves 6–8 as a side dish.* Be prepared to give friends the recipe.

POLLY'S POTATO SALAD

Naomi Judd once said: "If anyone knows her way around a kitchen, my mama does. She's my favorite cook in the whole world. Every time I go to Mama's I know I can find her potato salad in a green bowl on the second shelf of the refrigerator."

Now you can put Polly Judd Rideout's Potato Salad in your refrigerator, too, but it won't stay there long.

> **4 medium Idaho baking potatoes**
> **Homemade Tangy French Dressing (page 212)**
> **1 cup diced celery**
> **1 cup diced sweet onion**
> **1/2 cup sweet pickle relish (at least)**
> **1 tablespoon yellow prepared mustard**
> **1/2 cup light mayonnaise or salad dressing**
> **2–3 hard-boiled eggs, cubed**

Boil potatoes in their jackets until tender when pierced with a long-pronged fork—about 15–20 minutes. Remove from heat, drain the water, and let potatoes cool until they can be handled. Peel and cube in about 1/2-inch squares.

Pour French dressing over the potatoes and toss to coat them well. Cover and refrigerate for an hour.

Then dice celery and onion and mix with potatoes. Add at least 1/2 cup of pickle relish, maybe more if taste tells you the salad needs it. Mix 1 tablespoon yellow mustard with light mayonnaise or salad dressing and mix with potatoes until it's all well coated and moist. You may need to add a bit more salad dressing.

Peel eggs, cube, add to salad, and mix lightly but well. Chill thoroughly and let the flavors have a chance to "marry" before serving. *Polly says this is enough for 4 and a little left over for the next day.*

HOMEMADE TANGY FRENCH DRESSING

1 six-ounce can tomato paste

1/2 cup olive oil

1/2 cup honey

1 tablespoon yellow mustard

1 tablespoon horseradish

1 teaspoon celery salt

1/2 cup rice vinegar

1 garlic clove, sliced

1 teaspoon salt

1 teaspoon Worcestershire sauce

Put everything in the blender and blend until a creamy consistency throughout. Store in refrigerator. *Makes about 1 pint.*

MINE AND MAMA'S POTATO SALAD

Sam Bush, hot picking multi-instrumentalist and a country boy by birth, once said that all the world could be divided into two camps: those who eat Kraft Miracle Whip Salad Dressing and those who swear by Hellmann's Mayonnaise.

Like Bush, I came from a family of Hellmann's devotees and like my mother, I wouldn't dream of making potato salad without it—or another equally good mayonnaise.

But like Sam Bush—who made his name by taking the traditional form of bluegrass music and adding modern innovations to put his own distinctive stamp on the sound—I've taken my mother's traditional salad and added some of my own twists.

My mama has never made a potato salad with skins on the potatoes—but I think it both adds a subtle textural touch and enhances the flavor. And while my mother was always content to stand in the kitchen chopping and thin-slicing whole dill pickles by hand, I've found that if you take the time to find a prepared dill relish with firm, crisp texture and fresh dill taste, it works just as well and saves plenty of time. (Claussen's and Sechler's are the two brands I've found best in my neck of the woods.)

My husband, meanwhile, not afraid of a little innovation on his own, insists that my version of this salad is not pickly enough. So I serve it with a bowl of relish on the table so he and any other budding improvisationalists can add at will.

> 7 medium Idaho potatoes
>
> 4 hard-boiled eggs
>
> 1/2 teaspoon salt
>
> freshly ground black pepper
>
> 1 medium onion, chopped finely
>
> 1 cup celery (about three stalks), chopped finely
>
> 1 cup dill relish
>
> 1 tablespoon dijon mustard
>
> 1 cup mayonnaise

Wash the potatoes carefully and cut out any eyes and blemishes. Cut each in half and put in a pot with a lid, covering with water. Bring water to a boil, then turn to a lively simmer and cook the potatoes 20–25 minutes until centers are tender when pierced with a fork. Don't let them cook until they're mushy. Drain and let potatoes chill thoroughly.

While potatoes are cooling, hard-boil eggs by covering with water and bringing to a boil, then turning down to barely simmer for 15 minutes. Peel eggs and let them cool.

When potatoes are cooled, cut them into 1/2-inch cubes. Sprinkle with salt and freshly ground pepper to suit your taste. Chop onions and celery finely and add to the potatoes, tossing lightly to mix. (You want the ingredients to mix well, but be careful not to stir too vigorously and make mush of the potatoes.)

Add the cup of crisp dill relish with its juice and toss lightly again. Mix mustard into the cup of mayonnaise and stir into the potato mixture. The result should hold together creamily. You may need to add a bit more mayonnaise to get it just right. Chop eggs and mix them in lightly at the last. *Serves 6 with some left over for the next day.*

MACARONI SALAD

Long before there were pasta salads of fusilli and rotini, country cooks would whip up simple, delicious macaroni salads for church suppers and reunions. Here's one we often have. Double the portions for your next potluck, using one sweet red bell pepper and a green one for more color.

3 quarts water
1 tablespoon olive oil
1 teaspoon salt
8 ounces dry elbow macaroni

1 cup finely chopped red onion
1 finely chopped green pepper
4 1/2-ounce can chopped
black olives

1 cup mayonnaise
1 tablespoon honey
1 tablespoon red wine vinegar
1 tablespoon dijon mustard
1 teaspoon celery salt
several grinds of black pepper

In a big pan, bring water to a boil, add oil, salt, and macaroni. Cook 12 minutes until macaroni is al dente. Drain, run cold water over the pasta, drain again, and let cool.

When macaroni is cooled, add chopped onion, pepper, and olives and toss together to mix well.

Combine the rest of the ingredients in a blender and process until well blended. It's a thick mixture, so I have to blend for a few seconds, then turn the machine off, stir it with a spatula, and then blend again. When the sauce is well blended, pour over macaroni and mix until everything is coated. Refrigerate for about an hour before serving. *Serves 8.*

JERRY'S SLAW

I have never determined for sure if Louisa (pronounced Loo-eye-zee) was my cousin by blood, or if she simply was a friend who lived with my parents and grandparents often enough to become a "cousin" by association.

Sharing your home with friends and relations was the custom in Appalachia. It was a custom that migrated with the people of the region when they went north to more industrial cities looking for jobs. And the house I grew up in in Louisville had an ever changing assortment of fascinating, occasionally odd characters from "back home." They ranged from my magnificent

His 'n' Her Gardens

Dwight Yoakam remembers with tender amusement that there were two gardens at his grandparents' house in Betsy Layne, Kentucky.

"My grandma had about an acre that she gardened," he said. "You'd walk two steps out the back door and then a couple of steps up the hillside. She grew her vegetables up there to feed the family not just in the summer, but to can for all through the winter. That was the main garden.

"But my grandad gardened, too. He had his own. They had separate gardens. I think she didn't want him meddling in hers and—aw—he just grew some things. It was his patch behind the garage. He had sweet potatoes that he grew down behind there and some other stuff he liked.

"I think they both maybe got in and worked each other's patches sometimes, but he did mostly one and she the other. And it somehow got titled that was 'Daddy's' down by the garage and the girls—my mother and her sisters—would come home in the summer and say: 'Well, what's daddy got growing down there this year?' "

Aunt Minnie, who made me hot fried apple pies and a whole layette of baby doll clothes, to Bill Moore, a drifter and distant relation my father took in for a while who looked like Popeye, walked with a limp, and taught me how to cheat at 500 Rummy.

Louisa was before my time, however. My mother said she had always been an itinerant part of the family, living for a month or so at a time in my grandparents' house in Corbin and then moving on, only to come back a few months or years later. When my parents married, custody of Louisa went to them much as my grandmother's china cabinet did.

Louisa's longest stint with my parents came in the late 1930s soon after my sister was born, and she earned her keep by taking on much of the cooking chores from the beleaguered new mother. Louisa was, by all accounts, a remarkable cook—but it is her one consistent disaster that has become the stuff of family legend.

It seems that Louisa worked for a time as a cook in the restaurant of a London hotel (London, Kentucky, that is) and in that restaurant she made coleslaw—by the vat. When she left the restaurant to cook at home, she was able to reduce most of the ingredients to fit the moment, cutting cabbage in just the right proportions for whatever size crowd she was feeding. But both my parents swore that no matter how much slaw Louisa was making—enough for three or twenty—she always added the same amount of mayonnaise she'd used at the restaurant. Her slaw was often so slathery as to be inedible—no matter how much good cornbread you might have to sop it with.

But if Louisa's slaw didn't directly contribute much to the Lundy family palate, it added immeasurably to our vernacular: For years we referred to anything too slippery to grasp as "slicker than Louisa's coleslaw."

And I feel confident that it was Louisa's slaw that indirectly led to the development of one of my mother's most impressive dishes: a coleslaw that is simple and sublime.

The secret to my mother's coleslaw is not an easy one to imitate since it's not in the ingredients or the timing—as with most recipes—but purely in the wrist. My mother shaves delicate strings of cabbage from the head with a touch and patience very difficult to imitate.

My theory is she developed the technique in those early years of house-keeping as a defense against Louisa's slaw.

"Here, Louisa," I imagine her saying. "Let me make the coleslaw for dinner tonight, because you know Pap just loves the way I cut the cabbage."

I have tried with only limited success to imitate my mother's coleslaw. I learned the hard way that grated cabbage doesn't work. The pieces are too small and release too much pungent cabbage juice for the right flavor. And although I have friends who swear by their food processors, I can't get one to come close to my mother's style.

With years of trying, however, and attention to a few details my mother has provided, I can cut the cabbage pretty close to make a delicious slaw that pleases everyone except those raised on my mother's. Here is her recipe including her tips on how to get the cabbage shaved just right. My bet is you still won't be able to get it quite like my mother's slaw, but it won't be Louisa's, either.

6 cups of cabbage, most of one medium head

2/3 cup mayonnaise

2 teaspoons half and half

1/4 teaspoon salt

1/4 teaspoon sugar

a few grinds of black pepper

green pepper (optional—and arguable)

You want a very fresh, very firm head of cabbage with tightly packed leaves. You can tell a head that is tightly packed because it will feel heavier for its size than its loosely packed counterpart. Do a little comparative balancing in the produce department to pick the best.

At home, peel the loose outer leaves from the cabbage until you get to the lighter, tighter, moister ones. Cut cabbage in half and cut hand-sized chunks from it, avoiding the thick, solid core.

(When I was little my treat was to get to eat the core with a little sprinkle of salt on it while dinner was being prepared. My daughter likes the same treat now. If you don't have an innocent bystander to dispose of the core, however, save it for vegetable soup.)

To shave the cabbage, hold it firmly in your left hand (or vice versa if left-handed) with the outer leaves against the palm, your thumb securing it. With a very sharp, thin knife, begin shaving super-thin slices of cabbage from the top of the piece until the piece is too small to shave any more. Pop remnant in your mouth, don't put in slaw. Do this until 6 cups have been shaved.

My mother says: "And it takes a lot of time to shred cabbage right. When you're cutting it up, you think you've got a lot, but when you put your mayonnaise on there, it goes down quite a bit."

One trick to the shaving is a very sharp paring knife with a short, thin blade. The one my mother uses is about 2 1/2 inches long, tapering from 1/2 inch wide at the base to 1/8 of an inch at the tip. I thought the proper knife had to be curved mid-blade as well because the one I remember Mother using in my childhood was. But when I asked her she just laughed and said, "No, that started out as a straight edged blade, but it just got worn in the middle from use."

The tip finally broke off that knife and she used the less than 2-inch remaining blade for a few more years to make slaw before it was lost in a move and she got the current one. Whatever knife you choose, my mother says, it must be "sharp, sharp, sharp."

Shave the cabbage into a good sized bowl and then sprinkle with salt, pepper, and just the pinch of sugar, tossing it well to distribute evenly. Add the mayonnaise and just a splash or two of half and half so that the dressing is smooth and creamy, but not runny. Taste and adjust salt or pepper if you want. You shouldn't actually taste the sugar. It's just there to bring the other flavors out.

From time to time my mother likes to put about a half cup of chipped green pepper in her slaw, but I hate it when she does. There's something about the pepper's bitter presence that ruins the slaw of my childhood memories. My mother says it's a good variation, though, and I'd better tell you about it. If you decide to add the green pepper, the operative word here is chipped, not chopped. My mother cuts her pepper in very small pieces, about 1/4 by 1/8 inch or smaller, and you should do the same.

This will make enough slaw for 4 if served with the Green River Style Fish Sandwich (page 81) and Best Ever Hushpuppies (page 240); or Mother's Roast and Good Brown Gravy (page 55) and Hot Water Cornbread (page 237); or the Fried Green Tomatoes (page 186) or just about anything else.

Lemon Slaw

I was always glad when my Aunt Ariel came to visit because she smelled like perfumed face powder and wore a little fur jacket that she wasn't afraid to let small children rub their cheeks up against. I was also glad to see her because whenever she came my mother would fix roast beef and this lemon-flavored, gelatin slaw—Aunt Ariel's and my favorite. Fresh-juiced lemons give it a zip that perfectly complements the vegetables' crunchy zing.

1 cup cold water

2 envelopes gelatin powder

1/2 cup sugar

1 1/2 cups boiling water

1 cup fresh lemon juice

1 cup seeded and thinly chopped cucumber

1 cup thinly sliced celery

1 cup grated carrot

1 cup thinly sliced cabbage

Put 1 cup of cold water in a large bowl and sprinkle the gelatin powder over the top. Let sit undisturbed for a minute. Mix sugar and boiling water and when sugar is dissolved, add to gelatin and stir well.

Let cool while you juice the lemons (about 6), grate the carrots, and chop the other vegetables finely. When gelatin is at room temperature, stir in the lemon juice, then add the vegetables and mix well. Pour into a 2 1/2-quart dish and refrigerate until set, about 4 hours. *Serves 8–10.*

Deviled Eggs

Some folks think you make deviled eggs just by popping out the yolks, mashing them with a little mayonnaise, and putting them back in the whites with a splash of paprika for dash. But I don't see anything sinfully enticing

"When I was a little boy around the table at home I remember very well when company would come I would have to be right still until the whole crowd ate My mama always said to me, 'Just take a tater and wait.'"

"Take an Old Cold Tater (and Wait)" by E. M. Bartlett

Shuck Beans, Stack Cakes, and Honest Fried Chicken

220

in that. These are truly deviled eggs with a taste so wickedly good you can't stop eating them. Take them to a potluck or reunion to share the burden of guilt.

> 1 dozen hard-boiled eggs
> 1/8 teaspoon white pepper
> 1/4 cup dill pickle relish
> 1 green onion, minced
> 1/4 teaspoon horseradish
> 1 tablespoon dijon mustard
> 1/4 cup mayonnaise

Cut the eggs in half lengthwise and carefully pop out the yolks into a small mixing bowl. Reserve the whites, throwing out any that are torn.

Sprinkle yolks with pepper and then mash well with a fork. (The mayonnaise and mustard are salty enough without adding any.) Mix in relish and green onion (be sure to mince it very finely). Then add horseradish, mustard, and mayonnaise and mix until smooth and creamy.

My sister, Pat, cousin Jessie, and my mother at a Grinstead family reunion in the early 1950s. Jessie was one of my favorites. She could cook as well as my mother and tell funny stories as fast as my father. Grinstead family reunions began with everyone around the table eating until they hurt and lasted long into the night with everyone still around the table, laughing as hard as they could.

My father's favorite tale of Jessie involved Boy, a pet parakeet she kept in her kitchen. She talked to the bird constantly and at night the two would make kissy noises until it was time to go to bed. Then Jess would cover the bird cage with a cloth, and head off to her bedroom where she'd put her dark hair up in pin curls and slather cold cream on her face.

In the mornings, she usually made sure the cream was off, the pin curls out, and her hair brushed before she came into the kitchen to get a cup of coffee and take the cover off Boy's cage to let the day begin.

But one day she was too hurried or harried to get things in order. She came into the kitchen still in those pin curls, got her coffee, and then pulled the cover off the cage.

Boy popped open his eyes, took one look at Jessie's huge-eyed, sharp-nosed, pin-curled visage right outside his door and promptly fell over dead.

Using a teaspoon, fill the cavities of the egg whites with big dollops of the yolk mixture. Spread some out over the top. Be generous. Don't worry if you have a couple of whites left over when you run out of yolk. Just pitch the extra whites. It's better to have well-filled eggs with lots of flavor than lots of eggs with not enough.

Chill until it's time to serve and try to keep from eating them all before dinnertime. *Serves one dozen, if no one commits the sin of gluttony.*

CHRISTMAS FRUIT SALAD

"Back during the Depression we saw an orange about once a year," recalls Chet Atkins. That once a year was likely to be Christmas time and that orange was such a rarity it most often ended up as a gift tucked in the toe of a stocking.

When I was growing up in the city several decades later, fruit was more common, but the old traditions persisted. My Christmas stocking usually had little toys, geegaws, and jewelry in it but always, at the top, there was a banana peeking out; halfway through an apple; and in the toe, every year, an orange.

And every year my mother made her traditional fruit salad. In fact, she made the salad twice a year—at Thanksgiving also—because she firmly believed a body couldn't eat turkey without it. But somehow—perhaps because the fruit in my stocking got contributed to the process—I always thought of this as her Christmas Fruit Salad.

She said this was how her mother made fruit salad also and when we had a houseful of company for Christmas, she would make nearly double the amount here and serve it in the big glass punch bowl from the china cabinet, just as her mother had done.

My special treat while she was making it was to drink the drained juice from the pineapple chunks out of a small jelly glass, but some folks like to use the juice to make a dressing that's served on the side with fruit salad. I have included a recipe for the dressing, although my family always thought the undressed fruit salad was good enough.

You can add or subtract ingredients to suit your own tastes, of course.

"To me, the more grapes and bananas and nuts you have in it, the better it is," is what my mother says.

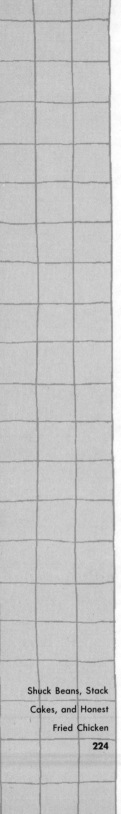

1 large, red delicious apple

1 firm-fleshed pear

2 or 3 navel oranges

1 pound red grapes, halved and seeded

1 20-ounce can pineapple chunks, drained

1 8-ounce can crushed pineapple, with juice

2 nectarines if available, or 1 16-ounce can peaches

1 1/2 cups pecan halves

4 firm bananas, not too ripe

Quarter and remove stem and core from apple and pear. Cut into slices about 1/2–3/4 inch wide at the arc and cut small bite-sized pieces into a large bowl. Over the bowl, peel the oranges, using a knife so you get all the white pith off and so all the juice runs over the apple and pear. Cut oranges into small bites also, being careful to remove any seeds.

My mother usually uses red Emperor grapes that nave seeds, which means that after she cuts each in half, she uses the tip of her knife to flick the seed out. She prefers the flavor of the Emperor, but in recent years has found the convenience of the seedless red grapes, now commonly available, even more attractive. But even if you use the seedless grapes, you still have to cut them in half. If you toss them in the salad whole "it doesn't get everything near as juicy and good tasting" my mother says.

Drain juice from can of pineapple chunks and set aside for dressing, if you want—or pass on to your favorite little kid to drink if not. If chunks are too big, cut in half. Cut nectarine in pieces like pear and apple—or if using canned peaches, drain and cut them into pieces that size.

The pecan pieces you can buy in groceries already broken up are actually too small to be good, my mother says. Pecan halves, of course, are too large. So what you have to do now is take the 1 and 1/2 cups of pecan halves, break each one in half across the middle, and toss it into the salad.

Just before you're ready to serve, peel bananas and add to salad in slices about 1/4 inch thick. Toss everything together gently but well and put in big serving bowl. Pass salad dressing on the side. *Serves one dozen.*

CHRISTMAS FRUIT SALAD DRESSING

1/2 cup sugar

2 tablespoons flour

1/8 teaspoon salt

1 egg, beaten

reserved pineapple juice

1 tablespoon butter

1 cup cream, whipped

In a saucepan, mix together the sugar, flour, and salt, then stir in the beaten egg and pineapple juice. Put over medium heat and cook, stirring constantly until it begins to thicken. Remove from heat, add the tablespoon of butter, and stir until it's dissolved and mixed in. Refrigerate for one hour.

When you're ready to serve, whip the cream until it's fluffy, then fold chilled pineapple juice mixture into the cream, blending it well. Serve in a bowl next to the fruit salad, letting folks spoon on dressing if they desire.

AMBROSIA

This sweet fruit salad is a southern tradition, and was most often made in the simplest of ways—just sliced orange sections layered with fresh-grated coconut and left for a bit in the refrigerator while their flavors married.

Over the years, any number of variations on that theme have come along—and the name Ambrosia has been given to several kinds of fruit salad that have oranges, coconut, and something creamy to hold them together. Most Ambrosias these days usually have canned mandarin oranges and pineapple, coconut, whipped or sour cream, and marshmallows. My version is as rich as that one, but with ripe summer fruits and a wonderful homemade dressing to keep them together. Although this is called a salad and is traditionally served as such with the meal, it's rich and sweet enough to be dessert.

1/2 cup sugar

1/8 teaspoon ground ginger

1 tablespoon cornstarch

1 20-ounce can of pineapple chunks

3 beaten egg yolks

3 small oranges

1 1/2 cups apricots or bing cherries

2 peaches

7-ounce package sweetened coconut

Drain the juice from the can of pineapple and set the chunks aside to go in the salad later.

While water is coming to a boil in the bottom of a double boiler, mix sugar, ginger, and cornstarch in the top, away from heat. Add pineapple juice and beaten egg yolks and whisk until blended. (If you're wondering what to do with the leftover whites, see Pecan Angels, page 318).

Then heat the mixture over boiling water, stirring constantly, until it's thick enough to coat the back of a wooden spoon. Pour into a cool bowl and refrigerate while you prepare the fruit.

Peel the oranges with a knife, removing all the white. Slice into three rounds, then section, removing the pith and seeds. Slice apricots in quarters or cherries in half and remove seeds. Peel the peaches and cut into bite-sized bits. Mix all the fruit, including the pineapple chunks, with coconut. If dressing is not cooled yet, refrigerate fruit until it is.

When dressing is cooled, pour over the fruit and toss lightly until everything is well coated. Keep chilled until ready to serve, but serve soon since this salad does not keep well. In addition to being a good addition to a chicken or turkey dinner, Ambrosia makes a lightly sweet teatime snack with Sally Lundy Bread (page 266). *Enough for 12.*

Ham or Smoked Turkey Salad

This salad is wonderful piled in ripe tomatoes or avocado halves, or served on dark rye bread. It's also great made with smoked turkey which has a hickory-rich flavor similar to ham.

> 1 pound cooked ham or smoked turkey with fat removed
> 1/2 cup sliced celery
> 2 tablespoons minced white onion
> 4 heaping tablespoons sweet pickle relish
> 1/2 teaspoon coarsely ground black pepper
> 1 tablespoon country-style, coarsely ground dijon mustard
> 1/2 cup mayonnaise
> 3 hard-boiled eggs, chopped

Chop the ham or turkey into small chunks, but don't mince. Add celery, onion, relish, and pepper and mix together well. Add dijon and mayonnaise and mix until all is well moistened, then chop eggs into salad and mix lightly. *Makes 6–8 sandwiches.*

Mama's Chicken Salad

Chicken salad is the fundamental southern luncheon food. New variations on the theme arrive every decade or so ranging from the basic sandwich spread with gherkins to the more exotic curried chicken salad of recent years.

This grape and pecan chicken salad surfaced in our family in the late 1960s and has been a solid favorite since. This is how my mother makes it still and she usually serves it as salad with a bread on the side since it's too chunky to spread. But if you want it in a sandwich of sorts, it fits nicely into a pita half.

"Turkey in the straw, haw, haw, haw. Turkey in the hay, what do you say? Roll him up and twist him up—a high tuck a-haw And hit 'em up a tune called 'Turkey in the Straw.' "
"Turkey in the Straw," Traditional

8 small chicken breasts

1 stalk celery

1/2 teaspoon salt

water

1 cup thinly sliced celery

2 cups green or red seedless grapes, halved

1 cup chopped pecans

1 cup mayonnaise

1 tablespoon dijon mustard

1/2 teaspoon celery salt

black pepper

Wash chicken breast and put in saucepan with celery, salt, and water to cover. Bring to a boil, then turn heat to low and simmer for 20 minutes, until chicken is done. Remove chicken from broth and when cool enough to handle, remove skin and bones. (I usually put them right back in the pot and simmer everything for another hour or so, then strain and put the broth in the freezer for future use.)

Chill chicken. When cold, cut into small bite-sized chunks. Put chicken, celery, grapes, and pecans in a bowl and toss until well mixed.

In a separate small bowl, blend together mayonnaise, mustard, and celery salt. Mix with dry ingredients until everything is moistened and holding together. You may need to use a little extra mayonnaise. Add black pepper to taste. *Serves 6–8.*

Tuna Waldorf

Tuna salad was the old reliable of summer. Any well-stocked pantry had a can of tuna that could be mixed with mayonnaise, celery, and relish on a moment's notice. But while canned tuna salad could be depended on, it didn't really excite.

With fresh tuna so readily available now, though, you can make an unusual, light, and crunchy salad combining the fundamentals of Waldorf salad with a chilled, grilled tuna steak. The steak itself is delicious hot, so what you may want to do is to cook and serve several of them, then use the leftovers for salad the next day.

This salad is very chunky, and if you want to make a sandwich of it, you'll have to put it in a pita pocket. You can, however, make a delicious and more spreadable variation substituting mayonnaise for the oil and lemon dressing.

3/4-pound tuna steak, about 1 inch thick

juice of half a lemon

1 teaspoon olive oil

1/4 teaspoon salt

1/2 cup chopped apple

1/2 cup sliced celery

1/2 cup broken walnuts

juice of half lemon

1 tablespoon olive oil

salt and pepper to taste

Coat tuna with mixture of lemon juice, oil, and salt and let refrigerate for at least 1 hour. Grill over red-hot charcoal, about four inches from coals, until well browned on one side (about 10 minutes) and then for 5 minutes on

Churning Song

"I don't remember how she made it," Chet Atkins said, "but my mother made cottage cheese all the time when I was a little boy. And it was really good. Better than the kind you buy in the store.

"And she made butter, too, and it tasted better than any butter you could buy. She'd let me churn for her when I was a little boy. And I learned to sit there and sing and churn like she did, and hum. You know how women will sit and churn and twist the ladle as they churn, and hum: 'Dee, dee, dee, dee,' and churn some more."

the other. Refrigerate again until thoroughly chilled.

When it's chilled, chop tuna into bite-sized pieces. Chop apple and celery finely and break walnut halves into four pieces. Toss together with lemon juice and olive oil. Taste and add salt and pepper to suit. *Serves 6.*

MANDARIN CREAM CHEESE

This fruity sandwich spread is nice on melba toast but decadently divine on a sweet bread such as banana, applesauce, or brown bread.

8-ounce package cream cheese

11-ounce can mandarin orange slices

8-ounce can crushed pineapple

1 cup raisins

1 cup pecan pieces

Soften cream cheese at room temperature in mixing bowl. Drain juice from oranges and pineapple. Beat cheese until creamy with an electric mixer—about one minute. Then add orange slices and beat another minute until they're shredded and mixed throughout.

Remove bowl from mixer and add pineapple, stirring it in well with a spoon. Add raisins, then pecans and stir until all are mixed in. Chill for several hours. *Makes one dozen sandwiches.*

BENEDICTINE CHEESE

I was born in Corbin, Kentucky, but I was raised in Louisville, and no good Louisville girl would leave you without a recipe for that city's classic tea sandwich spread, Benedictine Cheese.

The cucumber blend gets its name from the turn-of-the-century hostess who popularized it, Jenny Benedict. It gets its distinctive light green color from a couple of drops of food coloring which you may decide to omit, if you prefer, but please don't put Jenny's name on the recipe if you do.

Classically, Benedictine Cheese is spread thinly between pieces of soft white bread with the crusts trimmed, then cut into diagonal fourths and served on a doily-covered platter. That recipe uses just the juice from the cucumbers and onions to make a very smooth spread.

Recently, though, local cooks have started to add the drained, grated cucumber back into the mix. One Louisville restaurant also makes a fat, earthy benedictine with small chunks of unpeeled cucumber and pieces of red onion through the flavored and colored cheese. The chunkier spreads go well with hearty, whole wheat bread. Some folks also like to add strips of bacon to a benedictine sandwich.

The recipe here is for the classic, smooth benedictine—a wonderfully cool treat on a hot summer's day.

8 ounces cream cheese, softened

3 tablespoons cucumber juice

1 tablespoon onion juice

1 teaspoon salt

a few grains of cayenne pepper

2 drops green food coloring

To get the juice, peel and grate a cucumber, then wrap in a clean dish towel and squeeze juice into a dish. Do the same for the onion. Mix all ingredients with a fork until well blended. Using a blender will make the spread too runny. *Makes enough for half a dozen sandwiches.*

"Only two things that money can't buy: That's true love and homegrown tomatoes."

"Homegrown Tomatoes" by Guy Clark

BREADS

REAL CORNBREAD

If God had meant for cornbread to have sugar in it, he'd have called it cake.

Real cornbread is not sweet. Real cornbread is the fundamental building block of good Appalachian eating. Crumble it in a bowl and cover it over with hot Soup Beans (page 121), serve a slab of sweet onion and maybe a little pickle relish on the side, and you've got the ultimate supper. Cornbread served with Killed Lettuce (page 204) makes a fine dinner out of nothing more than bread and greens. And speaking of greens, you simply can't serve Greens with Pot Likker (page 190) unless you've got a big wedge of cornbread to soak up all that good juice. And you don't want a bunch of sugar, flour, or baking powder in there fighting with the other tastes.

What you want is cornbread that pops out of a cast-iron skillet flat and browned, steam rising from the gash when you cut it to serve. Real cornbread is sunny tasting and golden crispy, thin with a high ratio of crust to center—that's why cornsticks are so prized among mountain people. It tastes of drippings (bacon grease or butter are the best) and corn. It's about the most American food I know of, and it's a shame that you can't seem to get it—made right—in a restaurant. On the other hand, you can get it just perfect at home if you follow this recipe for Real Cornbread, just like my mother made it all my life.

4 tablespoons drippings

2 cups finely ground white cornmeal

1 teaspoon salt

1/2 teaspoon baking soda

1/2 teaspoon baking powder

1 large egg

1 1/2 cups milk or buttermilk

The secret to really great cornbread is the crust, and the trick to making the crust just right is to heat the pan and drippings good and hot in your oven before you put the cornbread batter in it. So before you so much as get out a bowl to mix up the batter, turn the oven to 450 degrees.

In a 9-inch, round cast-iron skillet (or reasonable facsimile thereof), put

"Boil 'em cabbage

down and down

Turn them hoecakes

round and

round . . . "

Traditional dance tune

about 4 tablespoons of drippings. Bacon grease is the traditional choice and gives cornbread a distinctive flavor. Butter is tasty and about a tablespoon of butter along with a bland vegetable oil will still give you a good taste with less saturated fat to feel guilty about.

Pop the skillet, grease and all into the oven. Please note, you can't accomplish what you want by heating the skillet on a burner on top of the stove. Doing that will make hot spots in the bottom of your skillet which in turn will make your cornbread stick to the pan.

While the grease is getting good and hot in the oven, mix cornmeal, salt, soda, and baking powder in a big bowl. Add the egg and milk or buttermilk, and stir until just blended.

Remove the skillet from the oven and very, very carefully (don't burn your hand!) swirl the grease around in the skillet so it coats the bottom and the lower half of the sides.

Now pour the hot grease into the cornmeal mix and if everything is perfect it will snap, crackle, pop, and bubble invitingly. (Even if it doesn't, there's no problem. It just means your grease wasn't quite hot enough and you should leave it a smidgen longer the next time. But don't leave it too long and start a fire.)

Mix lightly until the grease is just blended in, then pour the cornbread batter into the hot skillet and put it back in the oven for 20–25 minutes until the bread is firm in the middle. If the crust isn't browned on top, pop the pan under the broiler for just a few seconds to get it crispy golden. Serve from the skillet, or turn the skillet upside down on a big plate and the cornbread should slip right out.

If you want to make cornsticks, use the same recipe, but pour the batter into greased cornstick pans and bake for half the time.

If you should have any left over, check page 241 for what to do next. *Recipe will yield 6 hefty wedges of cornbread from the pan, or a dozen cornsticks.*

HOT WATER CORNBREAD

My mother learned to make this recipe from our neighbor, Bert Harrison, who always served it with fresh fried fish. Bert would put out the golden, meal-dipped fish filets on one platter and the golden cornpones on another. And she'd also put out a plate of sliced white bread for anyone foolish enough to prefer a sandwich.

Once her cousin came in, snatched a cornpone instead of a piece of fish, slapped it between two pieces of white bread with catsup, and pronounced it the lightest, best-tasting fish sandwich he'd ever had.

These cakes are that delicious indeed, but I recommend you eat them with soup or a good, hearty stew instead of trying them as fish sandwich filling.

2 cups finely ground white cornmeal

1 teaspoon salt

4 teaspoons white all-purpose flour

2 cups boiling water

vegetable oil for frying

Put a kettle of water on to boil. Mix the cornmeal, salt, and flour together in a bowl. When water is boiling, measure out 2 cups. Add the water to the cornmeal slowly, mixing well. The 2-cup measure is approximate. Some meal may require more, some a little less. You want the mixture to be thoroughly moistened and firm enough to hold together, but you don't want it soupy like a batter.

Heat a heavy skillet, then pour in oil 1/2 inch deep and let it get very hot, but not smoking.

Now here comes the part where you must be very, very careful. Put a big spoonful of the hot cornmeal mixture in your hand and pat into a pone that's about 3 1/2 inches long, 2 inches wide, and 3/4 of an inch thick in the middle. If your hands are very sensitive to heat, you may want to rinse with icy water first, dry quickly but completely, and then pat out the pones.

The Mason-Dixon Cake Line

Chet Atkins has this to say about real cornbread:

"Mark Twain wrote a chapter on it once that there's something about people born above the Mason-Dixon line, when they get in the kitchen making cornbread, they think they're making cake and they always put sugar in it.

"And my wife will say, 'There's a Yankee in the kitchen!' when we go in a restaurant, you know, and they have something sweet in the cornbread.

"They just don't seem to be able to make cornbread, and a lot of it is the receipt on the bags suggesting you put a lot of stuff in it. Sweeteners and everything, I guess a Yankee makes up that receipt."

Lay the pone carefully into the hot oil being careful not to burn your fingers. Some people put the pone on a spatula and use that to transfer it to the oil. It's safer, but stickier than the hand method. (Please note: If you didn't dry your hands completely back when you rinsed them in cold water, any water that drips into the oil now will pop and can burn or blister you badly.) Make enough pones to cover the surface of the pan, but not crowd one another. If the pones touch each other, they're likely to stick and crumble.

When the pones are golden on the bottom (1–2 minutes), flip over for another minute to turn the other side golden. Lift out of oil with a slotted spoon or spatula and put on paper towels to drain. Keep making pones and frying until all are done.

The boiling water steams the meal in the cornpone, giving it a delicious, creamy texture but a fresh, popcorn-like taste. They should be eaten while hot, but it's a good idea to break the first ones open and let the steam out before taking a bite. *This recipe makes about a dozen, which is enough for 4 greedy people.*

HATTIE DICK'S CORN MUFFINS

This recipe comes from the recipe box given to Blanche Pedigo of Anchorage, Kentucky, by her grandmother. The recipe is attributed to Hattie Dick, the Little Colonel of Annie Fellows Johnston's quintessentially southern books. Both Dick and Johnston lived in Pewee Valley, Kentucky, and when Blanche's father, Peyton Hoge, was a little boy, his family lived in a house on Johnston's land.

"When my parents would go to town, Mrs. Johnston would baby-sit me," he recalled. "What a privilege that was for me! She was a one-of-a-kind character and often she thought more like a child than a grown-up. We'd sit on her veranda and she had names for all the little chipmunks and squirrels and we'd watch them and talk to them. She had one she called Heliotrope— because it sounded so pretty, I guess. I found out later this wasn't quite a proper name for a squirrel."

This is a proper recipe for a corn muffin however—one with no sugar to fluff it up.

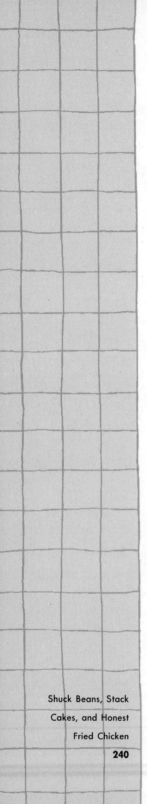

2 cups cornmeal

1 teaspoon salt

2 cups boiling water

1 teaspoon butter

1 beaten egg

1 cup milk

1 heaping teaspoon baking powder

Mix cornmeal with salt. Add boiling water to cornmeal, stirring constantly so it doesn't lump. Add butter and stir vigorously, then let cool. When cooled, add beaten egg, milk, and baking powder. Mix well. Grease muffin tin and put in 400 degree oven until it's hot. Remove and pour batter in. Return to oven and bake for 20 minutes until browned. Serve hot with plenty of butter. *Makes 12 big muffins.*

Best Ever Hushpuppies

As a rule, I don't like hushpuppies, but this recipe is one to break the rules for. Not sweet like most commercially made pups, these have a tangy bite from the chives and buttermilk, and are truly sensational if the onion used is a sweet Vidalia.

2 cups white cornmeal

2 tablespoons flour

1 teaspoon baking powder

1 teaspoon salt

1 medium onion, grated

3 tablespoons chives, chopped very finely

1/4 teaspoon freshly ground black pepper

2 eggs, beaten

1 cup buttermilk

canola oil

Mix cornmeal, flour, baking powder, and salt together, add grated onion with juice, chives, and pepper and mix lightly. Add the egg and buttermilk and mix until just blended.

In a heated skillet or other heavy pan, pour oil an inch deep and when it's really hot drop hushpuppies in by the tablespoonful. Let fry until golden brown all over, turning once. It only takes a minute or two. (Use a slotted spoon to skim the grease of any batter nubbins after each batch so they don't burn and make your pups taste charred.) Drain on paper towels and serve hot. *Makes enough for 6.*

Leftover Bounty

Any leftover cornbread can be used to make Kentucky Cakes (page 277) or Cornbread Dressing (page 20). But when I was growing up, leftover cornbread at our house hardly ever made it to the next day.

My daddy always had to have a little bite of something before he went to bed at night. Sometimes it was a dish of ice cream or a bowl of cereal. But if there was cornbread in the house, what he liked best was to crumble it up in a tall glass, pour milk on it, and eat it with a long-handled spoon. He's not alone. About the only disagreement concerns whether it is better to use sweet milk or buttermilk. Either is great.

If a piece of cold cornbread did manage to see the light of the following day, my mother would split it in half, put slivers of butter on it, and pop it under the broiler to make a toast that we'd eat with jam. Or if the cornbread had accompanied her roast the night before, then she'd serve it the next night for dinner with Mother's Hash (page 57) on the top.

Grace Rainwater, down in Georgia, said all of her children, including Brenda Lee, liked their toasted cornbread with cane syrup poured over it.

And Jean Ritchie said that "the main best eating there is" would be to take a piece of cold cornbread in one hand, a fistful of black walnut meats in the other, and to trade off bites of each with a glass of cold milk on the side.

"No corn in the crib, no chicks in the yard. No meat in the smokehouse, no tubs full of lard. No cream in the pitcher, no honey in the mug. No butter on the table, no 'lasses in the jug."

" 'Leven Cent Cotton, Forty Cent Meat" by Bob Miller and Emma Denver

RICED CORNBREAD

Nothing went to waste in a good country kitchen and cooks looked for clever ways to mix a little bit of this and a little bit of that to create a recipe that yielded a lot of good eating.

This bread is one—a fine way to use leftover rice with a bit of cornmeal. I use brown rice at my house, because that's what we most often have left over. It gives this bread both a creamy quality and a chewy subtext. And if you don't eat all this cornbread for dinner, you can make a glorious breakfast the next morning on leftover wedges split open, toasted, and served with thick jam or Sorghum Butter (page 348).

2 tablespoons butter

1 cup yellow self-rising cornmeal

2 eggs

2 cups buttermilk

2 cups cooked brown rice

Put butter in a 10-inch, cast-iron skillet and place it in oven with temperature turned to 450 degrees. While the butter gets hot and crackling, mix cornmeal, eggs, and buttermilk in a large bowl. Add cooked rice and mix.

Butter should be bubbling in the skillet by now, so take it out of the oven and swirl it gently to coat the bottom and a bit up the edges of the skillet. Be careful not to burn yourself, though.

Pour hot butter into the cornbread batter and mix. Pour batter back into

the skillet, put the skillet in the oven, and bake at 450 degrees for 25 minutes—or until bread is firm in the middle and browned on the sides. Turn out into a large plate and serve immediately. *Serves 6.*

SPOON BREAD

Spoon Bread, much beloved in the South, is really just company cornbread all gussied up in its Sunday best. It has a more delicate flavor and creamy texture and is best, as its name suggests, served with a spoon from its steaming hot pan. It used to be quite a production to make it when all the beating had to be done by hand, but with an electric mixer, it's very simple.

3 cups low fat milk

1 1/4 cups cornmeal

3 eggs

1 teaspoon salt

1 3/4 teaspoons baking powder

3 tablespoons butter

Bring milk to a boil in a large, heavy pan. Stir in cornmeal in little batches, being careful not to let it lump or stick. (I use a whisk to keep down lumps.) When the mixture thickens—usually very quickly—remove from heat.

In a large electric mixing bowl, beat eggs for 2 minutes on high. While you're doing that, put butter into a large cast-iron skillet and place skillet in a 400 degree oven until butter melts.

When eggs are beaten, add the hot cornmeal to them a large spoonful at a time—adding salt and baking powder during the process. When all the cornmeal is in, pour butter from the skillet into the batter.

Beat batter on medium for 10 minutes, scraping the sides of the bowl regularly. It will be quite thick but very creamy. Turn out into buttered skillet and bake in 400 degree oven for 25 minutes. Serve straight from the oven, piping hot with butter on the side. The consistency is like a supremely thick pudding and you will have to use a big spoon to serve it. *Serves 6.*

The Care and Curing of Cast Iron

Old cast-iron skillets, Emmylou Harris says, are "like an old pair of shoes or a pair of jeans that you just can't part with."

She has some from her mother, Eugenia, who in turn inherited quite a few from her mother.

"And then I had a good friend who gave me a fortune of cast iron," Eugenia said. "Because you can't scrub them with dish soap, she felt they were too oily and greasy, so she just gave them to me. And they were already blackened and a little crusty looking, and you know that's just when they're getting good. That's the joy of cooking with them."

Cast iron is porous and that's one reason why it's traditional never to use soap to clean it—the detergent can flavor your pan. If your skillet is well seasoned to begin with, cornbread and the like won't stick to it, so you can just wipe it clean with a cloth after baking. I've got one skillet that I use strictly for making cornbread, so I don't ever have to worry about cleaning something else off.

If you have to give a skillet a scrubbing, use table salt rubbed around the surface with a clean dishcloth, then rinsed with plenty of hot water. Or if it's a stubborn cleaning job, use a plastic scrubber. After you've rinsed the skillet, dry it thoroughly. I put mine on a burner to vaporize any moisture out.

The simplest way to season a new cast-iron skillet—or one that has lost its seasoning from a scrubbing—is to turn your oven to 450 degrees. When it's good and hot, pour a couple of tablespoons of vegetable oil into the skillet and rub it into the surface well with paper towels. Put the skillet in the oven and turn the oven off. Let sit for 30 minutes to an hour. Use paper towels to wipe out any excess oil that may not have been absorbed.

But while the oven method is the easiest way to season cast iron, it's not the best way, avers Bucky Harris, Emmylou's dad.

"It takes about a week to break one in correctly," he says.

"I burn mine in out in the backyard. What you do first is oil the pan down good (with a vegetable oil). Then I build a fire in a big grill we have in the backyard, and I put the skillet on and just let it smoke. And then I wipe off the fluffy stuff that forms on the surface and I let it cool down. And then I oil it again. It's a process that takes about a week and I burn it three or four times a day.

"The whole idea when you burn them in is to get a solid coating of carbon inside the pores of the cast iron, just worked into the pores. And a lot of the newer cast iron isn't as porous as the old. They closed up all the old factories because of the EPA and all of them now use electric furnaces rather than the open-fire hearths they used to use and I think that makes a cast iron that's not as porous.

"But if you work at it hard, you can get a good coating."

CHICKEN FIXINGS

Southerners are famous for their hospitality and southern mountain people even more notorious for their willingness to share a meal with anyone, friend or stranger.

I was fully grown before I learned it wasn't considered an unbearable breach of etiquette to have someone visit your home without feeding them. In my parent's house, as soon as company crossed the threshold, my mother offered them coffee, tea, Coca-Cola and the entire contents of her Frigidaire and pantry.

And if someone arrived close to the time for supper or dinner, she insisted they stay and share whatever was destined for the table, no matter how much or little there might be. I watched my mother invent some amazing dishes for four out of three pork chops or stretch a couple of minute steaks into an hour's worth of good eating for family and friends.

CHICKEN EXTENDERS

Old-time country cooks were ingenious at stretching a modest entree into a bounteous feast. Perhaps one of their cleverest and tastiest inventions was Chicken Extenders—little fingers of mush or dough fried in the skillet after the chicken had been taken out to give them a crisp, golden crust and the meat's luscious flavor.

The humblest Chicken Extenders were made from cold cornmeal mush (page 170) sliced into slabs about 1/2 inch thick, one slab to a customer. Then each slab was sliced into pieces about 3/4 inch wide and the pieces laid in the hot skillet just as soon as the chicken was taken out. They were fried on medium-high heat until golden brown on both sides. And while they might be plain food, they were plain delicious when covered with cream gravy.

Chicken Starfish

The "company coming" version of Chicken Extenders was something more like a fried biscuit. You can make them using most any biscuit recipe, but I like this rich egg and broth dumpling one best for its full flavor.

Some cooks roll the dough out, slice it in strips and cut or pinch off squares to fry; but we have a little star-shaped cookie cutter, about 1 1/2 inches from point to point, that I use. And that's given rise to a whole new name for these tasty little morsels. My daughter, Meghan, likes to call them Chicken Starfish and likes to eat them just as fast as she can.

> 2 cups flour
>
> 1 tablespoon margarine
>
> 1/2 cup boiling homemade chicken broth
>
> 1 teaspoon salt
>
> 2 teaspoons baking powder
>
> 1 egg, beaten
>
> oil from chicken frying

Put 1 cup of flour in a bowl, make a well in the center, and put margarine in it.

Pour boiling broth into the well and stir until smooth.

Mix salt and baking powder with the second cup of flour, then add to the moist flour mixture. Add beaten egg. The dough should be stiff enough to roll out. If not, add more flour a little at a time until it is.

Turn dough out onto a floured board and knead very lightly (about five times), then roll out 1/2 inch thick.

Cut into desired shapes.

When chicken has been removed from the frying pan, turn heat to high and drop the biscuits in the oil and drippings. Fry to golden on one side, then turn and fry until golden on the other. (Be careful not to burn them; reduce heat if necessary.)

Drain on paper towels and serve on a platter with chicken. Eat the biscuits split open with gravy poured over them, or with apple butter.

Makes about a dozen and a half bite-sized biscuits.

LIGHT BREAD

When I was growing up there were three regular kinds of bread in our house: biscuits, cornbread, and light bread. Biscuits and cornbread were made from scratch and most of the time you had one with breakfast, the other with supper. Light bread was bought from the store, wrapped in cellophane and already sliced. It was used primarily for sandwiches. I had no great-aunts or cousins who specialized in making yeast breads or rolls. And it seemed an unnecessary effort when hot biscuits or steaming, hearty cornbread could be had with a smidgen of the time and effort.

As I got older, though, I realized that bread from the store was "light" in more ways than I'd thought—especially lacking in flavor and nutrition. And so I set about teaching myself how to make a good, rich loaf of whole wheat bread. My instruction in the art of bread making was from Edward Espe Brown's *Tassajara Bread Book*, and learning from Espe was something like learning from a Zen hillbilly uncle. His methods are based as much on the spirit in which you bake as the technique and ingredients—an attitude that didn't seem at all alien to the way my mother and aunts had taught me.

When it came to technique, I liked most of all Espe's recommendation that you make a sponge and let it practice rising before mixing up the full bread batter. And I've incorporated that step into this recipe given to me by a friend many years ago.

As whole wheat loaves go, this one is notably airy and delicate—easy to slice and deserving of the term "light bread" used as praise.

3 cups warm water

2 tablespoons yeast

1/4 cup sorghum molasses

1 beaten egg

5 cups whole wheat flour

1 tablespoon salt

1/4 cup canola oil

2–3 cups whole wheat flour

Dissolve yeast in warm water in a big bowl. Add the molasses and stir gently to dissolve. Add egg, then add the 5 cups of flour a cup or less at a time, stirring well after each addition. When all the flour has been added, beat briskly about 100 strokes until batter is smooth.

Cover the bowl with a damp towel and put it in a warm place (90–100 degrees) to rise. If you have an oven with a pilot light, this is a good place. Or you can heat your oven slightly for a few minutes, turn it off, and put the bread in it to rise. Don't let the temperature get over 100 degrees though, or you run the risk of killing the yeast.

Let rise for approximately 1 hour—depending on the heat of the rising place, it may take more or less time. It should be close to double in bulk from its original size, although a bit less is acceptable.

When sponge has risen, sprinkle salt and pour oil over it. Mix the two into the dough by "folding in." You do this by moving the wooden spoon around the edge of the dough, lifting and folding it into the center. Try not to cut through the sponge.

Fold in the rest of the flour this way as well, adding it about a half-cup at a time. Some breads may take more, some less. The dough is ready to knead when it holds together and can be easily turned out of the bowl in one piece. Place on a floured board and knead until elastic and firm.

Lightly oil the bread bowl and return the dough to it, turning the dough over in the bowl to coat the surface with oil. Return to a warm place and let rise for 45 minutes.

Punch down the risen dough by gently pushing your fist into it to let out the air. Divide in half, knead a quick four times each, then roll up and put into 2 large (9 1/4 x 5 1/4 x 2 3/4 inches), oiled loaf pans. Let rise the final time for about 20 minutes. Use a sharp knife to make a few slits in the top of the bread.

Bake at 350 degrees for approximately an hour. Bread is done when top and sides are golden brown and the loaf gives a nice hollow thump when you rap it with your knuckles. Remove from pans immediately and let cool thoroughly before slicing if you want nice, even, not-too-crumby slices. Or decide you don't care and eat it warm with butter melting right away. *Makes 2 loaves.*

John Lair started broadcasting the Renfro Valley Barn Dance out of Cincinnati in 1937 on a 500,000-watt channel that some farmers swore they picked up on barbed-wire fences and milking machines. Determined to set up a more genuine country version of the radio variety show than those he'd been involved with in Chicago and Cincinnati, Lair eventually moved his barn dance to the small Kentucky town it was named for. Lair tried to create a spontaneous, homey feel, including occasional early morning broadcasts from around a breakfast table like the one pictured here. While some cast members dug into biscuits and gravy, others picked up banjos and mandolins and played. Lair presided over all, seated at the head of the table with a microphone in front of him. He liked to call the slice-of-life breakfast shows "reality broadcasting."

SALT-RISING BREAD

Once I'd started baking bread, it wasn't any time at all before my mother began hounding me to bake her a loaf of good Salt-Rising Bread. This is one of the most cherished of homemade breads, but also one of the most difficult to accomplish, based as it is on a starter made from scratch. To make the starter you soak either sliced potatoes, rough cornmeal, or both in warm liquid with a bit of sugar and then coddle it for several hours until it begins to bubble and ferment like a natural yeast.

The problem is that such a starter is unpredictable and downright skittish. Sometimes it bubbles, sometimes it won't—and even slight variations in temperature will send it into a slump.

And if you're lucky enough to succeed and get a good starter going, you'll be rewarded with a house that smells overpoweringly like a hamper of ripe gym socks—the distinctive aroma of a good salt-rising starter. So why would any loving mother goad her child into this experience? Why would anyone go to the trouble (and endure the smell) of making salt-rising bread at all?

Because once it's baked, it has the finest flavor of any bread imaginable—light but tangy with a whisper of sweetness at the end. Sliced and toasted, it may be the best bread ever invented.

And Lord knows, I tried to bake such a loaf for my mother. Every time I'd run across a new recipe or technique that purported to be foolproof, I'd get out my bread pans. Blessedly, heaven didn't let such efforts go unrewarded. No, I didn't one day hit upon the perfect starter and turn out golden loaf after golden loaf, but fate eventually allowed me to buy a house not too far from Bussman's, a local bakery that turns out perfect salt-rising bread every Thursday—often enough to satisfy both my mother and me.

But Bussman's only makes enough bread for the local folks. And in the interest of science and this cookbook, I decided it was imperative that I come up with a workable recipe for salt-rising bread. So I gathered every cookbook, piece of folklore, and article I could and after a few false starters I came up with this recipe—which works for me—and some general pointers.

1. Forget the potatoes. About half the recipes for salt-rising starter used thinly sliced or grated potatoes mixed with cornmeal, the rest just plain

cornmeal. I never had any success with the potatoes and peeling, slicing, and then later draining the starter from them was just extra trouble.

2. Use the most unrefined cornmeal you can get. Some cooks recommend stone-ground or water-milled. Avoid those that are degerminated. I had my best success with organic cornmeal bought from the local health food co-op. It doesn't matter if the meal is yellow or white, as long as it's got gumption.

3. Warm everything that comes in contact with the starter—the vessels you mix it in, the spoons you mix it with, the measuring cups. I made sure my cornmeal and flour were room temperature also. And don't work in a kitchen where there are drafts or where a fan is operating.

4. When you leave it to ferment make sure the starter stays at a constant temperature between 90–100 degrees. Everyone I talked to who has had successful starter and has a gas stove with a pilot light set the starter over the pilot light to ferment. I have an electric stove, though, and for a few attempts tried placing the jar with starter in my stock pot filled with warm water. Doing this, though, requires monitoring the water with a thermometer and reheating it very, very carefully when the temperature dips.

The best success I had came after I read in Bernard Clayton's *New Complete Book of Breads* that he sometimes uses an electric yogurt maker for starter. Voilà! Mine was gathering dust in a cabinet, but when I'd gotten it out and cleaned it up a bit, it worked like a charm. It has five cups in it and I divide the starter ingredients in half and use two to make the starter for this recipe.

3 teaspoons sugar

4 tablespoons organic cornmeal

1/2 cup scalded milk

2 cups warmed milk

1 teaspoon salt

2 teaspoons baking soda

2 cups flour

1/2 cup oil

4–6 cups flour

Mix sugar and cornmeal together, then pour scalded milk over them. Mix well and then put starter, uncovered, in a warm place (90–100 degrees) for

10–12 hours. If your starter is working, it will be foamy or bubbly on top and have a sweetish, sour smell (the worst of the smell comes in the next step). If your starter isn't working, pitch it and try again.

When starter is ready, in a large bowl mix warmed milk with salt and soda. Add the starter and blend. Then using a big wooden spoon to stir, mix in the 2 cups of flour about half a cup at a time. Beat until smooth. Cover bowl with plastic wrap or a plate on top and place somewhere warm to rise for 2–4 hours, until bubbling and nearly doubled in bulk.

(For this rising, I turn my oven on for one minute at 200 degrees, turn the oven off, put the bowl with the sponge in it, and close the door. This is where your faith will be tested, because it's during this sponge-rising stage that the smell gets really potent.)

When sponge has pretty near doubled and is bubbling along merrily, remove from warm place and pour oil over the top, then fold it in to the batter. Begin to add flour to the mix about 1/4 cup at a time. Use a spoon to mix at first, but as it gets stiffer, flour your hands and get them into the act.

The dough is ready to turn out and knead when it begins to hold together in a mass that is not too wet. Turn out on a floured board and knead for 8 minutes, incorporating flour as you do. This dough is a soft one, and it will become elastic as you knead it.

Divide dough into two parts, and use a rolling pin to roll each into a rectangular shape. Fold each in half and pinch edges together. Put each loaf into a lightly oiled, large (9 1/4 x 5 1/4 x 2 3/4 inch) loaf pan with the seam side up, then roll it so the seam side is down for baking. (This will give a light coating of oil to the top.) Press it into the pan, then cover with waxed paper, and let rise in a warm place for 45–60 minutes, until dough has doubled.

Bake at 375 degrees for 45 minutes, until top and sides are golden, and the loaf makes a nice, hollow thump when you thwack it with your knuckles. Turn out and cool thoroughly before slicing. *Makes 2 loaves.*

"I smell your bread
   burnin'
Turn your damper
   down
If you ain't got a
   damper,
Turn your bread
   around."
"Mule Skinner Blues" by
Jimmie Rodgers and
George Vaughn

Breads

253

FREEDOM BREAD

Sheila Joyce Pyle and her husband, Ken, used to run a little club in Louisville, Kentucky, called the Storefront Congregation. Sheila dished up savory soup beans and cornbread from a back room. Ken served cold beer in plain Mason jars from the bar. And up front on a little rickety wooden stage with a mural of heavenly folks ascending on song behind it, bluegrass music was played like never before.

The progressive bluegrass movement was born at the Storefront Congregation in the early 1970s, spawned by a band fronted by Sam Bush and called the New Grass Revival. This is where Tony Rice got his start, first with the Bluegrass Alliance and then with J.D. Crowe's New South. It was there that someday country music stars Ricky Skaggs and Keith Whitley sang pure bluegrass harmony as boys still wet behind the ears in Ralph Stanley's band.

Those were heady days, fueled by the music and Sheila's good cooking. Along with those soup beans, she also served fine country ham and when the spirit struck her and the yeast would rise, a sturdy, delicious loaf called Freedom Bread.

The Storefront was torn down at the end of the 1970s to make way for a drive-thru chili parlor and a bank. But progressive bluegrass became a powerful force on the acoustic music scene. And Ken and Sheila started a new place where you can hear bluegrass, rockabilly, serious blues, reggae, or Afro-pop most any night. Called the Rudyard Kipling, it's a full-service restaurant with soup beans still on the menu along with hearty burgoo, meat pasties, vegetarian red beans and rice and, when the spirit hits her and the yeast will rise, Sheila's Freedom Bread.

Sheila said this recipe had another name when she saw it in a newspaper "oh, about umpteen hundred years ago." It also had some other ingredients and they didn't go together quite this way. She kept changing it a bit each time she made it and eventually ended up with the recipe here (with lots of options recommended in case you feel like changing it, too).

"I named it Freedom Bread because it has sweet potatoes in it," Sheila said. "Sweet potatoes come from Africa, you know. And I thought Freedom Bread worked really well because after you eat this wonderful, rich, brown bread you'll be free of white bread forever."

1 cup wheat germ (may substitute 1/4 cup oats, bulghur, or cracked wheat for equivalent amount of wheat germ)

2 cups water

2 medium sweet potatoes (1 pound cooked—you can also use cooked pumpkin, carrots, squash or pinto beans)

2 tablespoons yeast

1/2 cup water

1/4 cup honey or brown sugar

1/4 cup oil

1 tablespoon salt

5 cups bread flour

3 cups whole wheat flour

Three hours before you're ready to begin baking, cover wheat germ with water and leave to soak. Bake sweet potatoes, peel and mash until very soft and smooth. Sheila sometimes uses canned sweet potatoes, drained.

When you're ready to bake, dissolve yeast in warm water and add honey or sugar and stir until dissolved. Add potatoes, soaked wheat germ, oil, and salt and blend together. (Sheila says you're welcome to use less salt if that's a concern, but she cautions that the bread won't brown as prettily if you do.)

Add flour a bit at a time, using a spoon first, then working it in with your floured hands. The dough may not require all the flour here, or it may need a little more. It should be a soft dough, but one that isn't gummy. When it's ready it shouldn't stick to you, Sheila says.

Turn out on a floured board and knead it for 5–8 minutes until it feels firm but elastic. Return to bowl, cover, and let rise in a warm place until nearly doubled—usually 45 minutes to an hour.

Punch dough down gently. Divide dough into 3 parts and fold each one into a loaf shape. Put each into a well-greased, large (9 1/4 x 5 1/4 x 2 3/4 inch) loaf pan. Cover and let rise again in warm place for 45 minutes.

Bake in a 350 degree oven for 30–40 minutes. Bread is done when it's nicely browned and gives a good hollow thump when thwacked with your knuckles. *Makes 3 loaves.*

POLLY RIDEOUT'S YEAST ROLLS

2 packages dry yeast

1/2 cup warm water

2 teaspoons salt

1/2 cup white sugar

1/3 cup shortening

1 cup cool water

1 egg, beaten

4 2/3 cups sifted unbleached white flour

Dissolve the yeast in the warm water. Add salt, sugar, shortening, the cool water, and the beaten egg. (You want warm water to activate the yeast, but then you add the cool water so the egg won't curdle.) Gradually add flour, mixing very well. Place dough in greased bowl, punch down gently several times with your fist, then cover and let rise at room temperature until doubled, about an hour. Punch mixture down a second time, cover, and refrigerate for at least 2 hours, but no more than 12.

When ready to bake, turn the dough out on a floured surface, knead lightly three or four times, then roll out to about 1/2 inch or less in thickness. Use a 3-inch-diameter, round biscuit cutter to cut rolls. Brush the top of each lightly with melted butter.

Use the dull edge of a table knife to crease each roll across its diameter taking care not to cut through the roll. Fold the halves together to make a roll that looks like lips. Give each roll a little nudge as you place it on a greased pan. Let the rolls rise there for an hour, then bake in a 425 degree oven until golden brown. *Makes about two dozen.*

Baking Powder Power

"Those yeast rolls were always a big favorite of Naomi's and of all the rest of my kids," Polly Rideout, Naomi Judd's mother, says.

"They were a big hit when I was cooking on the river barge, too, but I don't know if they were any more popular than cornbread or biscuits. A lot of the fellas working on the boats are country boys, and you set a country table. And there's nothing they like better than hot cornbread or hot biscuits.

"It took me a long time to learn how to make good biscuits but I'm glad I did, because by the time I was cooking on the boat—well, a lot of the time you were practically making biscuits in your sleep."

The first breakfast serving was at 5:30 A.M. and that meant Polly was up at 3:30 or 4 A.M., frying, baking, and making biscuits.

"There are two tricks and the first is learning to judge how much milk. It varies from batch to batch and what you want is to just put in enough so that it holds together. The second trick is fresh baking powder and enough of it. I learned if my biscuits weren't rising to add more powder. And if that didn't work, then throw the powder out and get a fresh can."

A good way to test your baking powder before you put it in a batch of biscuits is to put 1 teaspoon in 1/3 cup of hot water. If it's good it will fizzle and bubble to beat the band. If it doesn't, pitch it.

BUTTERMILK BISCUITS

Southern food guru John Egerton suggests that the southerner's proclivity for soft, hot biscuits at breakfast—contrasted to the northerner's preference for harder rolls or bread made into toast—likely came about because of the types of wheat grown in each region. While the northern states produced a hard, protein-rich wheat, southerners grew a softer winter variety, better suited for light cakes and airy biscuits. Those of us southerners who grew up waking to the smell of biscuits hot out of the oven are awful glad that's how things worked out.

Like many a southern cook before him, South Carolinian Louis Osteen, owner/chef of the famous Louis's Charleston Grill, says that of all the soft flours milled in the South, the best for biscuits is White Lily, from a small mill down in Knoxville.

But Osteen, who bakes fluffy, butter-rich biscuits at his restaurant, admits also to a fondness for Martha White flour "because it makes an excellent biscuit, too, and because the company sponsored Lester Flatt and Earl Scruggs for all those years." Osteen, you see, loves his bluegrass with his biscuits.

If you can't find Martha White or White Lily flours at your grocery, settle for a good cake flour which will give you the requisite fluff and puff. I guess because they make biscuits so very often, southerners also love flour that is self-rising (or in the case of Martha White, equipped with "Hot Rize").

But the recipes here start at scratch and have baking powder or soda added to them. Osteen says that the secret to a great biscuit is a light hand in the mixing and he's right. Just mix flour and shortening until it starts to hold together. You want to have little lumps of butter in the mix. Stir milk into it just enough for everything to combine and when you fold the dough on the board, pat it but don't knead it.

2 1/2 cups soft flour

1 1/2 teaspoons baking powder

1/2 teaspoon baking soda

1 teaspoon salt

1/2 cup slightly softened butter

1 cup buttermilk

Sift flour, baking powder, soda, and salt together twice. Cut butter into the flour mixture and use fingers to lightly mix together. Dump buttermilk into flour all at once and mix quickly and lightly until dough holds together. Turn out on a well-floured board, pat dough out, and fold it over a few times. Roll out lightly to about 3/4 inch thickness and cut with a straight-sided biscuit cutter. Place on a greased cookie sheet and bake at 350 degrees for 15–20 minutes, until tops are golden brown. Eat hot with Sorghum Butter or Instant Black Walnut Grape Jam (both on page 348). *Makes 12–16 biscuits.*

EARLENE'S BISCUITS

Dwight Yoakam's grandmother kept her bacon grease in a small brown ceramic pitcher. She kept her flour, already sifted, in a big green porcelain pan that, when she wasn't using it, sat in the bottom of an old, wooden Hoosier cabinet in her kitchen. From these two simple vessels with their plain ingredients, she made biscuits that her daughter, Ruth Ann Rankey, remembers as being "the smoothest in the world. They were lighter than any biscuits I've had since—not as short as most people make them. And that little dab of bacon grease she put on the top of each one gave them such a good flavor."

Nowadays when a cook decides to make biscuits from scratch, it's a big event in the kitchen that requires getting out the mixing bowl, rolling pin, measuring spoons and cups. But for Earlene Tibbs, biscuit making was an everyday occurrence and she mixed each batch up right in the flour pan.

"A Hoosier cabinet is one of those big, old kitchen cabinets with a shelf to work on, a flour sifter built in and storage above and below," Ruth Ann explained.

"I can still see that big green pan. Mother would pull it out from the cabinet when she was ready to make her biscuits and make a little nest in the flour and put her rising agents and bacon grease and whatever liquid in it that she needed and work the flour into the nest right there in the pan until it was right. Then she'd lift the ball of biscuit dough out of the pan (the rest of the flour and the pan went back into the cabinet to wait for the next day's biscuit making) and she'd squeeze it in her hands to make the biscuits. She never rolled the biscuits and cut them. 'Choking the biscuits out' is what she called it."

Plenty of country cooks opted for the quicker methods of "dropped" or "choked" biscuits as opposed to the more time- and space-consuming process of rolling the dough and cutting it. But while biscuit batter dropped from a spoon bakes up with a nubby, crunchy crust, choked biscuits come out nearly as smooth and satiny as the rolled ones.

Crusty Biscuits

Musicians have many meals on the road and that's not a pleasant prospect when you travel by bus at odd hours and have to rely on fast food and chain restaurants to get by.

But Emmylou Harris says things have gotten brighter ever since the food chains discovered the South's best breakfast secret—biscuits.

"My mother made real biscuits and I just loved them. And now hot scratch biscuits are all the phenomenon at drive-in window and chicken places. They're not my mother's biscuits, of course. But they're good. The rest of the country has discovered what we had in the South for as long as I can remember and I tell you, I couldn't be happier—unless maybe they also discovered grits."

But Brenda Lee says she still isn't satisfied. Seems like everybody makes their biscuits too big for Little Miss Dynamite.

"Little bitty, fluffy biscuits, now that's what I like," she said. "A lot of people like great big biscuits, wide as a saucer. But my mother makes the little fluffy ones with crust all golden on the bottom and crust on the top and just a bite of fluff inside."

How does she get them that way? Grace Rainwater, Brenda's mother, says, "A lot of people cut their biscuits, but I don't. I roll mine in the palm of my hand and then I flatten it out. Put a little flour in your hand to keep the biscuit from sticking and roll and flatten it until it's just a little bigger than a silver dollar. It'll rise about an inch or so. I'm the type that don't like a whole lot of the inside of a biscuit."

Ruth Ann remen [...] g sheet, ready to go in the ove [...] e bacon grease pitcher and bl [...] savory drippings.

"I know it's not g [...] he says.

Here is a recipe ad [...] ts, with bacon grease for the sho [...] uits out just right. The bacon g [...] Butter (page 348).

Sift flour, salt, and ba [...] l. Add bacon grease and work int [...] ur into the grease lightly until it's [...] k a bit at a time, and continue to w [...] e flour will require a little more, s [...] hen it all sticks together easily and [...] sticky. If you get it too wet, add a [...]

Pick up a big handful [...] n your left hand (if right-handed) and pat it smooth lightly, then squeeze about a third of the dough through the circle made by your thumb and forefinger, pushing gently from the back with your right hand. Put the biscuit on an ungreased baking sheet, with the rough broken surface down. Continue to make all biscuits this way until done. Leave plenty of space between the biscuits on the baking sheet.

When biscuits are made, put your finger in the bacon grease and dot each biscuit with a little dab on top—just a streak of grease for flavor, not a big dollop.

Then put the baking pan in a 400 degree oven, baking for 15 minutes until just beginning to brown. Serve hot. *Yields about 9 biscuits, each the size of half a tennis ball.*

GRIT BISCUITS

What a scrumptious way to use up leftover breakfast grits—and what an excuse (as if I ever needed one) for making hot biscuits of an evening. Mix your batter up while the grits are still warm in the morning, cover, and put in the refrigerator until about an hour before you're ready to bake. Then put in a warm place and let rise. Or cook up a cup of grits according to package directions expressly to make these crunchy, wholesome biscuits.

> 1 package yeast
>
> 1/3 cup warm water
>
> 1/4 cup molasses
>
> 1 cup warm, cooked grits
>
> 1/2 cup margarine
>
> approximately 1 cup flour, half whole wheat and half white

Dissolve yeast in warm water and mix with molasses. Add to grits and cut in margarine. Add enough flour to make the dough stick together. Cover and let rise 30 minutes. (You can refrigerate for up to 8 hours if you don't want to bake right away—just let rise in a warm place for an hour after removing from the fridge.)

Roll dough out on a heavily floured board, folding it over on itself three or four times. Cut biscuits (they'll be very moist and need to be handled delicately) and place on a greased cookie sheet. Let rise for another 30 minutes, then bake at 350 degrees for 20 minutes until browned. *Makes a dozen.*

BEL CALAS

Biscuits weren't the only hot breads popular on southern mornings. Bel calas were the poor man's version of the New Orleans airy, yeasted, and fried pastry, the beignet. The bel calas were made from leftover rice and at the turn of the

Granddaddy's Honey on Granny's Biscuits

Dwight Yoakam's family would leave Columbus, Ohio, on a Friday night when his daddy got off work and drive all night down Route 23 to his grandparents' house in Betsy Layne, Kentucky. The kids would tumble, sleepy, from the car into Luther and Earlene Tibbs's arms, and then get trundled into bed still more than half asleep.

"In the morning," Yoakam recalls, "I'd wake up in Kentucky and it was like a dream, but I knew just where I was, listening to the sounds of my grandmother. It's about 5:30 in the morning but she and my granddaddy would be up at 5, banging around. And I'd wake up to the aroma of sausage and eggs and her singing out there in the kitchen, humming hymns to herself.

"And that was a pretty charming way to wake up as a kid.

"I also remember she'd cook the eggs in the skillet that the sausage had been fried in and there'd always be that kind of good sausage taste on the fried egg. It was like an additional season.

"And biscuits. My granny's biscuits. Honey on those biscuits—that was something else. We always had raw honey because my granddad had hives. He had a lot of beehives up on the hill out behind the house. And he'd go up there in his gloves and mask and smoke the bees out. Rob the bees of honey. We rarely ever bought store honey. And we'd chew the comb. My mother taught us that, because she chewed the comb growing up in lieu of chewing gum.

"In the mornings, you know, after eating a plate just full of her eggs and sausage you'd still have to have one more of my grandmother's biscuits and some of Granddaddy's honey on that."

"Bake 'em biscuits, bake 'em.
Bake 'em good and brown.
When you get them biscuits baked
We're Alabammy bound."
"Pig in a Pen," Old-time fiddle song

"You make the best biscuits with lard or bacon grease," Bobby Bare says.

"Bacon grease is heavier and you get better biscuits—real old-fashioned ones with a texture to them. First thing I do is I take the skillet and put bacon in the skillet and fry it cause you gotta have grease for anything.

"Then I start mixing up my biscuits. Always use buttermilk. And you've got to have an iron skillet to bake them in. An iron skillet is the only thing that will make the bottoms right on either a biscuit or cornbread. An iron skillet is a must to get them perfect, if you're going for perfection. You can put them in pans, those little thin, nonstick baking pans and they'll be okay, but the iron skillet is really the thing.

"Sometimes now I use a low-cholesterol shortening instead of grease in my biscuits and they come out pretty good—a little too light, but good. But of course, you've still got to take a spoon and put bacon grease on the tops before you put them in the oven. And of course, put grease into the pan before you put them in to keep them from sticking. That makes them perfect."

Here a little girl in Andrews, Texas, in 1945 adds a dollop of bacon grease to make biscuits just like the ones Bare describes.

century in the French Quarter you could hear black women calling out their musical name as they peddled them, steaming, from napkin-covered baskets.

This recipe came to me from Blanche Pedigo of Anchorage, Kentucky, who inherited it from her great-great-grandmother, a Le Clerc from St. Louis whose family background was Louisiana Cajun. Even without a pedigree, though, it would be equally scrumptious. And what a way to use leftover rice.

> **2 cups cooked rice**
> **1/4 ounce dry yeast**
> **1/3 cup lukewarm water**
>
> **3 eggs**
> **1/4 cup sugar**
> **1/8 teaspoon nutmeg**
> **1/2 teaspoon salt**
> **1/2 teaspoon vanilla**
> **1/4 cup sifted flour**
>
> **canola oil**
> **confectioners' sugar**

Mash the rice well. Dissolve yeast in lukewarm water and mix with the rice. Cover and leave in a warm place to rise overnight.

The next morning, beat the eggs, then add all ingredients except the canola oil and confectioners' sugar to the yeasted rice. Beat well with a wooden spoon. Cover and let rise again for 20 minutes.

Pour canola oil 2 inches deep in a heavy saucepan and heat to 360 degrees. Test batter by dropping a tablespoonful quickly into the oil. If it breaks apart or scatters, add flour a little at a time until it will hold. (Remember to remove the test drops immediately so they don't burn and taint the oil.) Don't add too much flour, though, because the secret of great bel calas is their lightness.

When batter is suitable use a large spoon to drop fritters into the oil, frying only 4–6 at a time. Turn once and remove when golden brown on both sides, draining on paper towel. After they're drained, but while they're still hot, sprinkle confectioners' sugar on them and eat them as soon as you can. *Makes 12–18.*

"I smell your bread

burnin'

Turn your damper

down

If you ain't got a

damper,

Turn your bread

around."

"Mule Skinner Blues" by
Jimmie Rodgers and
George Vaughn

SOUTHERN SHORTENING BREAD

Mammy's little baby loved shortening bread in keeping with a southern tradition for savoring sweet breads and little tea cakes. This butter-rich biscuit falls in that last category and is almost sweet enough to pass for a cookie. It's simple to make and wonderful served with an afternoon pot of tea.

1/2 cup butter
1/4 light brown sugar
1 cup flour

There is no liquid in this recipe so you want your butter to be very, very soft (not melted, though). Cream it with the brown sugar, then add flour a bit at a time and mix well. Roll out on lightly floured board to about 1/2 inch thickness. You can cut with a biscuit cutter, but I prefer to roll the dough out in a rectangle, slice it in half with a sharp knife, and then cut the shortening bread in about 1 1/2-inch, ladyfinger-like slices from that.

Put the biscuits on a greased pan and bake at 350 degrees for 20 minutes, until just beginning to brown. Cool completely before lifting from pan. *Makes about a dozen and can be eaten plain or with jam.*

SALLY LUNDY BREAD

Legend has it that Sally Lunn bread, a light, sweet, and golden loaf served more often as a tea snack or dessert than as a dinner bread, goes back to the earliest colonial settlers. One thing is for certain: The bread is enormously popular in the South, especially in Virginia where it is often made when company is coming.

One afternoon I decided to whip up a batch of Sally Lunn bread for my own special company—a teatime visit from my sister and my mother. But starting from the recipe given in *Welcome Back to Pleasant Hill*, a fine little cookbook from the restored Shaker village at Pleasant Hill, Kentucky, I soon encountered both the need, and inspiration for, improvisation.

My sister couldn't eat wheat flour at the time, so I resolved to use rye instead only to discover after the mixer was creaming the butter and sugar that I had only half the amount called for in the recipe. No problem, however, with a box of rolled oats at hand to fill out the measure.

For flavor's sake I opted for brown sugar instead of white, and in honor of the new cake's more humble ingredients, I baked it in a lightly greased, cast-iron skillet instead of the more formal loaf or Bundt cake pan.

The resulting tea cake was downright delicious and deserving of its own birthright, so I christened it Sally Lundy Bread to acknowledge its hybrid background.

It's best served warm with fresh cream butter on the side. You can set a pot of jam on the table, too, but the bread is sweet enough on its own. It's also delicious made into a summer shortcake sliced down the middle with fresh, sweetened peaches slathered inside, and whipped cream flavored with just a bit of brown sugar and vanilla on the top.

2 eggs, beaten

2 tablespoons butter

1 scant cup brown sugar

1 cup milk

1 1/2 cups rye or whole wheat flour

1 1/2 cups rolled oats

3 level teaspoons baking powder

Put eggs, butter, and sugar into mixer bowl and cream with electric mixer until smooth and fluffy. While that's creaming, sift the flour with baking powder and then mix in the oats. Alternate adding the flour-oat mixture and the milk to the creamed butter in small increments, beating all the time. When all has been added and thoroughly mixed together, pour into lightly greased, 9-inch skillet and bake at 350 degrees for 30 minutes. *Serve in wedges; yields 8.*

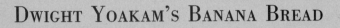

DWIGHT YOAKAM'S BANANA BREAD

Not all recipes are handed down from parent to child. This is a recipe that Dwight Yoakam sent to his mother for a California-style banana bread—one with no refined sugar. It's simple to make and the taste is strong and earthy.

1/2 cup butter or margarine

2 eggs

6 very ripe bananas

1 cup raisins

2 cups whole wheat flour

1 teaspoon baking soda

1/2 teaspoon salt

1 teaspoon cinnamon

3/4 cup chopped pecans

1 cup raisins

Put butter, eggs, bananas, and raisins in a blender and whir on high speed until liquified. Sift together flour, soda, salt, and cinnamon and mix with the liquid. Add nuts and raisins and spread into a well-buttered, large loaf pan. Bake at 350 degrees for 1 hour. Or you can make muffins and bake them at 350 degrees for 25 minutes. *Yields one large loaf or a dozen big muffins.*

COWBOY COFFEE CAKE

Amy O'Brien said this cake really doesn't have a thing to do with cowboys, Indians, or the wild West. She first dreamed it up, then dreamed up the name to convince her children, including country singer Tim, to eat it. But it's hard to imagine any little buckaroos or buckarettes would need persuading to tie into its warm sweet goodness.

Amy uses white flour, but I substituted a half-and-half mix of whole wheat and white to give it a homey, brown color and hearty taste.

2 1/2 cups half whole wheat and half white flour

1/2 teaspoon salt

2 cups brown sugar

2/3 cup shortening

2 teaspoons baking powder

1/2 teaspoon baking soda

1/2 teaspoon cinnamon

1/2 teaspoon nutmeg

1 cup buttermilk

2 well-beaten eggs

Mix together flour, salt, and sugar, then cut in shortening and work lightly with your fingers until it's blended throughout. Set aside half a cup of the mixture. Add baking powder, soda, and spices to the rest and mix very well. Pour buttermilk and beaten eggs into center of the flour and mix quickly and lightly with a spoon. Pour mixture into 2 greased 8-inch cake pans. Sprinkle the 1/2 cup of flour mixture over the top of each. Bake at 375 degrees for 25 minutes. *Serve warm to 8 hungry children or adults.*

Mystery Morning Cake

These days breakfast breads are more likely to be festive food than daily fare. This Mystery Morning Cake could have been designed for the holiday season, since its secret ingredient is one you're likely to have in the refrigerator following a big family dinner. Bake it on the morning after Thanksgiving or Christmas to keep the festive glow aglimmer.

As for the "mystery" ingredient, well, my mother took about three bites then decided it had to be cream cheese. Noting this cake's unusual combination of a light, airy texture and a close-your-eyes creamy taste she surmised that the only thing that could make a pastry that good was something bad for your waistline and heart.

Mama isn't wrong much, but this time she was. The secret here is a cup of mashed potatoes left over from supper the night before to create a cake that is airy and rich.

"What I have always maintained is that nobody can have a real conversation for more than five minutes without mentioning food. At least, not one you'd want to listen to, anyway."
—Amy O'Brien

Breads

1/2 cup white sugar

1/4 cup oil

1 cup leftover mashed potatoes

1 1/4-ounce packet active dry yeast

1/8 cup warm water

1 1/3 cups flour

1/4 cup brown sugar

2 tablespoons butter

nutmeg

The night before you want to serve, mix sugar and oil, then cream in mashed potatoes. Dissolve yeast in warm water and add to potatoes, mixing thoroughly. Add flour, 1/3 cup at a time, mixing with a wooden spoon. The result should be a stiff batter. Cover the bowl and put in a warm place to rise overnight.

In the morning, heat oven to 375 degrees and grease a medium-sized baking pan (approximately 11 by 7 inches or its equivalent). Turn dough out into baking pan using a rubber spatula to scrape out any that sticks to the side of the bowl, and to smooth it evenly into the pan.

Butter the tips of your fingers and use them to press dents all over the top of the dough. Sprinkle brown sugar, then nutmeg, over the top, and dot with butter. Bake for 30 minutes, or until the dough is firm and golden brown on top. Serve warm.

You may also want to sprinkle walnut or pecan pieces on the top, or to change the spice to cinnamon.

Makes 6 polite servings.

STACK PIE

"Stack pies" such as this were often served as noon meal desserts back in the old days when men and women worked heartily all day and ate the same. But this "pie" is really sturdy enough to serve as a meal in its own right. It's become a breakfast favorite around our house, especially in the fall of the year when tart apples and black walnuts hit their stride, so I'm including the recipe here along with the muffins, pancakes, and other breakfast breads. If company is coming and you want to make a full brunch out of it, serve the pie with a big skillet of fresh eggs, scrambled with shredded sharp cheddar cheese, and hot coffee.

Fried Apples (page 194)
2 cups flour
3 teaspoons baking powder
1 teaspoon salt
1/2 cup black walnuts
1/2 teaspoon vinegar
2/3 cup milk
1/2 cup cooking oil

Make the recipe for Fried Apples. While apples are cooking, sift flour, baking powder, and salt together into a large bowl, add the black walnuts and mix. Add vinegar to milk and stir, then pour into dry ingredients along with the oil. Stir until the dough hangs together, then place on floured board and knead quickly one dozen times. Divide the dough into three equal parts and round into balls.

Turn oven to 375 degrees. Place 1/4 pound butter in a 10-inch cast-iron skillet or round pan, and put the pan in the oven until the butter melts. While butter is melting, roll one ball of dough on a floured board in a circle to fit in the bottom of the skillet. When butter is melted and you take the skillet out of the oven, swirl the butter to cover the bottom of the pan and at least halfway up the sides. Put the circle of dough in the skillet, return to oven and bake 12 minutes.

While it's baking, roll the second circle of dough to fit. Remove skillet from oven when the 12 minutes are up and slather half the Fried Apples over the first layer of biscuit crust. Place the second circle of dough on top of the apples and return to the oven for another 12 minutes. Roll third circle of dough while waiting and repeat the stacking process, slathering the rest of the apples on the second crust, placing the third crust on the apples and putting the whole thing back in the oven for another 12 minutes. If the top crust isn't browned when the 12 minutes are up, run it under the broiler for a few seconds to tint it golden. Serve the whole thing piping hot, sliced in wedges from the pan at the table. *Serves 6 amply.*

From Gid Tanner and the Skillet Lickers to Hot Rize, plenty of country bands have taken their names from foods. Along with the Skillet Lickers, early country string bands had names such as the Fruit Jar Drinkers, the Possum Hunters, and the Chuck Wagon Gang. And early entertainers included Pie Plant Pete and the Cackle Sisters—who did a mean chicken imitation.

Before he became a Texas Playboy, cool country swing king Bob Wills (who grew up in Turkey, Texas) was a Light Crust Doughboy. One of the most popular Fort Worth bands during the Depression, the Doughboys, pictured here, took their name from their sponsor, Light Crust Flour.

Some performers didn't adopt the name of their sponsors but became so closely identified with them that they might as well have.

"Oooooooh, that's corny," means Homer and Jethro and Kellogg's Corn Flakes to the first television generation. And Lester Flatt and Earl Scruggs will be forever linked to Martha White Flour, the company whose theme song was central to their act. In the early 1970s, when a young Colorado-based band playing updated Flatt and Scruggs–style bluegrass went looking for a name, they settled on Martha White's secret ingredient, Hot Rize.

RICE PANCAKES

Eugenia Harris is a marvelous cook. Her daughter, Emmylou, can rattle off dozens of dishes her mother makes that set her mouth watering simply with the remembering of them. But her father Bucky has had some memorable moments in the kitchen also—especially when it comes to breakfast.

"I remember when I was about ten, Mother was in the hospital and Daddy cooked for us every morning, fried bologna and rice," Emmylou said.

"And now that might sound funny, but it was delicious. It was rice pancakes that Daddy would make with leftover rice and it makes the pancake batter real crispy—my favorite pancakes. The bologna wasn't bad either."

Bucky said he first had bologna for breakfast in the Marines.

"They used to serve fried bologna in the morning at regular intervals in the Marine mess hall. Of course, we called it tire patches or inner tube patches back then. We had a lot of bad names for food."

His tip on frying the perfect tire patch?

Niftier Sifter

My mother had a metal flour sifter. I know, because it made a nifty rhythm instrument, and I would sit on the floor and play with it and her measuring cups and spoons while she made cornbread, biscuits, and the like without them. Like most country cooks, she measured by eye and added things until batters "looked right." And I'm pretty sure it was from her that I learned to sift with a wooden spoon and a big metal strainer. That's what I use still.

Oh, I had a sifter with the wires that spin around when you grip and release the handle and it worked just dandy—once. But I washed it and didn't get it dried well and next thing I knew had a worthless, rusty contraption on my hands—it couldn't even scrape out a good rhythm anymore. Since then I've stuck to my strainer, which rinses easily, dries promptly, and sifts every bit as nicely.

"You've just gotta hit it or it curls up. You've gotta sort of hit it on the edge and several areas. And of course, you want to be sure to take off that cellophane."

Meanwhile, here's a recipe for crispy Rice Pancakes.

> 1 cup cooked brown rice
>
> 1 cup whole wheat flour
>
> 1 teaspoon salt
>
> 1 teaspoon baking powder
>
> 2 tablespoons sugar
>
> 2 eggs
>
> 2 tablespoons oil
>
> 1 1/2 cups milk
>
> oil for frying

Put rice in bowl and break up with your fingers so it's not in lumps. Sift flour, salt, baking powder, and sugar together, then mix with rice until rice is coated. Mix eggs, oil, and milk and add to dry ingredients and mix. Grill in cakes about 3 inches across. *Makes 1 1/2 dozen.*

QUICKIE SOURDOUGH PANCAKES

Pancakes are just skillet relations of muffins—a quick bread that, like a good mule, works better the less you beat it. So remember when mixing these just to get the dry ingredients moist with the wet, then plop them in the pan.

That pan would best be a cast-iron griddle or skillet because it heats hot and evenly, and will turn your cakes a toasty color in a short time.

When cooking pancakes, heat the pan first and then splash in a little oil. Tradition insists you follow the ritual of making one cake first "for the pan" to see if the griddle is too hot or cold and to soak up any extra grease. You want the oil just to make a very, very thin film in the pan. A paper towel wadded up and wiped gingerly across the pan (don't burn your hand!) will also absorb any excess oil. I find it works best to have the pan very hot when I

Raising Cane

"We raised sorghum cane and that was the big joy in the fall, to run the sorghum mill and make it into molasses," Chet Atkins remembers.

"The sorghum making was always a kind of social gathering with the neighbors. It was a chance for all the kids to get together and play. And it was a chance for the adults to visit and talk politics, cuss the Democrats. Where I grew up in East Tennessee is pretty Republican—at least 50-50 and probably more Republican. They didn't have slaves up there during the war, so that made for a good many Republicans and talking politics was what the adults would do.

"We kids now would get to feed the sorghum cane into the two big rollers that crushed it. And then you'd take the liquid that came out and put it in a vat over a big fire, and boil it and boil it and boil it. And then skim it and skim it and skim it.

"You'd throw the impurities over after you'd skimmed it, and we kids were always barefoot and getting in the skimmings. It was awful.

"And there was always an opinion about 'Is it done yet?' Sometimes it'd be a more heated discussion than about politics. Because if you boil it too much, it'd be too thick and on cold mornings you couldn't get it out of the jars. But if it was too thin, of course, it'd run all over your damn plate and you'd have to hem it up with two or three biscuits."

"Wake up, Jacon,
     day's a-breakin'
Fryin' pan's on an'
     hoecake bakin.'
Bacon in the pan,
     coffee in the pot.
Git up now and git it
     while it's hot."
Traditional cowboy song

put the first cakes in, then immediately turn it down to a medium-high flame for cooking thereon out.

Ladle or spoon the batter into the pan—enough to make cakes that are about 3 inches in diameter. Flip pancakes only once—when the bubbles start to form in the batter on top and the edges of the cake get firm and glazed.

To test and see if cakes are done, press your finger lightly against the center of the cake. If the cake feels wet and squishy inside, it needs to cook more. If it feels spongy and springs back a bit at your touch, holler "Come and get it!"

Sourdough pancakes start the day with a perfect balance between the sour tangy taste of the cake and whatever sweetness you choose to lavish on top. In the country, plenty of good cooks were known by their sourdough starter, passed down from generation to generation and replenished by the regular rituals of bread and pancake making. But for those of us who don't bake bread with regularity, sourdough starter is a thing of the past. This recipe makes an "instant" sourdough that turns plain pancakes into super flapjacks overnight.

3 slices dry whole wheat bread

1 cup sour milk

1 envelope dried yeast

1 cup flour

1 tablespoon sugar

1/2 tablespoon salt

1 teaspoon baking soda

2 eggs, beaten

1 tablespoon oil

1 cup buttermilk

splash of oil

The night before you plan to serve these, place broken-up pieces of whole wheat bread in a big ceramic or glass bowl, sprinkle yeast on top then pour lukewarm sour milk over. (To make sour milk, add a teaspoon of white vinegar to a cup of milk and stir.) Cover and let it sit at room temperature overnight.

In the morning, sift flour, sugar, salt, and baking soda and mix with the bread mixture. While pan is heating, add eggs, oil, and buttermilk and mix together. Put a splash of oil in the pan, make a test cake, and then cook up the rest, turning the heat to medium high. *Should make a dozen three-inch cakes.*

If you don't use all the batter up, refrigerate and add an egg and a splash of milk to the leftovers the next morning for sourdough cakes redux.

Kentucky Cakes

There are plenty of good ways to dispose of cold cornbread (see page 241), but one of the best is in this recipe for hot cakes. See Quickie Sourdough Pancakes (page 274) for general information on making pancakes.

1 cup cornbread

1 cup milk

1 cup flour

1 teaspoon salt

1 teaspoon baking powder

2 tablespoons brown sugar

2 eggs

1 tablespoon oil

1 cup buttermilk

Fried Apples (page 194)

bacon (optional)

Break the cornbread into pieces and combine with the milk and let sit in the refrigerator overnight. In the morning, sift flour, salt, baking powder, and brown sugar together and then mix in with the cornbread. Beat the eggs, oil, and milk and mix with the cornbread-flour and fry.

Serve these with Fried Apples on top—or if you're in a hurry, you can heat a jar of natural-style applesauce with a couple of spoonfuls of brown sugar in it, but it's not as good.

A good variation is to fry 4–6 pieces of bacon really crisp and crumble them into the pancake batter when you add the liquid.

You don't have to have exactly a cup of cornbread to make these. If you've got a little more or less, just estimate the liquid up or down to match. *This recipe also makes about a dozen three-inch cakes—and you can reuse leftovers as described in sourdough cakes.*

DESSERTS

MEAL PIE

COUNTRY PIE

POLLY'S CHOCOLATE PIE WITH NO-WEEP, NO-SHRINK MERINGUE

GREEN TOMATO PIE

SHAKER LEMON PIE

DOWN-HOME BLUEBERRY PIE

DECADENT FRUIT PIE

COBBLER

COMPANY COBBLER

FRIED PIES

IVA'S CHRISTMAS CAKE

Eugenia Harris's Chocolate Pound Cake

Kentucky Jam Cake

Red Velvet Cake

Rebbie's Spice Chocolate Cake with Flamingo Icing

Pear Cake

Depression Cake

Apple Stack Cake

Peach Shortcake

Peach Dumplings and Brown Sugar Whipped Cream

Gingerbread Men

Pecan Angels

Homemade Vanilla Ice Cream

Snow Cream

Snow Pudding

Plum Pudding and Hard Sauce

Woodford Pudding and Whiskey Sauce

Sea Foam

Peanut Butter Fudge

MEAL PIE

Chess Pie is the belle of southern pastries, her delicate flavors and unforgettably sweet personality popping up at every important social event from Derby parties and debutante balls to Alabama football tailgate dinners.

There are almost as many "authentic" recipes for Chess Pie as there are authenticated explanations for its mysterious name. (My favorite is that it's a Yankee interpretation of hearing some faux modest southern cook explain that this unbelievable delicacy she had just served up was "jes' pie.")

I'm not going to add to the plethora of Chess Pie recipes or stories by offering another one here. Besides, I much prefer Chess Pie's more wholesome country cousin, Meal Pie. Meal Pie is not nearly as sweet, but is all the more delicious because it has the rich, buttery flavor of cornmeal in each bite.

I experimented with a couple of recipes before settling on this one, which comes about as close to Mrs. Forest Stice's Lone Oak Pie (see page 282) as you can get without taking the interstate.

> 1/2 cup softened butter
> 1 1/2 cups white sugar
> 2 tablespoons white cornmeal
> 1 tablespoon flour
> 1/4 teaspoon salt
> 1/3 cup buttermilk
> 3 eggs, beaten
> 1 9-inch unbaked pie crust

Cream butter and sugar. Add cornmeal, flour, and salt and cream again. Add buttermilk and beaten eggs and mix well. Pour into unbaked pie crust and put in 375 degree oven for 15 minutes. Turn oven down to 325 and bake for 35 minutes more. Allow to cool before cutting. *Serves 8.*

"Just like old Saxophone Joe When he's got the hogshead up on his toe. Oh me, oh my. Love that country pie."
"Country Pie" by Bob Dylan

The Secret of Mrs. Forest Stice's Meal Pie

The best Meal Pie I've ever eaten is dished up by Mrs. Forest Stice at the Lone Oak Restaurant in Bowling Green, Kentucky.

Being just a hop, skip, and a side road from Nashville, the Lone Oak has seen its share of country music stars pass through its screened front door, but none has shone as brightly as this humble homemade pie which finishes off the all-you-can-eat, you'll-eat-til-you-bust family-style meals served there.

But while Mrs. Stice was more than generous with her recipe for Lone Oak Squash (page 175), she regretfully refused to part with her Meal Pie recipe.

"I'll tell you just how I came to get that recipe and then you'll understand why," she said.

"Several years ago there was a woman worked at another restaurant here and made the best meal pie anybody'd ever tasted. People would come from everywhere just to have a piece of that meal pie. So I asked her for the recipe, but she wouldn't give it out at all. I think maybe she was afraid that I'd serve it here in my restaurant, which is just what I wanted to do.

"But there was another woman worked both here and at that woman's restaurant and she said, 'If you want that recipe, I think I can get it for you.'

"And sure enough, one day that woman who made the meal pie wrote the recipe out to give to her daughter. And that woman who worked for me was there and when nobody was around to see, she took the recipe down off the shelf and copied it out for me.

"But when she brought me the recipe, she made me promise on my honor never to give it to another single person; and so you see, I'd be breaking my word if I told that secret recipe to you."

But of course.

COUNTRY PIE

The fundamental principle of country pie holds that you mix some kind of sugar, eggs, and thickener, add whatever you've got in the kitchen, pour it in the pie shell and bake it up for dessert. From that premise you get the delicious simplicity of Brown Sugar Pie, tart Vinegar Pie, kissing cousins Meal and Chess pie, southern royalty Pecan Pie, and the humble Poor Man's Pie in which a cup of oatmeal both thickens the filling and makes a chewy top crust.

Variations on the theme of Pecan Pie are numerous and often regionally associated. The folks in Louisville, Kentucky, like to make a pie with pecans, chocolate chips, and bourbon around Derby time and although the name Derby Pie is copyrighted by a company in Louisville that bakes and sells such a pie, other folks call their versions by any number of names associated with the world's most romantic horse race: Churchill Downs Pie, Thoroughbred Pie, Kentucky Pie.

This pie is out of that same bloodline, born one dark and stormy night when I had a great hankering for a Thoroughbred Pie but not a drop of whiskey or a pecan in the house. Black walnuts provided a suitably spirited taste, and oats gave this pie the stamina to go the distance. My bet is you'll find it a real winner.

1/2 cup melted margarine

1 cup sugar

1/2 cup oats

1/2 cup light corn syrup

1/2 cup sorghum molasses

3 eggs, lightly beaten

1 cup black walnut pieces

3/4 cup chocolate chips

1 9-inch pie crust

Melt margarine. Mix sugar and oats, then add margarine, syrup, and sorghum and mix well. Beat 3 eggs and add to mixture. Add nuts and chips and stir until well distributed. Pour into unbaked pie shell and bake at 350 degrees for 1 hour. *Remove from oven and let cool completely before slicing into 8 servings.*

POLLY'S CHOCOLATE PIE WITH NO-WEEP, NO-SHRINK MERINGUE

Naomi Judd has a wasp-thin waist that would make Scarlett O'Hara swoon with envy, so it's difficult to imagine her indulging in such a sweet sin as chocolate pie for breakfast. But her mother, Polly Rideout, says that's just what happens when Naomi and Polly's chocolate pie spend a night together at her house. In fact, Polly reports that all her children have been known to feast on leftover chocolate pie first thing in the morning.

"I guess when you think about it, it's not a bit different from eating a chocolate or jelly donut," Polly says.

Actually, it's quite a bit better when you consider the good, fresh ingredients Polly uses to make her pie. And fortunately this pie is also a real keeper—even the meringue doesn't lose an ounce of its appeal overnight with the special No-Weep, No-Shrink Meringue recipe she uses.

PIE

1/3 cup flour

1 cup sugar

1/4 teaspoon salt

2 cups milk, scalded

3 slightly beaten egg yolks

2 1-ounce squares unsweetened chocolate

2 tablespoons butter

1/2 teaspoon vanilla

1 baked 9-inch pastry shell

In the top part of a double boiler, mix flour, sugar, and salt; then gradually mix in the scalded milk. Cook over medium heat, stirring constantly until thickened. Add a bit of the hot mixture to the egg yolks, stirring constantly, to gradually warm the yolks without curdling. When they're warmed, stir the yolks back into the hot mixture in the double boiler, still stirring all the while. Add the chocolate and cook for 2 minutes, stirring constantly.

Remove from heat and allow to cool a bit, then add butter and vanilla, stir again, and pour into the baked pie shell.

Meringue

1 tablespoon cornstarch

2 tablespoons sugar

1/2 cup water

3 egg whites

dash of salt

6 tablespoons sugar

Mix the cornstarch, 2 tablespoons sugar, and water and cook over low heat until mixture is clear. Remove from heat. In a bowl, whip the egg whites until peaked and then slowly add the heated cornstarch-sugar-water mixture. Beat until creamy. Add salt and the 6 tablespoons sugar and beat again until fluffy. Pile on the pie and bake in a 350 degree oven until the meringue is gold tinged (usually 20–30 minutes). *Makes 6–8 slices.*

Green Tomato Pie

I was intrigued when I started running across recipes for Green Tomato Pie, but my expectation was that such a recipe was concocted more for novelty's sake than for taste. How wrong I was. The green tomatoes give this pie a wonderfully tart kiss of flavor, but a creamy texture—like some exotic variety of apple pie.

Some recipes call for a quarter cup or so of brandy or whiskey in the pie, but not this one since, I think, the flavor of the tomatoes and brown sugar get along quite nicely without it.

None I saw called for the addition of a green apple, but I think it enhances the flavor of the tomatoes without being the least bit assertive itself. And as for novelty, this is indeed the pie to serve to skeptical friends who will find themselves gobbling gluttonously after a first tentative bite.

"Put 'em on the side, put 'em in the middle. Put homegrown tomatoes on a hotcake griddle."
"Homegrown Tomatoes" by Guy Clark

1 cup brown sugar

1/2 cup flour

pinch of salt

2 tablespoons margarine

4 small green tomatoes (about 2 1/2 cups)

1 medium tart green apple

1 tablespoon apple cider vinegar

2 9-inch pie crusts, one for the lattice

Mix together sugar, flour, and salt and put half the mixture in an unbaked pie shell. Dot with butter. Slice unpeeled tomatoes very thin. Quarter and core apple and slice thinly. Spread half the tomatoes over the flour mixture. Lay the apple slices over that and top with the rest of the tomato slices. Sprinkle with the vinegar and spread the rest of the flour mixture over all. (The filling will be mounded higher than the crust, but will sink during baking. To make the lattice top for the pie, roll out the second crust in an oval shape. Cut 16 long strips about 1/2 inch wide. Lay 7 strips in the same direction across the top of the pie, about 3/4 inch apart. (Use shorter strips on the side and the longest strip in the middle.) Then turn every other strip back on itself halfway. Lay the longest strip of remaining pastry across the middle, perpendicular to the strips already there. Return the folded strips to their original places and fold back the other strips. Place the next perpendicular strip across, then unfold the cross strips back to their original place. Continue this process until the pie is crisscrossed completely, reserving two strips. Trim the lattice ends flush to the pan rim with a knife. Lay two extra strips around the edge, over the lattice ends, to seal. Pinch down with fingers or crimp with fork. Bake the pie in a preheated 375 degree oven for 50 minutes. Serve warm.

SHAKER LEMON PIE

The essence of country cooking is to make clever and delicious use of every ort and morsel at your disposal. No one was better at this than the Shakers.

Formally known as the United Society of Believers in Christ's Second Appearing (the name "Shakers" came from the frenzied, trancelike dancing

When Polly Rideout cooked on Ohio River barges for a living, she'd make as many as half a dozen of her chocolate meringue pies at once. It's a time-honored tradition. Here a cook on the Union Barge Line towboat *Neville* sets out her wares in June 1946.

that accompanied their services), they were a strange but fascinating offshoot of the Quakers. The sect flourished briefly in rural eastern United States in the 1800s. But by the beginning of the 20th century, they had practically died out.

This was hardly a surprise since the Shakers practiced celibacy. They also lived communally, trying to avoid much truck with the outside world, although their Christian spirit caused them to be known as exceptionally hospitable hosts to anyone who ventured into their community, believer or not.

The Shakers were known to set an impressive table. Extraordinary cooks, the Shakers' fundamental belief was to maximize the minimal. The restored Shaker Village at Pleasant Hill, Kentucky, has a restaurant specializing in just that sort of fine, fresh country fare. And every day the restaurant serves lemon pie made from an authentic Shaker recipe that perfectly captures the spirit of the sect by using the entire lemon (except the white center pith and seeds) for distinctive flavor and texture.

It's a labor of love to make this pie, for you must slice the lemons paper thin and that will take a lot of time and Shaker patience. But guaranteed, one taste and you'll be a convert for life, never able to countenance one of those flabby, quivery meringue-topped, gelatinous ordinary and secular lemon pies again.

2 thin-skinned and juicy lemons

2 cups white sugar

4 eggs

2 crusts for a 9-inch pie

Begin several hours, or even the day before, you want to serve the pie. Don't be seduced by big lemons with thick skins. You want two that are medium sized, have thin, shiny skins, and feel good and juicy. Wash them and cut off knobs on either end. Slice in half lengthwise, remove the white pith from the center, and discard seeds. Lay the lemon half, pulp-side down, on a cutting board and using a knife that will cut thinner than thin (I use a medium-sized serrated blade) slice the lemons into paper-thin slivers. The slices should be so fragile they will drape over your knife blade. (Okay, okay—if you must, you can use a food processor to slice them super thin, but it won't make you feel half so virtuous.)

Put the lemon slices and their juice in a glass or ceramic bowl and pour the sugar in, mixing the two together until every shred of lemon is coated with sugary sweetness, and every jot of sugar is sunny yellow from the lemon. Cover and let sit at room temperature for at least 3 hours. If you want to let the lemons sit overnight, put them in the fridge and then bring them to room temperature the next day before proceeding.

When you're ready to bake, preheat oven to 450 degrees. Put one crust in the bottom of the pie pan. Break the eggs into a small bowl and beat until buttery yellow, but not foamy. Blend eggs with lemon and sugar until all is mixed well and pour into the pie crust. Top with the second crust, trimming and crimping it closed, then slashing several air vents.

Pop the pie into the oven for 15 minutes, then turn down the heat to 375 degrees and bake for 20 minutes more—or until a knife blade inserted near the edge comes out clean. Remove from oven and let cool thoroughly and absolutely before slicing. *Serves 8.*

Down-Home Blueberry Pie

The Down Home Diner in Middletown, Kentucky, used to serve the most spectacular blueberry pie I've ever tasted—a cross between cheese cake and cobbler. But the Down Home went the way of so many good home-cooked country food diners a few years ago, and closed its doors. The recipe for this pie, though, had already become a favorite among family and friends.

> 1 cup sour cream
>
> 2 tablespoons all-purpose flour
>
> 3/4 cup sugar
>
> 1 teaspoon vanilla
>
> 1/4 teaspoon salt
>
> 1 egg, beaten
>
> 2 1/2 cups fresh or frozen blueberries
>
> 1 unbaked 9-inch pie crust
>
> 3 tablespoons all-purpose flour
>
> 3 tablespoons soft margarine or butter
>
> 3 tablespoons chopped pecans

With an electric mixer, beat sour cream, the 2 tablespoons of flour, sugar, vanilla, salt, and egg until smooth—about 5 minutes. Remove from mixer and fold in blueberries. Pour into the pie crust and bake at 400 degrees for 25 minutes.

When time is up, combine the 3 tablespoons of flour, margarine, and pecans, mixing well. Sprinkle that over the top of the pie and return to hot oven for 10 more minutes. Let cool and then chill in refrigerator completely before serving. *Makes 8 servings.*

DECADENT FRUIT PIE

One summer I spent my birthday with my friend Annie Laurie Wheat and her family in Sturgis, Michigan. Annie's grandmother offered to make me anything I wanted for my celebration and when I requested peach pie, she whipped one up from fat, fresh peaches and a butter-rich, cookie-type crust. It was unforgettable. This is not her recipe, but one that comes terrifically close. And it works marvelously with strawberries, blueberries, or other fresh, firm fruit for the filling. The crust is very difficult to work with but, because it is so short, also very forgiving if you have to pat it back together in the pan. I always do since mine invariably breaks in the transfer from board to pan— but it's never made a bad pie yet.

THE CRUST

1/2 cup cold butter

1/4 cup sugar

2 teaspoons beaten egg

1 cup plus 2 tablespoons all-purpose flour

THE FILLING

1 cup sugar

3 tablespoons cornstarch

1/8 teaspoon salt

1 cup water

4 cups chopped fresh fruit

1 tablespoon butter

Cut butter into little pieces. Mix sugar with butter using two forks or a pastry fork. Add egg and mix until just combined, then add flour and mix until it all resembles coarse cornmeal. Pat into a ball and then flatten ball into a disc, cover with plastic wrap and refrigerate for 30 minutes.

After chilling, roll dough out on floured piece of waxed paper to fit a 9-inch pastry pan. Transfer to pan, dusting off flour as best you can. If dough breaks, use fingers to press and patch it back together. Crimp edges.

Cut a round of aluminum foil to fit in the bottom of the pan, butter a side and place on pie crust. Weight down with dried beans or pie weights and bake for 10 minutes in 350 degree oven. Sides should be firm and turning golden. Remove from oven and gently remove foil and weights, then prick the bottom of crust with fork all over and bake again for about 7 minutes until lightly brown.

Let pie crust cool thoroughly. In a heavy saucepan, mix sugar, cornstarch, and salt. Put 1 cup of water and 1 cup of fruit in a blender and blend to make a watery puree. Add to the saucepan and stir well, while heating on medium. When very thick, add the rest of the fruit, mix well, and pour into pie crust.

Chill until the filling is set. Serve with unsweetened whipped cream or sour cream on top. *Serves 6.*

COBBLER

Emmylou Harris's grandmother made cobbler almost every day of her life, but never from a recipe. Eugenia Harris, Emmy's mother, recalled: "Sometimes she couldn't even tell you what she was doing even while she was doing it, her cooking came so naturally."

But watching her mother, Eugenia devised her own recipe for cobbler— one that tastes much like her mother's when the flour used is self-rising. That gives the cobbler a puffier, biscuit-like crust. Mrs. Harris also makes it with plain flour, for a more pastry-like crust, and it's grand either way.

Never a Timer, Always a Cobbler

"Some of my best food memories are of my mother's mother cooking on her old stove.

"Mother said she didn't even have a timer on it. My grandfather kept trying to buy her a new stove, but she wouldn't have it. Said she knew her stove, and I guess she did.

"And it seemed like there was always a cobbler sitting on the back of the stove, that day's cobbler just waiting for you to come along and take some. She had an old beat-up cobbler pan, too, that looked like it had been through the wars. Well, of course, I guess it had. And Nanny would just make up that pastry on the spot and throw whatever fresh fruit she had—green apple, cherry, peach, blackberry—into the pan and into the oven. The way people now just throw something in the microwave, she would just throw things together from scratch and onto the stove or oven and the next thing you know something delicious would be there."—Emmylou Harris

THE CRUST

2 cups flour (plain or self-rising)

(1 teaspoon salt, but only if using plain flour)

2/3 cup plus 2 tablespoons shortening

4–5 tablespoons ice water

THE FILLING

4 cups fresh fruit

1 1/2 cups sugar

2 cups water

4 tablespoons butter

Mix salt well with flour if you're using plain flour and not self-rising. Cut shortening into flour using two forks until mixture is blended and crumbly. Add ice water, mixing lightly until pastry holds together. Divide pastry into two portions, pat into balls, and chill while you prepare fruit.

Peel, pit, and slice fruit such as peaches, or simply rinse berries. In a heavy saucepan, bring fruit, sugar, water, and butter to a boil and let boil for about five minutes, stirring often to keep from sticking.

Roll out one ball of pastry to pie-crust thickness and cut into inch-wide strips. Pour half fruit mixture into a 12 x 9 x 2 inch pan and lay the strips across the fruit in rows. Roll out and cut second ball of pastry, pour the remaining fruit mixture into the pan and lay the rest of the pastry strips over it. Bake in 400–450 degree oven for 45 minutes. *Serves 8.*

COMPANY COBBLER

Late one summer many years ago my mother found herself with a house full of unexpected company and not a thing to make for dessert. But our neighbors had a gnarled old pear tree in the backyard that yielded hard green pears by the bushel-load. And they regularly offered us as many as we would take. So my mom sent me over with a dishpan to fill. When I got back, she peeled them, pitted them, laid them out in halves in baking pans, sprinkled them with brown sugar and butter, and baked them into tenderness. My cousin Rodney swears to this day it was one of the best desserts he's ever had. This cobbler is a variation on that simple theme, only a bit fancier in preparation and equally memorable.

THE CRUST

1 cup whole wheat flour

1/2 cup shortening

ice water

THE FILLING

2 firm pears

2 tablespoons brown sugar

1 tablespoon water

1/4 cup butter

1/2 cup brown sugar

2 eggs

"When it's peach

pickin' time in

Georgia,

Apple pickin' time in

Tennessee

Cotton pickin' time in

Mississippi

Everybody picks on

me . . ."

"Peach Pickin' Time in

Georgia" by Jimmie

Rodgers and Clayton

McMichen

Cut flour into shortening using two forks, then add ice water by the teaspoonful until dough sticks together well enough to be patted into a ball. Refrigerate for an hour. When chilled, roll out to fit in a 9-inch, deep-dish pie (or cake) pan.

Cut pears in quarters, peel, and pit. Lay them on the crust with the pitted side up, fanned out in a circular pattern. Sprinkle 2 tablespoons of sugar and 1 of water over the pears. Bake in 400 degree oven for 15–20 minutes until pie crust is golden and pears are softened. (If the ridge of the crust is quite done, you'll want to make a little collar out of strips of aluminum foil, shiny side out, to protect it during the final, broiling part to come.)

While pears are baking, cream butter and sugar, then beat in eggs. Pour this mixture over the baked pears, then place under broiler until the sauce crusts on top and turns golden brown. Serve immediately. *Enough for 8 delicate eaters or 4 hearty ones.*

FRIED PIES

I've always held you could tell mountain southerners from all other southerners by the kind of fried pie they prefer. My father, raised up in eastern Kentucky, wouldn't have turned down any form of hand-sized, fruit-filled pastry so perfect for a workingman's (or schoolgirl's) lunch. But he believed that ones made with dried apples were the peak of perfection.

Emmylou Harris, with Alabama roots, says simply, "It's got to be peach to be a real fried pie. Peach is the only way to go."

As for me, well I thought my Aunt Minnie's fried apple pies, hot from her cast-iron skillet, were just about the best things ever invented. I couldn't imagine anything to equal them until we stopped one day at Sprayberry's Barbecue down in Newnan, Georgia. There the pies were fat, half-moon shaped confections, stuffed and oozing with golden brown dried peaches infused with the sweet scent of a Georgia summer. They were as good as my memory of Minnie's—and I had to declare a draw.

But wait, one night I ran out of dried apples and turned to some dried pears instead. Mashed with brown sugar, their flavor was higher pitched yet more delicate than either apple or peach. The pies made with them were as good as any I've ever had. So it's up to you to figure out which you would prefer.

2 cups flour

1 teaspoon salt

1 teaspoon baking powder

1/2 cup shortening

3/4 cup hot skim milk

2 cups dried apples, peaches, or pears

2 cups water

1/2 cup brown sugar

oil for frying

Sift flour, salt, and baking powder together. In a large bowl, use a spoon to mix shortening and milk. You want some of the shortening to dissolve while the rest breaks up in little lumps. Add the flour a bit at a time and blend with a fork. When just blended, pat together into a ball and refrigerate for at least 2 hours. It will keep overnight.

Cover fruit with water, bring to a boil, turn down and simmer for an hour, adding more water if necessary to keep fruit from drying and sticking. Add brown sugar and mash together until a very thick, jamlike consistency.

When you're ready to fry, divide dough into 12 small, equal balls. Flatten each into a disc and roll out on lightly floured board until about 6 inches around.

Put about 2 heaping tablespoons of the dried fruit mix in the center of the lower half of the dough circle, and fold over to make a half-moon shape. Press and crimp edges together securely to seal. Make sure the edges are well sealed, otherwise the filling may seep out and cause the hot oil to splatter dangerously.

In a wide, heavy skillet, heat oil about a half inch deep until a little piece of dough dropped in it will dance around and slowly turn golden brown. Put pies in the oil a few at a time, being careful not to crowd. When they turn golden on one side, turn over carefully with a spatula and fry until second side is golden brown. Remove from oil and let drain on paper towels. These are pretty good the next day, but are finest when eaten as soon as they've cooled enough to bite into. *Makes one dozen.*

IVA'S CHRISTMAS CAKE

In our dining room is a piece of furniture my daughter and husband like to call "the sacred china cabinet." A tall half-cylinder made of inexpensive wood and curved glass, it probably would not bring a premium price in an antique store, since there is little about it that is ornate or expensive (except the curved glass, perhaps, which is near impossible to replace these days). But sacred it is to me. It belonged to my maternal grandmother, a woman I never met but nevertheless feel connected to through the stories and memories my mother passed along.

Iva Grinstead Fore was, my mother recalls, both an extraordinary cook and a generous hostess. Like the house I grew up in, my mother's childhood home was filled with family and friends gathered most often around a table creaking with the weight of Iva's generosity.

Holidays were celebrated at Iva and Bill's home and at Christmas she would remove everything from the sacred china cabinet and fill each of its four crescent-shaped shelves with the cakes, cookies, and candies she made. There were jam cakes, coconut cakes, fruitcakes, and countless other sweets. But of all the cakes Iva baked, the family favorite was her sixteen egg white pound cake.

It seems a simple enough cake at first bite, almost plain in fact. But its beauty is that it is at once unbearably rich and unbelievably light. My Aunt

Lib says you only have to slice a sliver for each guest to satisfy, it's that rich.

Although she remembered it well and lovingly, my mother did not have the recipe for this cake. For all her brilliance at the stove, she has never been a baker. And most of Iva's cake recipes were passed on instead to mother's cousin Jessie who seemed to have inherited Iva's white thumb. Jessie, in turn, gave those recipes to her daughter Jodie who shared them with me.

Like most family recipes, this one had an odd piece of information missing, though. Jodie couldn't tell me how long she bakes the cake, saying "I've never actually timed it. I guess I'm just one of those old grandma cooks who keeps checking until it looks right. I know it's ready when it gets light brown on top and cracks open a bit."

1 pound butter

2 cups sugar

1 teaspoon vanilla

4 cups flour

16 unbeaten egg whites

Let butter soften, then using an electric mixer, cream well with sugar and vanilla. Add flour and egg whites in alternating increments and mix until all is well blended. Pour into a greased and floured tube pan and bake at 350 degrees for 50–60 minutes, until a cake tester comes out clean. Cake should be golden brown and cracked open on top. Cool completely before cutting. *Serves 12–15.*

EUGENIA HARRIS'S CHOCOLATE POUND CAKE

"Tradition is a funny thing," Emmylou Harris said. "Not long ago my daughter needed a cake for a bake sale. Now I'm a real meat and potatoes cook. I don't make a lot of fancy things. And a cake is something that—other than a Duncan Hines mix every once in a while—I just never make.

"But all of a sudden I realized that what I really wanted to make for this sale was my mother's chocolate pound cake. It's not just a scratch cake, but one of the toughest, most impressive cakes that Mother makes, with frosting and everything.

"And I even had to go out and buy a mixer because if you try to do it with one of those hand mixers, you burn the motor out, my mother told me. She said she just burned up a little hand mixer once trying to make this cake with it.

"So I did. I bought myself a mixer and I made the cake and I don't know why but when I was done, it gave me such a great feeling. Maybe a sense of connection between my mother and me and my daughter—and even my mother's mother, who was a great cook and baker. It was a lot more than just a cake."

> 1 pound softened butter
>
> 3 cups sugar
>
> 5 eggs
>
> 1/2 teaspoon baking powder
>
> 3 cups all-purpose flour
>
> 5 tablespoons cocoa
>
> 1 cup milk
>
> 1 tablespoon vanilla

Cream butter and sugar thoroughly, then add eggs and beat for 10 minutes. Sift baking powder, flour, and cocoa together. Add vanilla to milk. When butter and eggs are well creamed, alternately add flour and milk mixtures in small amounts, mixing well after each addition. Pour into a well-greased and floured 10-inch tube pan and bake at 325 degrees for about 1 1/2 hours, until cake tester comes out clean. Remove and cool completely before frosting.

FROSTING

> 3 cups confectioners' sugar
>
> 1/3 cup butter
>
> 3 tablespoons half and half
>
> 1 teaspoon either vanilla or coffee

Sift the confectioners' sugar into a large bowl. Heat butter, half and half, and flavoring of choice until butter is melted. Add to sugar and beat until mixture is very smooth and spreadable. *Serves 10–12.*

KENTUCKY JAM CAKE

My Aunt Ariel used to sour a half pint of whipping cream for ten days to make her jam cake for Christmas and Lundy family reunions. But her daughter, Billie, just uses a cup of commercial sour cream and the result is still the best jam cake in the world.

2 cups sugar

1 4-ounce stick margarine

1 cup sour cream

24 ounces homemade or good quality seedless blackberry jam

1/2 teaspoon allspice

4 squares semi-sweet chocolate, melted

2 1/2 cups cake flour

2 teaspoons baking powder

1 pinch soda

1/4 teaspoon salt

4 large eggs

1 cup chopped pecans

Cream together butter, sugar, and sour cream. Add jam, spices, and melted chocolate and mix together well. Sift flour together with baking powder, soda, and salt. Add a bit at a time to the jam mix, beating after each addition. Beat the eggs and add them to the batter, again beating until well mixed, then mix in pecans. Pour into a 9 x 12 x 2 inch cake pan that has been greased and floured. Bake at 350 degrees for an hour, or until cake tester comes out clean. Let cool completely before frosting.

Frosting

1/2 cup margarine

1 cup light brown sugar

1/4 cup milk

1 1/2 cups confectioners' sugar

Cook margarine, sugar, and milk over medium heat, stirring all the while, until slightly thickened. It just takes about a minute. Remove from heat and let cool to room temperature. Add confectioners' sugar and beat by hand until it gets creamy and thick enough to spread. *Serves 12.*

Bell Dinger Christmas Cake

Almost every family that celebrates Christmas also has a Christmas cake tradition. When Tim O'Brien was growing up in Wheeling, West Virginia, it was the Christmas Eve "Bell Dinger" cake.

"Mom would make this cake with a little metal bell dinger hidden in it and whoever got the bell got to be king or queen for the next day. And then you could sit around and say things to your brother like, 'Jim, go get me a Coke.' Or, 'Mollie, make my bed.' It was great. That was my favorite cake."

But his mother, Amy, says it was just a simple white cake with white frosting—one that she loved, but was afraid her children might not like "with all those other holiday goodies and more elaborate cakes around.

"So I was standing there in the kitchen with the recipe and wondering how I would get the kids to touch it once it was made. And I saw that dinger on the window sill and I thought, 'instant tradition.'

"What they didn't know was I marked it with a toothpick so I always knew what piece it was in and could make sure that a different one got to be king or queen every year."

RED VELVET CAKE

Red Velvet Cake was my favorite childhood dessert. It always showed up at family reunions and I was enchanted by the mysterious red color of its layers contrasting with the butter-cream white of its icing. The two together have a rich, creamy texture that truly recalls the fabric it's named after. Nevertheless, it's a simple cake to make and every country cook worth her cake pans has a recipe for it.

"Everybody hurry
'cause them folks will
be here soon.
Oh, we've got
company comin',
company comin'
I saw company comin'
up the road."
"Company's Comin'" by
John Mullins

Mine comes from my mother's best friend, Sarah Johnson, who, for many years, would go into a baking frenzy right before Christmas, filling her kitchen with cakes, cookies, and candies of all flavors and stripes. Then she'd pack a big dress box for our family with slices and samples of all neatly and individually wrapped in plastic so we could indulge at our leisure.

Her Red Velvet Cake is matched only by my cousin Jodie's. Their recipes are very similar except Jodie uses shortening instead of butter and only one tablespoon of cocoa.

1/2 cup butter

1 1/2 cups sugar

1 teaspoon vanilla

2 eggs

2 ounces red food coloring

2 tablespoons cocoa

1 teaspoon salt

2 1/2 cups cake flour

1 cup buttermilk

1 tablespoon white vinegar

1 teaspoon soda

With an electric mixer, cream sugar and butter until smooth. Keep beating as you add first the vanilla, then one unbeaten egg at a time. Mix cocoa and red food coloring and add to the creamed butter mix. Sift flour with salt and add a little at a time, alternating with buttermilk. Mix soda and vinegar, add and beat until everything is mixed very well. Pour into two 9-inch cake pans and bake at 350 degrees for 30–35 minutes, until cake tester inserted in middle comes out clean.

Let the cake cool completely before frosting.

Frosting

1 cup milk

5 tablespoons cake flour

1 cup sugar

1 teaspoon vanilla

1 cup butter

This, Sarah says, is the "gooey, goodie part."

In a heavy saucepan, whisk together milk and cake flour, leaving no lumps. Place on low heat and cook, stirring constantly, until it begins to really thicken. (So thick, Sarah says, that it "sticks to your spoon and you think you've got the awfullest glob that ever was.")

Remove from heat and if you've gotten any lumps in it while cooking (you shouldn't have if you stirred constantly, but you know how these things sometimes go) whisk again until they're mostly beaten out. Transfer to a small mixing bowl and put it in the refrigerator to cool.

When it's quite cool, beat it with an electric mixer for about a minute, until it begins to fluff a bit and get ridges. Then, in a larger mixing bowl, cream butter, sugar, and vanilla until they're very fluffy. Add a little of the flour-milk mixture at a time. Beat until it's creamy, fluffy, and very spreadable. Makes enough to frost two-layer Red Velvet Cake. *The frosted cake serves 10.*

REBBIE'S SPICE CHOCOLATE CAKE WITH FLAMINGO ICING

The first time I made this cake I was put in mind of a story Polly Rideout told me about the time she was cooking on an Ohio River barge and the cake she'd made for dinner fell flatter than a flitter.

"You can't really waste anything on a barge because you've only got so many ingredients to work with and you can't just run out to the store to get more if something doesn't go right," Polly remembers.

"So I put that cake on a plate and was standing there trying to figure something out when one of the men came in and looked kind of funny and said, 'What's that?'

"And I just looked back real surprised and said, 'Why, that's my special Flat Cake recipe. Now don't tell me you've never had Flat Cake? Why you don't know what you've been missing.'

"And by golly he and all the other fellows ate that cake up, every bite."

The first time I made Rebbie's cake I, too, ended up with a flat cake on my hands, this one in two layers. But while Polly's cake was the victim of fate, mine was the victim of my own ignorance. The recipe I was working from was

Things My Mother Told Me, Part II

"Is there a reason why the butter drawer is full of empty butter wrappers?" my husband asked early on in our relationship. It was then it occurred to me there were things my mother had told me that perhaps everyone else's mother had not told them.

One such thing was to save empty butter wrappers. Then when a recipe calls for a greased pan, all you do is pull out the wrapper, with butter still on it, and slide it around the inside of the pan until it's shining. Not only does an old wrapper provide the perfect amount for greasing (feel free to use two if it's not enough), but it keeps your hand from getting slicked up in the process. And it seems so economical.

a very old family one and like old family recipes it left out a lot of information such as time of baking and (crucial here) the size of the pan. Family recipes leave out these kinds of details because, of course, everyone in the family knows just how the cake is supposed to look.

Trouble is, it wasn't my family that this cake came from, but that of Blanche Pedigo of Anchorage, Kentucky, Rebbie's great-niece. Unfortunately, Blanche couldn't remember what size the cake had been either, so it took me a couple of attempts before I determined that my "brownie pan," a useful 10 3/4 by 7-inch pan, is just right for making dessert for a small family dinner.

The Flamingo Sugar Icing recipe also came with a minimum of directions—little more than "heat and beat" to guide me. But I decided that since it's called an icing, not a frosting, and since it has "Sugar" in its title, the coarse, sugary topping that results when you "heat and beat" it as described here is probably right.

CAKE

1/2 cup butter

1 cup granulated sugar

1 1/2 cups sifted flour

1 teaspoon allspice

1 teaspoon cinnamon

1/2 cup milk

2 eggs

1 teaspoon vanilla

1 heaping tablespoon cocoa mixed with enough warm water to make a paste

In a big mixing bowl, cream butter and sugar. Sift together flour and spices. Add flour and milk alternately. Add eggs, vanilla, and cocoa water and beat until all is well blended and somewhat fluffy. Pour into a greased 10 3/4 x 7 x 1 inch baking pan and bake at 350 degrees until done—about 25 minutes. Let it cool while you make the icing.

ICING

1 1/2 cups granulated sugar

2 heaping teaspoons cocoa

1/3 cup evaporated milk

1 tablespoon butter

1 teaspoon vanilla

In a medium-sized, heavy saucepan, mix sugar and cocoa, then add milk. Stir constantly over medium-hot flame until the mixture just reaches the boiling stage. Remove from heat and add butter and vanilla. Beat until it begins to thicken and hold together in the pan. Pour the thickened icing on the cake still in the pan and spread to the edges. Allow to cool before cutting. *Serves 6.*

Hillbilly Dustpan

Another thing my mother told me that yours might not have told you is how to make a hillbilly dust pan—perfect for cleaning up spilled flour or sugar at the end of a busy baking day.

First you sweep your mess into a tidy small pile on the floor. Then you take a double-fold sheet of newspaper and run the very top of it very quickly under the cold water faucet. You want to dampen it just about an inch deep—not too wet and not too lightly.

Then you lay the paper on the floor with the wet edge about an inch or two from your pile. Smooth it out so there's no humps or ridges, and the wet part sticks nicely to the floor. Then sweep the mess onto the paper in short light strokes, being careful not to drag your broom over the newspaper's edge. When all the mess is in the paper, roll it right up to throw it away. And if there are some ornery dust motes still on the floor, you can use the damp edge of the paper to blot them up.

PEAR CAKE

This cake made with dried pears comes from Eugenia Harris, and it's a richly flavored treat, especially satisfying on a blustery winter day.

3 cups dried pears

1/2 cup water

3 eggs, beaten

1 3/4 cups sugar

1 cup vegetable oil

1 tablespoon vanilla

1 1/2 cups whole wheat flour

2 teaspoons baking powder

1 teaspoon soda

1 teaspoon ground allspice

1 cup chopped pecans

Let pears simmer in water for about 15 minutes. Put about 1/2 cup at a time in blender and process at chopping speed until pears are coarsely chopped and jamlike.

Combine eggs, sugar, and oil and beat at medium speed for 10 minutes, then mix in vanilla.

Sift together flour, baking powder, soda, and allspice. Add to sugar mixture, alternating with pears and mixing with a wooden spoon after each addition. Stir in pecans, then pour batter into a greased and floured 10-inch tube pan. Bake at 375 degrees for 55–60 minutes, until cake tester comes out clean. *Serves 8.*

DEPRESSION CAKE

The Great Depression followed by the Second World War gave rise to a number of inventive recipes that had to do without some essential ingredients—like this delicious cake with no eggs, milk, or butter. Though those days are gone, I still like to call it Depression Cake because it's a great antidote for the blues—sweet and satisfying, but, as desserts go, not all that bad for you.

This recipe comes from the woman I call my mother-in-law-in-law, Mary Fryrear, the mother of my sister's husband. It was written out for me many years ago by my nephew Tad on a piece of lined stationery in the careful, rounded letters of a conscientious 10-year-old. Tad's all grown up now, goes

"Money was scarce and times was bad The groceries mighty plain. Was it to do over boys, I'd live them times again."

"Uncle" by Norman Blake

by his given name of David, and writes as illegibly as the rest of us adults. But he still loves the flavor of this simple, earthy cake.

1 cup brown sugar

1/3 cup vegetable oil

1 teaspoon cinnamon

1/4 teaspoon cloves

2 cups raisins

1/8 teaspoon salt

1 cup water

2 cups flour

1/2 teaspoon baking powder

1 teaspoon baking soda

3 tablespoons warm water

1/2–1 cup chopped nuts

Put sugar, oil, spices, raisins, salt, and water in a saucepan and bring to a boil. Turn heat down and simmer gently for 5 minutes. Remove from heat and let cool completely, but don't refrigerate.

Sift flour and baking powder. Add slowly to cooled sugar mixture, mixing well after each addition. Mix soda and warm water and add to batter, beating well to blend it in. Add nuts—we always use the full cup, but you may prefer a less chunky cake.

Put in a small tube pan which has been greased and lined with brown or waxed paper. Bake at 350 degrees for 50–60 minutes, until cake tester comes out clean.

Traditionally this cake was iced with a brown sugar or chocolate glaze with no butter in it. But we've gotten decadent and prefer this chocolate icing to all others.

ICING

1/4 cup butter

3 tablespoons milk

2 tablespoons cocoa

1 cup confectioners' sugar

1 teaspoon vanilla

In a heavy saucepan, bring butter, milk, and cocoa to a rapid boil, stirring as you do. Remove from heat. Add sugar and vanilla and beat until smooth and thickened enough to spread. *Serves 8.*

The Family Blessing

Some families say grace before every meal, but whenever some dish turned out exceptionally well, our dinners were also accompanied by a litany of all the people who should have been there to share in whatever happened to be on the table that night.

"I sure wish your Uncle Jack could be here to have some of this okra stew," my mother would say over such, only a slight twinkle in her eye since Jack—who refused to touch okra—nevertheless loved my mother's stew as long as no one told him what was in it.

Fried oysters invoked my cousin Reed and my great-aunts Johnnie, Minnie, and Rae. Fried green tomatoes would call forth a whole list of relatives, living and dead, near and far, who would delight in their tangy taste. Beef and noodles would bring up my niece, Abbey, while anything with Granny's good gravy was vouchsafed to my nephew Tad. And I know that every plate of shuck beans anyone in my family has eaten since I "left home" some 20 years ago has had my name spoken over it.

This was not just my mother's own unique tradition. Our names were often likewise invoked whenever my aunts or cousins sat down to something especially good that one of us was particularly fond of. And not a single stack cake was ever eaten down in Corbin by my great-aunts Minnie, Johnnie, or Rae without my father's presence being pined for.

APPLE STACK CAKE

Stack cake is the ultimate mountaineers' dessert—a not too sweet, but satisfying and complexly flavored dessert made of 4–6 thin layers of molasses-tinged, biscuit-like cake covered with a dark, rich dried apple puree. The cakes, once baked and stacked, are covered with a towel and put away to ripen for at least two and sometimes as many as seven days. When they're finally cut into, the juice and aroma of the apples have permeated the hard cake, making for flavor and texture unlike anything else.

My Aunt Rae had just deemed a stack cake ready for cutting one day when my cousin, Sparky Parkey, showed up at her door. Rae made him some coffee and as the two of them began to eat she sighed about what a shame it was my daddy, up in Louisville, couldn't have some.

Sparky not only agreed but said since he didn't have anything planned that afternoon and night, he'd just remedy the situation. Rae wrapped up the rest of the stack cake, Sparky jumped in his car and drove three solid hours to our door. There he had another piece of cake with Daddy, drank about a pot of coffee, told about an hours' worth of news and stories, and turned around and drove right back to Corbin and Aunt Rae with Daddy's thanks.

Here's a recipe for stack cake based on Aunt Rae's and worth a drive.

4 cups dried unsulphured apples, packed*

water

1 cup brown sugar

1/2 teaspoon mace

4–5 cups flour

1 teaspoon baking soda

1/2 teaspoon salt

2/3 cup shortening

1 cup white sugar

1 cup molasses

2 eggs, beaten

1 cup buttermilk

*Unsulphured dried apples are available at many groceries and most health or natural foods stores

Put apples in a heavy saucepan and add water to cover. Bring to a boil and then turn heat down and simmer for about an hour until the apples are soft enough to be mashed. You'll need to stir the apples down into the water at first, since they tend to float. And you'll need to stir them frequently throughout since they tend to stick. You may need to add more water as they cook so that they don't dry out and burn.

When apples are good and soft, mash them with a potato masher, making a lumpy puree. While mashing, add brown sugar and mace and continue to simmer for a few more minutes to mix the flavors, stirring all the while. The consistency should be like a chunky apple butter or applesauce. If the mix is too watery, continue cooking on low heat, stirring, until it is thickened.

Remove from heat.

While apples are cooking, sift together 4 cups of flour, soda, and salt. Cream together shortening, sugar, and molasses. Mix beaten eggs and buttermilk. In small, alternating increments, add flour and buttermilk mixes to creamed shortening and sugar. Mix well after each addition. Dough should be like that for biscuits. Use as much as necessary from additional cup of flour to get the proper consistency.

Pat into a ball and chill in refrigerator until apples are ready.

Divide dough into five roughly equal handfuls. Each of these will be a layer, and if you want and you have five identical cake pans, you can roll them out altogether and bake them all at once.

But the traditional way to make stack cake is to bake each layer one at a time in a well-greased and floured, black cast-iron skillet. I've done it both ways and although I can't give you a logical reason why, I believe the skillet method actually does taste better.

To do this, take one handful of dough and leave the rest refrigerated. Roll it into a ball, pat it into a disc, put it on a floured board and roll it a couple of times almost big enough to fit an 8–9 inch skillet. Lay the dough in the greased and floured skillet and pat it out to fit. Sometimes the dough is harder to handle than others and will tear. But you can pat it together in the pan— making sure not to leave any broken seams or gaps.

Bake each layer for approximately 20 minutes in a 350 degree oven. Keep an eye on them to keep them from burning. They're done when they're golden brown all over and pull away slightly from the edge of the pan.

Put the first layer on a large plate and while you're baking the next one, cover the top with 1 1/2 cups of the apple puree, spreading it evenly to the very edges of the cake layer.

Monroe's Birthday Cake

Bill Monroe, the father of bluegrass music, was born on the same day as my father: September 13, 1911.

Monroe has a reputation for being difficult to interview and he lived up to it the first time I talked with him for an in-depth profile for the *Louisville Times* in the early 1980s. During our first meeting in Nashville, he was gracious but perfunctory in his answers, telling me only the things—in nearly identical quotes—that he'd told countless interviewers before. At the end of our conversation, hoping for another chance to talk and dig a little deeper, I asked him if we might speak again when he came to a Louisville bluegrass festival that September.

Looking regal and removed, like the country shaman he is, he said he might talk to me again if I'd bake him a birthday cake.

I said I would and—almost as if he were giving me a test—he squinched his eyes and asked what kind.

"I stack 'em as I bake 'em and that's what gives them the best taste," my Aunt Rae says. You should do the same. Don't put any apples on the fifth, top layer though. When they're all stacked, let them cool, then wrap in plastic wrap and a clean towel and put in a cool, dry place for at least 48 hours before cutting. *Serves 12.*

PEACH SHORTCAKE

Peach shortcake is easier than pie and, the way we make it around our house, twice as satisfying. You'll need first to make up a skilletful of Sally Lundy Bread (page 266). Then you need to toss together 8 cups of fresh, ripe peaches,

Playing a hunch, I answered with my father's all-time favorite: apple stack cake.

Monroe's face broke into one of his rare smiles:

"Now apple stack cake, I don't think I've had a good one for years. And when I was a young man and my Uncle Pen would take me with him to play the dances up around Rosine, Kentucky, why the people would come from miles and miles away to hear us play. And they'd dance all night, sometimes up until the morning. And the women would make food and bring it. And there'd be tables of cakes and pies, but the ones I always went straight for were the apple stack cakes. Now there's nothing in the world quite like that flavor. You bring me a good one and we'll see."

So I baked him the cake from the recipe on page 310. He took it with a simple thank you at the festival that fall and never said if he found it good or not. But when I called a while later to set up another interview and reminded him of who I was by mentioning the cake, he invited me and my photographer to three more meetings—including one very long afternoon at his secluded Tennessee farm.

peeled and sliced bite sized. Refrigerate them while you wait for "bread" to bake.

When bread is done, let it cool for a bit before you slice it. While you're waiting, whip up a batch of the Brown Sugar Whipped Cream described in the recipe for Peach Dumplings (pages 314–15).

When you're ready to serve, cut bread into six wedges. Split each open like you're getting ready to butter a piece of cornbread, but instead put the bottom half on a dessert plate, pour a cup of peaches and their juice onto it, and put the top on that. Pour another third cup of peaches over this and top with whipped cream. *Do the same for each piece and serve 6.*

"When it's peach pickin' time in Georgia,
Apple pickin' time in Tennessee
Cotton pickin' time in Mississippi
Everybody picks on me . . ."

"Peach Pickin' Time in Georgia" by Jimmie Rodgers and Clayton McMichen

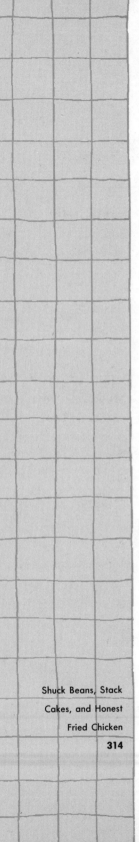

PEACH DUMPLINGS

Fruit dumplings were the ultimate quick treat in country kitchens. Faster even than cobbler, they were based on the same principle—dough cooked in a sweet fruit syrup—but were made on the top of the stove, the dough dropped into the syrup in little balls instead of rolled out into a crust. This slightly more elaborate recipe combines the best of both techniques to create an unforgettable dessert.

DUMPLINGS

2 cups whole wheat flour

1 teaspoon salt

2 1/2 teaspoons baking powder

6 tablespoons dark brown sugar

2 cups chopped fresh peaches (if frozen or canned, must be drained)

1/2 cup chopped pecans

2 tablespoons vegetable oil

2 cups buttermilk

In a medium-sized bowl, mix together whole wheat flour, salt, baking powder, and brown sugar. Add peaches and pecans and mix thoroughly. Mix oil with buttermilk and add all together, mixing until just blended. Refrigerate while you make sauce.

SAUCE

3 cups chopped peaches

2 cups water

1 1/2 cups sugar

3 tablespoons cornstarch

1/4 teaspoon salt

Blend peaches and water to make a watery puree with some peach lumps still in it. In heavy saucepan, mix sugar, cornstarch, and salt. Add peach puree and stir over medium heat until blended, taking care not to let the cornstarch lump. Heat until mixture begins to thicken.

Pour puree into a 9 x 13 inch baking dish. Using a large serving spoon, drop refrigerated dumplings into the peach sauce, leaving a little space between each dumpling. They can nest close to one another, but shouldn't touch. Bake in 375 degree oven for 30 minutes. Serve warm with brown sugar whipped cream. *Makes 6–8 dumplings.*

Brown Sugar Whipped Cream

1 cup chilled whipping cream
2 tablespoons brown sugar
1 teaspoon vanilla

Combine all the ingredients in a chilled mixing bowl and whip until cream is fluffy and stiff.

Gingerbread Men

Gingerbread men were a favored treat in the country kitchen. Their chubby human shapes with toes to be nibbled on and raisin buttons to be nibbled off were just the thing to please hungry children. And their wholesome taste—not too very sweet and made with abundant sorghum molasses—made them favorites with the cook as well. Plus they kept well when packed in a tin with a tight lid—although it's hard not to eat the whole batch in one sitting, they're that tasty.

This recipe makes a delicate dough, making the delicate art of getting the gingerbread man from the rolling board to the cookie sheet even more so. But the light and spicy taste of this cookie makes it worth the extra trouble.

When you're looking for a cutter for gingerbread men, try to find one that is an open form so if the dough sticks to the edges you can gently nudge it out with your finger from inside. And look for one that not only has a nice

> "One of my first memories is my mother would bake gingerbread cakes and she'd make me a gingerbread man with raisins for the eyes and decorations. I guess I was two or three years old then. And she would let me take the pan or the thing she mixed it up in—she'd let me clean that out after she got through, with a spoon. And I liked that almost as much as I liked that little baked man." —Chet Atkins

fat body, but fat arms and legs so his limbs won't be likely to break off in the rolling and transfer process.

Press raisins on the little men to make eyes, mouth, buttons, fingers, and toes before baking. Or you can also decorate them by making colored butter cream frosting and using it to "draw" on features after the men are thoroughly cooled.

3 cups flour

1/2 teaspoon baking soda

1 1/2 teaspoons ginger

1/2 teaspoon cinnamon

1/2 teaspoon salt

pinch ground white pepper

1/2 cup butter

1/4 cup dark brown sugar, packed

3/4 cup light molasses

1 egg

1 teaspoon warm water

1 tablespoon buttermilk

raisins or butter cream frosting

BUTTER CREAM FROSTING

1/4 cup butter

1 cup powdered sugar

1–2 tablespoons milk

food coloring

Sift together flour, soda, ginger, cinnamon, salt, and pepper. The pinch of pepper is just that, a pinch—less than 1/16 teaspoon.

In a large bowl, using an electric mixer, cream first butter and sugar, then add molasses and cream again. Add an egg and let the mixer beat on low until the batter is smooth and very creamy.

Remove from mixer (don't forget to scrape the creamed mix from the beaters into the bowl, maybe leaving just enough for a little helper to lick off). With a large wooden spoon, mix the flour into the creamed molasses a bit at a time. When you've used about half, add water and buttermilk to the mixture, then continue adding flour until it's all used up. Dough should be stiff but too moist to handle easily. Use a spoon to lightly push and pat it into a dome shape; then cover and refrigerate for at least 1 hour.

When you're ready to bake, turn oven to 350 degrees. Grease and very lightly flour a cookie sheet. Take half the dough from the refrigerator, leaving the rest to stay chilled until you're ready to work with it.

Pat the half you've removed into a smooth ball and—either on the cookie sheet itself or on a lightly floured pastry cloth—roll it to about 1/4 inch thickness. (You can make the men fatter, if you want, just increase the baking time a bit.)

A cloth-covered rolling pin, very lightly floured, helps to cut down on sticking. Cut out men and pull away excess dough if on cookie sheet—or lift with thin metal spatula and transfer to cookie sheet if on pastry cloth. Do the same with the second half of the dough.

(Put the excess dough after cutting back in refrigerator. You can roll it out again and make more gingerbread men, although the cookies it makes will be denser than the original batch.)

Use raisins to make eyes, etc., then pop pan of gingerbread men into oven and bake about 18 minutes. Time will vary depending on the size of the men. The time here is good for men about 6 inches tall. You want the dough to be firm when you press his tummy and just a smidgen brown around the edges.

Take sheet from oven and, with a spatula, remove men immediately to cooling racks.

You'll have the best results if you only bake one pan of gingerbread men at a time. *This should make 10–12 little men.*

To decorate with butter cream frosting, soften 1/4 cup butter and cream into it 1 cup powdered sugar. Add 1–2 tablespoons milk, a little at a time, until frosting is the right consistency. You want it "spreadable" but not runny.

Divide into bowls and make each bowl of icing a different color with drops of food coloring. Decorate completely cooled men using kitchen knives or spatulas to spread icing in broad strokes, or the tip of a chopstick to put it on in "drops."

We also like to make gingerbread cookies from this recipe in heart and star shapes, covering the top of each in prettily colored icing when cooled. Or my daughter and her friends like to create their own cookie shapes using the point of a steak knife to cut out free-form designs. The only rule is all the shapes must be close to the same size for each batch. Baking radically different sized cookies on the same pan results in some of the cookies being over or underdone while the others are just right.

PECAN ANGELS

Back in the olden days, little children would pray for a dinner recipe that called for the yolk of one egg. That meant the country cook, ever frugal, would have to use up the extra egg white, and that meant these heavenly, airy cookies.

1 egg white

1 cup brown sugar

1/8 teaspoon salt

1 tablespoon all-purpose flour

1 cup pecans, finely chopped

Beat egg white until peaks form. Gradually add sugar, salt, and flour and mix until well blended. Fold in nuts. Drop from a teaspoon onto a greased cookie sheet with plenty of room between each since they flatten out while baking. Bake at 300 degrees for 15 minutes. Let cool slightly before removing from cookie sheet with a spatula. *Makes two dozen.*

HOMEMADE VANILLA ICE CREAM

The secret to homemade ice cream is to get the day real hot and keep your ice cream real cold. You wait until August to be sure of the former. To accomplish the latter, you learn the principles of rock salt and ice.

Homemade ice cream makers (the real kind—big buckets with either a hand crank or a big, round electrical doojobbie on top that looks as if it's left over from a washing machine) use ice and rock salt in their outer basin to freeze the cream that's in the inner tub. The consistency of the ice and the layering of salt with it determine the freezing ability and the consistency of the cream.

To begin with, you want finely crushed ice to ensure that the cream is smooth. Those cubes they sell in grocery stores won't work—unless you take them home, wrap the bag in a big old towel, and bang the dickens out of them with a hammer to get them crushed just right. Or you can call your nearest ice supply outlet, tell them you want finely crushed ice, and then pick it up.

When you're ready to freeze the cream, you'll want to put a couple of inches of ice in the outer bucket, all around the inner freezing pan—not packing it, but pouring it in; then sprinkle a handful of rock salt evenly over that. Then add another layer of ice followed by rock salt and on until the layers reach the bottom of the freezing can's lid. You absolutely don't want to get the ice and salt any higher than that or it might seep into the ice cream, turning it briny.

After the cream is cranked to readiness and the paddle has been taken out, it has to "cure." Some folks put their ice cream in a freezer to do this, and I guess that's all right. But the best way to do it is to put it back in the freezer bucket and pack salt and ice all around it again, this time with a higher ratio of salt to ice, say a handful sprinkled around for every inch. The salt makes the ice melt faster than it would otherwise, and cools the cream both more quickly and more evenly.

Once you understand these proportions, you're ready to make ice cream.

2 eggs

1 1/4 cups sugar

3 cups whipping cream

2 cups milk

3 tablespoons vanilla

1/4 teaspoon salt

Beat the eggs lightly, then add the sugar and beat until stiff. Add the cream, milk, vanilla, and salt and mix the whole thing really well. Pour into freezer can, put in the paddle, put on the lid, and chill everything in the refrigerator for at least 15 minutes. Then put the can into the outer bucket of the freezer and layer finely crushed ice (about two inches or so) and rock salt (a handful evenly spread over each layer of ice) until it gets just to the under edge of the freezing can's lid. Begin to crank and as the ice melts down and runs off, continue to layer ice and salt in the same proportions into the bucket.

Crank until the ice cream is stiff and can hardly be cranked anymore. If you're using an electric machine, this usually takes about 20–25 minutes and the machine will stall when it's ready. (If your machine doesn't have an automatic shutoff, turn it off right away so you won't strip the motor!) If you're hand cranking, it takes a little longer and the human cranker may start to whine a long time before the machine's cranker is ready to stall. Avoid this by taking turns at the crank. When you're sure it's stiff enough, give it a few more cranks for good measure.

Take the freezer can out of the bucket of ice very carefully and wipe all the dribbles of ice, water, and salt off. Open the lid, take out the paddle and give to the nearest child or child-at-heart for licking. Put the lid back on securely. Drain any excess brine from the outer bucket and reinsert the freezer can, then pack it with more salt and ice, this time an inch of ice to each handful of salt. Wrap the whole shebang in newspapers and an old blanket or quilt and let it ripen for 1–2 hours. Eat it just as the sun goes down. *Makes 1/2 gallon.*

My sister, Pat (left), and (clockwise from top) cousins Hubertine, Mary Rose, and Charles Terrell slurp into the first watermelon of summer.

Emmylou Harris recalls, "You knew it was summer when DeDa, my grandfather, would bring home the first ripe watermelon.

"He always got the first one within a fifty-mile radius of Birmingham and he knew how to pick a ripe one. And we would have the watermelon and make fresh vanilla ice cream and that's when summer began.

"And the ice cream had to be the hand-crank type. Some people had these automatic electric ones, but I thought if you didn't do it by hand it didn't taste as good. And everybody had to take a turn at the crank.

"And you had to use the ice and the salt to cream it, not put it in the freezer. And the rock salt had to be put in just the right way. It was a ritual.

"And the ice cream itself, it always tasted best on the paddle."

SNOW CREAM

My mother could smell a snow on its way. Long before the weatherman had an inkling of what was to come on his radar, she would walk out on our back porch, turn her face to the night sky, twitch her nose a few times, then say: "I smell a snow coming."

Sometimes when the newscaster had gotten my schoolgirl's hopes raised with a prediction of real accumulation, the kind that could close school for a winter holiday, my mother would look puzzled, walk out and take a few sniffs, then come back in and tell me I'd better get my homework done anyway. There wasn't going to be a snow tomorrow, her nose said. I don't remember her ever being wrong.

She could also hear the snow in her sleep, I think, because whenever it began—at midnight, or two or three in the morning—she would pad softly out of bed and into my room to carry me, sleepy-warm and still dreaming, to my window. There she'd stand, holding me as we watched the flakes tumble down, making a crystal cold halo as they fell through the circular glow of the street light.

Snow was a joyous event in our house although we owned no sled and I never once made a decent snowman. But a good deep snowfall (which we managed to have about once every winter) meant that we would feast on snow cream. And snow cream is one of the most wonderful foods ever known to a child.

Unfortunately, as Chet Atkins pointed out when he was recalling the luscious snow cream he gobbled up as a small boy in Tennessee, it's something that it's not very wise to make anymore.

"I hear with the pollution and all in the air that folks say you shouldn't make snow cream these days," he said. "And you know, that's a real shame because it was a wonderful, wonderful thing to have every winter."

But in the hopes that we may someday soon find ourselves living again in a world where the air is pure as . . . the newly fallen snow, here is how you make snow cream:

In a big metal pan, mix together 1 beaten egg, 2 cups of milk, a cup of sugar, and a teaspoon of vanilla. Put on your boots and coat and gloves and take a great big spoon and the pan outside where deep snow has just fallen.

Look for a clean, protected patch and brush away the snow on the very surface. Now dip up big spoonfuls of the snow and put it in the pan and mush it lightly together with the milk. Work quickly as you keep adding snow and mixing until the snow cream is the thickness of soft homemade ice cream and all the snow is coated with the milk mixture. (Make sure that you don't dig so deep in the snow that you hit grass or dirt. Keep clearing patches if the snow isn't deep enough to fill your pan at one spot.)

Take the cream in the house and eat it right on the spot. It doesn't keep well in the freezer at all since the snow freezes into ice. But I never knew anybody who ever had leftover snow cream.

"My granddaddy didn't eat processed food his whole life—other than going down to get a custard.

"Custard is what he called soft ice cream. And when we'd be staying there with him and my grandmother in the summers, he'd say to us kids, 'You all want to run down the road with me here and get a custard?' And that's what we'd do of an evening, head on down to the Frosty Freeze."

—Dwight Yoakam

Desserts

323

SNOW PUDDING

When Eugenia Harris, Emmylou's mother, was growing up in Birmingham, Alabama, Snow Pudding was a traditional Thanksgiving dessert. It's a simple lemon gelatin whipped to a snowy-looking froth and then topped with an egg custard sauce. Mrs. Harris still makes the pudding for her family since it's become one of her husband's favorites.

And it's a favorite of ours, also, for I must confess that when I made Snow Pudding for the first time, I poured the gelatin into ten separate goblets to invite some friends over later to try it with us. As soon as the gelatin was set and the custard chilled, Ken, Meghan, and I sampled one just to make sure they were all right—then promptly sat down and ate all the rest.

PUDDING

1 envelope plain gelatin

1 cup sugar

1/4 teaspoon salt

1 1/2 cups boiling water

1/4 cup fresh lemon juice

3 egg whites

In a mixer bowl, mix together gelatin, sugar, and salt. Add boiling water and stir until gelatin is dissolved. Add lemon juice and let cool until it is as thick as unbeaten egg whites. Use a mixer to beat until fluffy, then add egg whites and beat together until mixture is thick enough to hold its shape. Spoon into individual serving bowls and refrigerate until firm. *Will make 8–10 servings.*

CUSTARD SAUCE

1 1/2 tablespoons cornstarch

2 cups half and half

3 egg yolks

1/2 cup sugar

1 teaspoon vanilla

Dissolve cornstarch in 1/4 cup of the half and half. Beat egg yolks until light and then combine with the cornstarch cream. In a heavy saucepan, heat the remaining half and half, being careful not to boil. When it's steaming hot, add the sugar and stir to dissolve. Pour about 1 cup of the hot cream mixture into the eggs, stirring constantly so it doesn't curdle them. Then return cream to low heat and slowly add the egg mixture to it, still stirring. Cook for 5 minutes on low heat, stirring constantly, until sauce is slightly thickened. Remove from heat, add vanilla and mix well, then cool. When you're ready to serve snow pudding, spoon custard over each serving.

Kitty's Surprise

Jean Ritchie, doyenne of mountain folk music, grew up in Viper, Kentucky, the youngest of Abigail and Balis Ritchie's fourteen children. Hers was a musical family, very conscious of its British roots. The evenings they spent on the old L-shaped porch of the cabin in the hills were filled with the British folk songs of their forebears interwoven with the homegrown songs of the region. And when they celebrated Christmas, it was with a feast of both the old and new worlds.

In her autobiography, *Singing Family of the Cumberlands,* Jean recalls: "We little ones always loved Christmas dinner because that was one day that nobody cared a hoot if you started out with cake and jam the first thing, and wound up the meal with a chicken leg, or whether you did or did not drink your milk. Of course, the baby ones'd get started off with someone poking into their mouths a mashed up mess of chicken livers and gravy over crumbled up biscuits and taters, but pretty soon that babe'd be sitting under the table with a chicken bone to gnaw, and a piece of butter cake in the other hand to change off on. Just so we weren't crying or showing off, that's all they cared—and we had a fine time.

"About the time we all had begun to push back our chairs and slow down a little bit, in came Kitty (Jean's sister) with her surprise, grinning away, her face all shining in the light from it—a great plum pudding, blazing and sizzling. Lord, how we all hollered!"

PLUM PUDDING

Few recipes are accompanied by such ritual and history as Plum Pudding. Like countless Appalachian folk songs, Plum Pudding's origins are in the British Isles. It made its way to the mountains of the southeastern United States with the early settlers. Over the years and in a new clime, it underwent changes and variations including, ultimately, the omission of plums. Nonetheless, the pudding tastes rich and strange and wonderful and looks spectacular when brought, flaming, to the table. For some Appalachian families, it was the only thing that could properly end a Christmas dinner already devoted to extravagance.

This recipe for Plum Pudding was devised by Dianne Aprile, a writer in Louisville, Kentucky, who decided that she wanted a rich Christmas tradition for her small family to call its very own. The annual making of the Plum Pudding, with both her husband and young son partaking in the ritual, has become just that.

1 cup raisins

1 cup dry sherry

1 cup butter, at room temperature

1 cup sugar

1 cup flour

1 teaspoon baking soda

1/2 teaspoon salt

4 eggs, lightly beaten

2 cups chopped dates

1 1/2 cups grated carrots

1 cup bread crumbs

1 cup milk

1 cup dark currants

1/4 cup dark molasses

1 tablespoon grated orange peel

1 tablespoon grated lemon peel

2 teaspoons ground cinnamon

1/2 teaspoon ground cloves

1/2 teaspoon ground nutmeg

1/4 teaspoon ground mace

1/4 cup brandy

You will need a large pot with a lid and rack, and a 2-quart mold with a tight lid that will fit inside the covered pot, on the rack.

Soak the raisins in sherry overnight.

The next day, grease the 2-quart mold heavily and well. In a big bowl, cream butter and sugar, then blend in flour, baking soda, and salt.

Add the soaked raisins with any sherry that's left and then add the rest of the ingredients except the brandy. Mix well after each addition. If you have children or friends in the kitchen, it's an old tradition in some families that each takes a turn stirring and gets to make a wish.

Carefully spoon pudding into mold, cover tight, and place in the pot on the rack.

Pour boiling water into the pot halfway up the side of the mold, cover, and steam in simmering water for 5 hours, adding hot water as needed to keep the same level. Sometimes a bit of the pudding seeps out of the top, but that's not a problem as long as the lid stays secure.

When the pudding is finished steaming, remove it carefully from the pan. Don't lift it by its lid because it may pull off and that would send the heavy pudding crashing back into the water. When it's out of the pot, remove the lid and allow to cool for 30 minutes.

When cooled, loosen edges with a sharp knife and turn upside down on serving platter. Let it stand until it slips easily from the mold. Just before serving, heat the brandy, pour it over the pudding and light.

Serve with chilled hard sauce on the side.

Serves 15–20.

HARD SAUCE

1/2 cup butter, at room temperature

1 1/2 cups confectioners' sugar

3 tablespoons brandy

1 teaspoon vanilla

1 teaspoon grated lemon peel

Mix ingredients together, beat until fluffy and chill. *Makes 2 cups.*

WOODFORD PUDDING

Though hardly as spectacular in presentation, and certainly much easier in preparation than Plum Pudding, Woodford Pudding comes with its own distinguished lineage. It's been made by cooks in Woodford County in the heart of the bluegrass region of Kentucky at least since the Civil War. Blackberry jam gives it a surprisingly rich taste. You can serve it warm with the same chilled Hard Sauce made for the Plum Pudding (page 328). Or you can let the pudding cool and serve it with the warm Whiskey Sauce here. Or you can serve it plain (but oh-so-comforting) by itself.

1 cup brown sugar

1/2 cup butter

3 eggs

1 teaspoon baking soda

1/2 cup buttermilk

1 cup flour

1 teaspoon cinnamon

1/2 teaspoon nutmeg

1 cup blackberry jam

Cream butter and sugar, then add eggs one at a time, beating after each.

"Little piece of pie,

Little piece of puddin'.

Gonna give it all to

Little Sally Goodin."

"Sally Goodin,"
Traditional

Dissolve baking soda in buttermilk and add. Sift flour and spices together and add; then mix in blackberry jam. Put in greased 9-inch cake pan and bake at 350 degrees for 40 minutes, or until center feels lightly firm and spongy. *Serves 6–8.*

WHISKEY SAUCE

4 tablespoons butter

1/2 cup sugar

1 egg, beaten

2 tablespoons whiskey

Let butter soften, then cream together with sugar and add well-beaten egg. Put in top of double boiler and stir until thickened over gently boiling water. Remove from heat and add whiskey. *Yields 1 cup.*

SEA FOAM

I tasted my first piece of store-bought divinity (Sea Foam's white-sugar cousin) at about the age of ten in a roadside Stuckey's outside of London, Kentucky. I could not fathom why anyone would want to throw good money at a confection so stale, so bland, and so stabilized when their mother could whip them up a batch of airy, sensual brown-sugar-flavored Sea Foam at home. At least, I assumed everyone's mother could since mine did, and often.

It was only when I got a little older and started trying to make my own Sea Foam (at the age of 11 to impress a little boy down the street with a sweet tooth and a winning smile) that I discovered making this great candy is more difficult than my mother made it look.

It requires little in the way of ingredients and comes together faster than most any candy I know. But you must have a good eye and a quick, steady, strong hand to make it. If you have both and follow the directions here, you'll have little pillows of airy, creamy sugar like a candy ocean's kiss. If it doesn't work (sometimes it's you, sometimes the weather) then you may just have to bake a quick chocolate sheet cake to ice with sea foam that won't quite set up. Or you may end up with coarser, slightly grainy pieces of candy which won't win you any prizes at the state fair, but will win praise from family and friends who gobble it up anyway.

One note: My mother never used a cooking thermometer in her life. We tested the Sea Foam syrup in that tried but not so true way, by letting drops fall in a cup of cold water and pulling the pot off to pour just when it reached the cusp between the firm and hard-ball stage.

It's a lot easier and more accurate to use a candy thermometer and remove the syrup from the heat just as the temperature reaches 250 degrees.

2 egg whites

1/4 teaspoon cream of tartar

1 cup white sugar

1 cup brown sugar

1/4 cup white Karo syrup

1/4 cup water

1/4 teaspoon vanilla

In a deep, heavy bowl, beat the egg whites with cream of tartar until they form stiff peaks. Lay out a piece of waxed paper about 18 inches long or lightly grease 2 dinner plates.

Put sugars, syrup, and water in a saucepan—one that has a handle and which you can easily pour from with one hand.

Bring to a boil while stirring. Put candy thermometer into the mix, stir occasionally to keep from sticking to the bottom, and when the syrup reaches 250 degrees, remove immediately from heat. (It gets there pretty fast, so don't wander off.)

Pour the hot syrup quickly in a thin, steady stream into the egg white mix, beating constantly as you do. (Sometimes the syrup doesn't "stream" but plops in glops into the egg white. This is all right. Just make sure you don't let the glops fall too quickly and curdle the eggs.)

When all the syrup has been added (you don't need to scrape the pan) begin to beat the candy vigorously and thoroughly. Although it doesn't take long, your arm will begin to feel as if it's going to fall off. Just about this time,

My mother says that to get the very best, creamiest texture from Sea Foam you need to put the candy in an air-tight tin and leave it overnight. She's right, but how she ever figured that out, I'll never know; when I was growing up no batch of Sea Foam ever stayed around that long.

And when she was growing up and making the candy for her father and her Uncle Hubert—who both loved it best of any confection—the Sea Foam disappeared even faster.

"Daddy and Hubert would sit at the kitchen table while I'd drop the Sea Foam out and as soon as it was off the spoon I swear that either one or the other would pick it up and put it right in his mouth," she remembered.

"Your daddy, though, used to say he liked the flavor but I'd put too much sugar in it. Can you imagine that? Too much sugar in a sugar candy?"

the candy should 1) begin to hold its shape a little and 2) lose some of its gloss. Immediately dip out in little mounds on wax paper or greased plate, using a teaspoon. (I use a second spoon to scrape the candy off the first—although you may want to use your finger if you can resist licking it.) *Makes 24 pieces.*

PEANUT BUTTER FUDGE

Here's what Dwight Yoakam remembers about fudge making in his youth:

"My mother made black walnut fudge, all-chocolate fudge with nuts in it, and that was pretty incredible. But when my Aunt Kay would come—that's her sister—she would whip up her specialty: peanut butter fudge.

"Now, you know how rich normal chocolate fudge is? Peanut butter fudge is like that multiplied. Peanut butter fudge is like artery lock.

"It is so rich, a rich where you . . ."

(And here his description becomes barely intelligible as he slaps his tongue to the roof of his mouth in an imitation of how things go when you eat peanut butter fudge.)

". . . can't hardly talk and you think to yourself, 'I get the feeling that anything to drink right now would be great. Milk. A glass of milk. That's what I need.'

"And your mouth, it's a convulsion of the mouth. The tongue goes into some sort of tongue lock with peanut butter fudge. And it's a kind of miserable ecstasy. Yeah, there's nothing richer in the inventory of confections than peanut butter fudge."

2 cups sugar

1/2 stick (4 ounces) butter

1/2 cup half and half

1/2 teaspoon vanilla

1/2 cup peanut butter

In a heavy saucepan, bring sugar, butter, and half and half to a boil. Cook until soft-ball stage (234–240 degrees). Remove from heat. Add peanut butter and vanilla and stir to mix peanut butter in, then beat energetically with a wooden spoon.

Ruth Ann Rankey, Dwight's mother, said the secret to the fudge she and her sister Kay make is that they "beat the daylights out of it. Beat until your arm feels like it's going to fall off and then beat some more."

Beat until the fudge loses its gloss and starts to thicken and set up some, then pour it immediately onto a buttered platter. Let cool before cutting. Store in covered tin for extra creaminess. And make sure you have something to drink handy (preferably cold milk) when you take your first piece. *Yields about 1 1/2 pounds.*

Condiments

Vidalia Onion Relish

Mama Nell's Catsup

Mrs. Ralph's Green Tomato Catsup

Cool Cucumber Sauce

Deane's Brown Sugar Bread 'n' Butter Pickles

Pickle Beans

Apple Butter

Pear Honey

Instant Black Walnut Grape Jam

Sorghum Butter

VIDALIA ONION RELISH

Most country cooks canned from necessity, but in the process they sometimes invented delicacies that are so good—and unmatched by anything available in stores—that it's worth the little bit of trouble it takes to make them still. This Vidalia Onion Relish is tangier and more complex in flavor than most commercial relishes. It will turn a hot dog cookout into a celebration—and it's super in meatloaf sandwiches.

Vidalia onions come from Vidalia, Georgia, and are firm and sweet enough that some folks swear they eat them like apples. If you can't get Vidalias, though, settle for the sweetest variety of white onion you can find.

4 medium Vidalia onions, chopped finely

2 cups shredded cabbage (about half a medium head)

1/4 cup salt

1 quart water

1/2 cup brown sugar

2 cups cider vinegar

1 tablespoon dried mustard powder

1/8 tablespoon turmeric

1/2 cup water

1/4 cup flour

2 teaspoons celery seed

2 teaspoons mustard seed

Chop onions and shred cabbage into a large glass or crockery bowl—not metal. Dissolve salt in 1 quart of water and pour over the vegetable mix. Cover and let soak overnight.

In the morning, turn the vegetables into a large colander and drain. In a large pot, dissolve the brown sugar in cider vinegar. Mix mustard and turmeric with water then add flour, mixing well to make a thick paste with no lumps. Add this to the vinegar and brown sugar mixture and stir to blend, again making sure there are no lumps.

Add celery and mustard and bring it all to a boil over medium heat, stirring to keep it from sticking. The mixture will thicken as it comes to a boil.

When it does boil, add cabbage and onions and continue to boil and stir for 5 minutes. (This mixture is very pungent and will clear your head in nothing flat while you stir.)

Put in sterilized jars, top with sterilized lids, and process in hot water bath for 15 minutes to seal. *Makes 1 1/2 quarts.*

MAMA NELL'S CATSUP

This comes from a box full of recipes that Anchorage, Kentucky, cook Blanche Pedigo was given by her grandmother, Mrs. George Weissinger Smith Hoge—also known as Mama Nell. Blanche serves it on the side with Country Ham (page 27). I've used up most of the batch I made slathering it on every type of potato imaginable—from home fries to leftover mashed-potato cakes. And it's no insult to pour this rich, resonant sauce on top of a perfectly grilled steak.

Mama Nell's catsup is something of a family elixir. Peyton Hoge, Blanche's father, recalls: "All during the war years, when we were living in chicken coops in Louisiana and our furniture was 20th Century fruit crates, Mother would send us catsup and beaten biscuits so we could survive."

Blanche says there are two secrets to the recipe and the first is to "just keep stirring from time to time, so it doesn't stick."

The second?

You should only make the catsup when the barometer is on the rise or at a steady high. If the barometer is dropping, Blanche warns, the catsup just won't set up.

4 quarts ripe tomato pulp

1 teaspoon salt

2 teaspoons ground black pepper

1/4 teaspoon ground cayenne pepper

1 teaspoon whole allspice

2 teaspoons Coleman's ground mustard

2 teaspoons ground horseradish

2 teaspoons ground ginger

1 tablespoon celery seed

2 teaspoons whole mustard

1 pint cider vinegar

1 clove garlic, crushed

1 chopped green pepper

1 chopped onion

1 dried red chili pepper

1 pound light brown sugar

Stem and peel tomatoes and chop into eighths in a very large and heavy pan. Squoosh the tomatoes lightly with hands or a potato masher to make a thick pulp. Add all the other ingredients except chili pepper and brown sugar. Put 1 cup of the liquid from the tomato pulp into a blender, shred the dried chili pepper into it, and blend until the pepper is liquified. Add to the tomato pulp and mix everything together well.

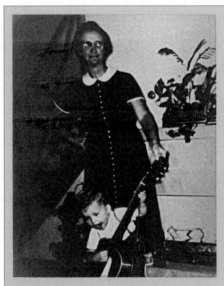

Earlene Tibbs witnesses the start of her grandson Dwight Yoakam's career at age three. Yoakam remembers, "My grandmother canned just about everything she raised and she raised about everything she could in her garden. She'd put by the beans and corn and tomatoes. And she had several different berry patches and she'd make her homemade preserves from that. We'd go down to visit and go home with jars of granny's good food and that was a real treat. But she didn't do it just to be a treat, now. That was how her family survived, from the food that she and my grandfather were able to raise and hunt and then put by."

Simmer on medium-low heat for 6–9 hours, stirring occasionally to keep the mixture from sticking. The time varies according to the juiciness of the tomatoes and the humidity of the day. What you're looking for is for the mixture to get very, very thick and cohesive and to turn reddish brown instead of clear tomato red. But remember that this is not a puree like commercial catsup. Mama Nell's will be a chunky paste. When it's thick enough to spread and not at all runny, add the brown sugar, mix it in and bring the whole thing to a boil.

Remove catsup from heat and pack into sterilized jars, top with sterilized lids, and process in a boiling water bath for 15 minutes to seal. *This makes about 3 quarts of rich, delectable catsup.*

MRS. RALPH'S GREEN TOMATO CATSUP

Ralph's grocery outside of Shelbyville, Kentucky, is a little bitty store sitting in a great big parking lot—which was fortunate the time Alabama pulled up in a big old tour bus to eat.

What brought Alabama and what brings a steady stream of locals to perch at the 13-stool counter in the back of Ralph Wade's store are the fresh, no-pretensions hamburgers flipped out from the grill there. In addition to Alabama, fans include retired publishing magnate Al Neuharth, and barbecue maven Vince Staten, co-author of *Real Barbecue* and a man who knows his meat.

Staten says the burger is great because Ralph, a retired A&P butcher, grinds the meat fresh every day. Ralph says the burger is great because of the gentle way they handle the baseball-sized mound of meat.

"You don't pat it too much, or it'll get tough," he advises.

But I say the real secret to Ralph's burger is the special homemade "catsup" they'll pull out from under the counter and let you slather on the burger if you're smart enough to ask.

Mrs. Ralph—Lillian Wade—makes the catsup from a recipe that belonged to her grandmother, Ada Gordon of Anderson County, Kentucky.

"Where she got it from, I have no idea," Lillian says. "My mother never did make the catsup very much and by the time I realized I wanted that recipe, my grandmother was gone. But I got the recipe from her sister. And the day I called my aunt up to get it she said, 'Why honey, there is no recipe. You just get you a peck of tomatoes, a head of cabbage and go from there.'

"And she put it in a pillow slip and hung it on the clothesline and let it drain all night. A group of ladies would get together with my aunt and cook it out in what she lovingly called 'the wash house.' "

But if her aunt didn't have a written recipe, Lillian has devised one over the years and that's what's reprinted here—enough to make 25 to 30 pints of catsup. By the way, you don't have to hang your pillow case outside. You can drain it over the sink or bathtub if you're brave enough. But Lillian holds her nose as she cautions that "between the green tomatoes and the onions, you got a real pee-yew."

> 5 gallons of green tomatoes
>
> 12 medium onions
>
> 1 large head of cabbage
>
> 5 green bell peppers
>
> 2 red bell peppers
>
> 3/4 cup coarse pickling salt
>
> 5 pounds sugar
>
> 2 quarts cider vinegar (approximately)
>
> 1 small box pickling spice

Wash, remove stems, and grind all the vegetables in a food grinder to a fine consistency. (Or use the metal blade on a food processor to fine-chop the food.) Mix the salt in well with the vegetables. Put the mixture into a clean pillow case you don't want to use on pillows any more, and hang it up to drain overnight—preferably outside.

The following morning, take the vegetable mix out of the pillow case; put it in a large pot; cover with cold water and then drain.

Put the vegetables back in the pot and add sugar and 1 quart of vinegar. The mixture should not be watery, but should be moist enough to spread. Add more vinegar if necessary.

Put the pickling spices into a spice infuser or cheesecloth bag and put that in the pot. Cook an hour or more over low heat, stirring to keep the mixture from sticking. Gradually the mixture will change from a fresh, bright green to a medium-khaki shade of green. When it changes color, it's ready to put up.

Sterilize jars and lids for 5 minutes in hot water, fill with relish, put on lids, and put in boiling water bath for 15 minutes to seal. *Makes 25–30 pints.*

COOL CUCUMBER SAUCE

This is great with just about any fish—a lighter, fresher variation of traditional tartar sauce.

> 1 medium cucumber
> 2/3 cup plain yogurt
> 1/3 cup "light" mayonnaise
> 1 teaspoon fresh or green dried dill
> 1/8 teaspoon salt
> 2 green onions, minced finely

Peel cucumber, remove seeds, and chop up finely. In a bowl, mix yogurt and mayonnaise well. Do not substitute salad dressing; it is too sweet. Hellmann's Light Mayonnaise is my preference because it is good and tangy.

Add cucumber, dill, salt, and onions and mix until blended. Chill until ready to serve. *Makes about 2 cups.*

DEANE'S BROWN SUGAR BREAD 'N' BUTTER PICKLES

You can get waxed, flabby forest green cucumbers in supermarkets year-round; but pickling cucumbers only show up in the summertime and are more likely to appear at seasonal fruit stands or farmers' markets than in the chain

Peanut Coke

At Ralph's grocery in Shelbyville, Kentucky, you can usually find Ralph sitting on a stool at the register where he has been known to give small children a complimentary piece of bubble gum on the way out. Ralph still sells "little Cokes" at his store and "nickel" bags of peanuts, too, so it's a great place to make a Peanut Coke.

And what, you may ask, is a peanut coke? As soon as you do, you will have betrayed that you were born and raised north of the Mason-Dixon line since the Peanut Coke is one of the most revered traditions of the South.

But whether you were born to it or not, making a peanut coke is easy as pie and, some folks swear, better.

First buy one nicely chilled small bottle of Coca-Cola of the classic variety—preferably from a country store like Ralph's in the dead of summer. Then buy one "nickel bag" of peanuts. Of course, you won't be able to buy the bag for a nickel anymore than you could get a candy bar for that price these days. But folks still call those little bags "nickel" ones—and if you can get them, Planters are the preferred variety with the festive, top-hatted, monocled and dancing Mr. Peanut on the pack.

Then open the Coke and take a good healthy swig. Tear the corner off the peanut bag with your teeth. Gently pour the peanuts into the Coke, swish the bottle just a bit to bring a few near the top, then proceed to sip and munch at the same time.

You'll employ the gentle swishing motion to get the peanuts to your mouth through most of the drinking of the Coke, but chances are when you get to the end, there will still be a number of peanuts in the bottom of the bottle.

It is proper etiquette to tip your head back and hold the bottle up for as long as it takes to get those last peanuts—provided you are careful and do not choke. Choking on a Peanut Coke simply isn't done in the South.

Making Soap with Mrs. Ralph

Green Tomato Catsup (page 338) isn't the only thing Lillian Wade cooks up each fall. In the nearly two decades that she and her husband Ralph have run their grocery in Shelbyville, Kentucky, she says she hasn't bought a box of soap yet. That's because she makes her own lye soap using the strained bacon and sausage drippings from the grill at Ralph's.

If you want to try it too, Lillian says to save enough drippings to "fill a 3-pound coffee can up to the second ring from the top. Put the can on a low flame and melt the grease, then strain it through cheesecloth."

Then set it aside and get a big metal pot to make the soap in, but be sure it's not aluminum. Lillian cautions that "the lye will eat an aluminum one up before your soap sets up."

Then she says: "Pour one quart of water into the container. Stir in one can of lye. As far as I know, they only come in one size and *Be Careful!* Stir it until the lye's dissolved. Gradually you pour the lukewarm grease into that. And then you add a tablespoon of Borax powder. Stir until it's the consistency of thick honey, then let it sit overnight. Turn it out of the container and let it cure a few days before using it.

"I still use a wringer washer because as greasy as we get here, you can put hot, hot water in it and your clothes come out right. I shave about a cupful—loose—of shavings from the soap to a load.

"You can even wash your hair in it."

stores. They are worth waiting for, though, both for plain eating and, unquestionably, for making pickles.

Pickling cucumbers are lighter green, smaller and knobbier. Their skins are never waxed, since waxed skins won't pickle properly. For this recipe you want firm, fresh ones six inches or less in length.

Deane Patton is the photographer who coined the phrase "chowl of billy" a few chapters back. Although her job is a full-time one, she still plants a garden each year at the house she and husband, Phil Wakeman, share in Westport, Kentucky. And every year she puts a large share of that garden by in jars of pickles, tomato sauce, and preserves.

This recipe is one she devised from several older ones—her most notable change is the substitution of brown sugar for white. It makes a mean-looking pickle; but I've never had one that tasted any better.

18 cups sliced pickling cucumbers

3 pounds small white onions

3/4 cup kosher or pickling salt

6 cups firmly packed brown sugar

1 1/2 teaspoons turmeric

1 teaspoon ground cloves

3 tablespoons mustard seed

1 1/2 teaspoons celery seed

6 cups apple cider vinegar

Wash and slice the cucumbers in 1/4-inch-thick rounds. Thinly slice the onions. Toss together by hand in a large bowl (not metal) with the salt. Cover and let stand for 3 hours, tossing occasionally.

When the time has passed, drain the cucumbers and onions. In small batches, rinse them well with cold water in a colander. Drain well again.

Sterilize enough jars and lids to hold 5 quarts of pickles and keep them in simmering water until you need them.

In a large stew pot, mix together the brown sugar, turmeric, cloves, mustard seed, celery seed, and vinegar. Bring slowly to a boil and let boil for 5 minutes. Add cucumbers and onions and heat to just below the boiling point, stirring occasionally to keep from sticking. With a slotted spoon, loosely fill the prepared jars with pickles to just below the point where the jar starts to narrow. Then, with a ladle, fill the jars to within 1/2 inch of the top with the pickling liquid.

Top with prepared lids and rings, and process in a hot-water bath for 20 minutes to seal. If any don't seal properly, put them in the refrigerator and eat them first. *Yields 5 quarts.*

PICKLE BEANS

Canning beans all afternoon long isn't something folks are much inclined to do these days when frozen foods are so easily available and tasty. But putting up a few jars of pickled beans—now that's another story.

"I'll tell you something that's just about one of the best things you've ever eaten and that's pickle beans," said singer Bobby Bare.

"But you cannot find them anywhere outside of the Appalachian area. It's not just that you can't get them anywhere else, but nobody knows anything about them.

"But I'm telling you, buddy, there is nothing in the world any better on a cold winter day than a big old skillet of pickle beans cooked in bacon grease. And it'll smell up your house, but you eat it with cornbread and you just won't care, it tastes so good."

Be warned, though, that Bare's passion is an acquired taste. Pickle beans have an acidic, briny flavor something like super-salty sauerkraut. And while Bare and other aficionados are willing to make a full meal on pickle beans, I like mine better as a side dish. They're good with anything normally accompanied by kraut—pork chops, soup beans, or spicy sausages, especially.

2 pounds green beans
water to cover

1 cup water
1/4 cup rice vinegar
4 tablespoons pickling salt

bacon grease

Remove strings and ends from beans, break into bite-sized pieces and rinse well. Put in a heavy pan, just barely cover with water, bring to a boil, cover, and turn down to simmer for 25 minutes. Remove from heat, let cool and refrigerate overnight.

The next day, sterilize four pint jars and lids, then pack the beans into them with enough juice to fill them about halfway. Put cup of water, vinegar, and pickling salt into a pan, bring to a boil and then pour over the beans, filling the jars. Seal tightly and store in a cool, dry place.

When the weather gets cold and you're ready to eat pickle beans, put about a tablespoon of bacon grease in a skillet over medium heat. When it's melted and hot, open a jar of beans and add it to the skillet. (Be careful of your hands since the brine will cause the grease to pop and splatter.) Some folks rinse the beans and drain them before putting them in the grease to cut the salty taste some. When beans are warmed through, serve. Be sure to have cornbread. *Yields 4 pints.*

APPLE BUTTER

Making apple butter used to be an all-day, community affair with the apples cooked slowly outdoors in a big copper kettle. Neighbors would take turns minding the big stirring spoon so the butter wouldn't stick and burn.

These days, even with the added convenience of a blender, it will still take you the better part of an afternoon to make a batch of apple butter. But slow baking it in the oven means you won't have to stand over a pot stirring all that time. I've been using my clay pot to bake apple butter and think it may keep a bit more of the flavor in, but you can make this in any 4-quart pot with a lid that will go in the oven.

Even so, you might wonder if it's worth the trouble for a product so easily found in the grocery store. Well, I can tell you that no grocery ever produced an apple butter as tart and full flavored as this one. But most of all, it's worth the making for the spicey, homey scent that fills your house as the apples slowly bake. My family fairly danced around all day the last time I made apple butter. It was as if the making was a formal celebration of winter's arrival and the holidays to come.

"And if that's not
loving you,
Then God didn't make
little green apples
And it don't rain in
Indianapolis
In the summertime."
"Little Green Apples" by
Roger Miller

Condiments

345

Speaking of holidays, little jars of apple butter make the perfect Christmas gift, and if you want to give them, you should put the hot butter in hot, sterilized jars and process in a water bath for 15 minutes. We eat ours so quickly, though, that I usually just put the jars in the refrigerator without sealing.

Be sure to buy a tart variety of apple; winesaps are good, as are green cooking apples. Those big, waxed, and glossy "delicious" apples offered in most groceries aren't worth your time and effort.

1 peck (8 quarts) of apples

2 cups apple cider

1 cup brown sugar

1 teaspoon ground ginger

1 teaspoon ground cloves

2 teaspoons cinnamon

Wash the apples very well and cut into eighths, discarding the core. Put about 6 slices of apple in a blender and add 1/4 cup of cider. Blend on high until smooth, and then using feeder opening, add apples a slice at a time. When you've got about 2 cups worth, add another 1/4 cup of cider. When you have 4 cups worth, pour into the baking pan and start again.

(A peck of apples will probably make more pulp than you can pack into a 4-quart pan, but we eat what's left as applesauce.)

When the pan is filled almost to the rim, cover, put it in a cold oven and turn the temperature to 250 degrees. If you're using a clay pot, soak it in water for 15 minutes before placing in a cool oven. Set temperature to 300 degrees. (See Clay-Pot Chicken, page 13.)

Bake sauce for 5 hours, stirring it well every hour or so to make sure none sticks to the bottom. Stir more frequently as sauce thickens. Remove from oven, add the brown sugar and spices and mix them well into the sauce.

Return to oven and cook an hour more until the sauce has a thick, buttery consistency. Cooking times will vary depending on how juicy the apples are.

Pack into hot, sterilized pint jars. Process 15 minutes in a water bath if you're going to keep in the cupboard—or let cool and refrigerate if you're not. *Makes about 6 pints.*

PEAR HONEY

Chet Atkins spent his early childhood living with his mother in the mountains of eastern Tennessee. But when he got a little older, he moved to Georgia with his father and stepmother and there discovered a whole world of foods he'd not had before—like grits, sugar cane syrup, and canned pineapple.

"My stepmother brought out some canned pineapple and I marveled at that. I'd never seen any of that before, in those rings and all. And she didn't do anything special with it—bake an upside down cake or anything—because it was special enough just by itself to me."

Atkins wasn't the only person delighted by the advent of canned pineapple. In country kitchens it quickly became an easy addition to the canning routine—mixed with other fruits to create preserves that were both easy to make and distinctive in flavor. My brother-in-law's mother, Mary Fryrear, for years made all of us beautiful little jars of rosy Christmas Jelly from maraschino cherries and pineapple.

My own mother's favorite was the simple, delicate Pear Honey.

4 cups pears

3 cups crushed pineapple

3 cups sugar

Wash the pears, core, and grate them. Put pears, pineapple (with its juice), and sugar in a heavy pan and cook over medium heat for an hour, stirring often to keep it from sticking. When mixture has thickened to a jellylike consistency, pour into hot, sterilized jars, seal and water process for 15 minutes. *Makes about 4 pints.*

INSTANT BLACK WALNUT GRAPE JAM

My aunts had a small grape arbor I used to play under when I was visiting down in Corbin. It had tiny little purple grapes too tart to please my tongue straight off the vine. But they made wonderful, jewel-like rosy jellies that I still remember.

My mother remembers that her mother made a thick, rich grape jam every summer and just as she was ready to put it up, she'd mix handfuls of black walnut pieces into it. Mother says that was absolutely the best thing you could ever dream of eating on hot biscuits.

But good grapes for making jams are hard to come by in groceries these days; the table grapes most frequently available don't have the right texture or flavor for a good homemade jam. Sometimes in the summer in the southeastern part of the country, you may come across a farmers' market or roadside fruit stand with a batch of muscadine grapes—those thick-skinned, musky-flavored beauties used for homemade scuppernong wine or jam. But those opportunities are rare.

My mother isn't one to easily give up treats she remembers so well from her childhood. So every autumn she invests in the best jar of commercial grape jam she can find, and then she gets a mess of black walnuts to mix in it a cup at a time. For each cup of jam, she adds between 1/4–1/2 cup of the nut meats, depending on her mood. She says it's not quite the same as her mother's, but it's still pretty great eating.

SORGHUM BUTTER

Candy is dandy, but sorghum molasses is what sweetening in the country is really all about. Sorghum "has a whang to it": This is how my mother describes the buttery, pungent backbite of this syrup.

The proper way to have sorghum—and any country girl or boy worth his molasses will tell you—is to mash it and cream it with a soft blob of butter until it makes a smooth gold-bronze spread which you then daub a bite at a time on hot biscuits.

I don't believe a recipe for this delicious dish has ever been written out. In fact, it seems to me I was just born knowing how much molasses to pour on how much butter. But in the interest of science, I've measured and come up with this formula: 2 teaspoons of butter + 3 teaspoons of sorghum = 4 small biscuits worth of sweetening.

(Unless you're a pig, of course, in which case the biscuit part of the equation will come out less.)

To make sorghum butter, you need to let the butter sit at room temperature until it's very, very soft, but not runny. Then you pour molasses over the top. Using the back of a fork's tines, mash and moosh and squish and squoosh and finally gently whip the butter and molasses together until it's a soft, creamy spread.

If you didn't get the butter soft enough, it won't cream, but will break into tiny globules. It's not perfect like that, but it's still pretty good. This is also good on pancakes, French bread, and hot or cold cornbread.

"I still fix my molasses that way with the butter," Chet Atkins says. "Oh yeah, yessir. I still do that. And I've gotten so I fix a little peanut butter with it too. Mix it up just like the butter. I've got to swear off sweets one of these days. But I think I'll continue that of a morning and quit having desserts instead."

"Bake 'em good and tender
Saw a little cane
Raise a pile of sorghum
Sweet little Liza Jane."

"Pig in a Pen," Old-time fiddle song

Condiments

349

MUSICIANS AND THEIR FAMILIES

CHET ATKINS was born in 1924 in the Clinch Mountain region of Tennessee. Called the dean of country music guitar, Atkins has a unique finger-picking style that has influenced players for decades. He's had an even greater impact on country music as a producer and executive. Atkins is one of the prime architects of the Nashville sound of the '60s, the commercial style credited with keeping the country music industry alive during the heyday of rock and roll. Since the early 1980s, his records have topped not only the country music charts, but jazz charts as well. He has won a blue-million Country Music Association Awards and several Grammys for his work.

BOBBY BARE hit the big time in 1963 with his recording of "Detroit City," a southern boy's aching lament for the rural home left behind when he moved north for work. Bare's earliest rural home was in the rolling hills of Portsmouth, Ohio, just over the river from Kentucky. There he developed his passion for fishing and for country fare such as pickled beans, bacon-grease-kissed biscuits, and fresh-caught, pan-fried fish. These days Bare is a mainstay in the country music scene of his adopted hometown, Nashville.

JETHRO BURNS was best known as half of the country comedy duo Homer and Jethro. But in musical circles he was revered as one of the greatest mandolin players. Deft at playing both country music and swing jazz, Jethro was a generous teacher. He was also a delightful raconteur with a raft of stories about the early days of his and Homer's careers. The recollections in this book are from an interview conducted in 1988, a year before Jethro died at the age of 69.

SAM BUSH, multi-instrumentalist and former leader of the New Grass Revival, provided much of the impetus behind the progressive bluegrass music movement that started in the early 1970s. More recently, Bush has been a featured player and singer in Emmylou Harris's Nash Ramblers. He grew up in the 1950s and '60s in Bowling Green, Kentucky, where he was nurtured on good country food and music.

EMMYLOU HARRIS, born in Alabama in 1947, served her musical apprenticeship, she says, "in the better hippie honky-tonks of the nation." She and the now-deceased Gram Parsons are credited with popularizing the country-rock sounds of the early 1970s. These days, though, Harris reigns in Nashville as the queen of the new traditionalist sound. She is a pure-voiced singer who interprets vintage country and writes her own songs.

EUGENIA HARRIS and WALTER "BUCKY" HARRIS are Emmylou's parents. Eugenia is known by family and friends as an extraordinary cook. Bucky learned how to fry bologna as a career marine and is an expert at seasoning a cast-iron skillet.

JOHN HARTFORD made his name and fortune as a singer/songwriter—the author of one of the most recorded songs in history, "Gentle on My Mind." He is capable of coaxing music from a banjo, fiddle, and guitar as well as from a piece of amplified plywood on which he dances. While music is his delight and livelihood, Hartford's greatest love is for the steamboats he has worked on since his boyhood in Missouri.

MARIE HARTFORD, John Hartford's wife, is known in Nashville as a fantastic country cook, a reputation she earned in the late 1970s when her kitchen table was often the gathering place for country music's most beloved outlaws: Willie Nelson, Waylon Jennings, Bobby Bare, Kris Kristofferson, and Tompall Glaser.

NAOMI and WYNONNA JUDD are the most celebrated mother-daughter duo in the history of country music—rising to sudden success with tradition-oriented harmonies in the mid-1980s and winning countless country music and Grammy awards for their work. There is another talented mother in the family as well: Naomi's mom, Polly Rideout, contributed several recipes to this book.

BRENDA LEE performed professionally by the age of five, signed with Decca Records in 1956 at the age of 11, and, in her teens, earned accolades as the best female singer in rockabilly. In recent years, Lee's musical successes have been charted in the country category; she is a star performer at Opryland. Her early childhood in Georgia, she says, was dramatically different from her later success. She remembers fondly the wood stove her mother, Grace Rainwater, used for cooking big dinners from the vegetables she and her children had grown.

LORETTA LYNN has been called the most honest of country music's queens. In 1972 she was the first woman to win the Country Music Association's highest honor, Entertainer of the Year. She was inducted to the CMA's Hall of Fame in 1988. Her girlhood in eastern Kentucky and her rise to country music fame were recounted in her autobiography and its movie adaptation, *Coal Miner's Daughter*.

BILL MONROE, born in 1911 in Rosine, Kentucky, is called the Father of Bluegrass music. He first appeared on the Grand Ole Opry in 1939 playing a jacked-up, high-powered, tenor-sung version of "Mule Skinner Blues," which became the model for bluegrass and an influence on country music and rock and roll.

TIM and MOLLIE O'BRIEN are singing siblings who grew up in the suburbs of Wheeling, West Virginia, during the late 1950s and '60s. Tim found fame as a member of the Colorado-based contemporary bluegrass band, Hot Rize, and as the leader of its alter ego country swing group, Red Knuckles and the Trailblazers. He works now as a solo singer/songwriter in country music. Mollie has just begun touring with her band, the Blue Tips.

AMY O'BRIEN contributed singer/songwriters Tim and Mollie to the world of music; she also contributed several recipes and much good advice to this book.

She lives in Wheeling, West Virginia, where her spreads for parties are legendary.

DOLLY PARTON is known for the platinum wigs, sequined skin-tight dresses and outrageous Hollywood style befitting a mainstream recording star and actress, but she has celebrated a different life in many of her songs. The strengths she gained and hardships she encountered while growing up in Sevierville, Tennessee, in the Smoky Mountains are the subjects of her classics: "Appalachian Memories," "My Tennessee Mountain Home," and "Coat of Many Colors."

JOHN PRINE was born in 1946 just outside of Chicago, but he says it might as well have been Kentucky, so attached was his family to the state where his parents and grandparents had been born. Prine immortalized the Muhlenburg County region they were from in his song "Paradise." In this book he has also immortalized the hash made by his mother, Verna Prine. Prine is one of America's finest songwriters, turning out works such as "Angel from Montgomery," "Hello in There," and "Sam Stone," which have the texture of well-crafted short stories. He now runs his own record company, Oh Boy Records, and has said that his next career move might be to "own a hot dog stand, one that makes *real* french fries."

GRACE RAINWATER knows a blue-million ways to cook a potato and make it delicious, says her singing daughter, Brenda Lee. Her recipe for Buttermilk Fried Chicken is also exceptional. Mrs. Rainwater lives in Lathonia, Georgia, where Brenda grew up.

RUTH ANN RANKEY, mother of hillbilly crooner Dwight Yoakam, is his link to the hills of eastern Kentucky. Ruth Ann shared several of her family's recipes and recollections of her parents, Luther and Earlene Tibbs, for this book.

POLLY RIDEOUT, mother of Naomi Judd and grandmother of Wynonna, grew up in a restaurant outside of Ashland, Kentucky—her grandmother's "Hamburger Inn." Her childhood, and her later experience cooking for a big family, prepared her for a mid-life career as a barge cook on the Ohio and Mississippi rivers.

JEAN RITCHIE brought the traditional Appalachian melodies she grew up singing to a larger audience at the first Newport Folk Festival in 1959. Legendary folklorist Alan Lomax called her "one of the finest pure mountain singers ever discovered." In her more than three decade career, she has been a powerful force in traditional music. Her songs have been recorded most recently by Emmylou Harris and Michelle Shocked.

EARLENE and LUTHER TIBBS were Dwight Yoakam's maternal grandparents. His song, "Readin', 'Rightin', Route 23" describes trips to their house in an Appalachian holler, and "Coal Miner's Prayer" is dedicated to his grandfather, who died in 1979. Earlene died in 1983.

DWIGHT YOAKAM was born in Pike County, Kentucky, in 1956, and although he grew up in Columbus, Ohio, he says that much of his early life was shaped by the weekends and summers he spent with his grandparents, Earlene and Luther Tibbs, back in eastern Kentucky. That Kentucky influence was most apparent in the hard-edged, hard-driving but traditionalist sound with which Yoakam starting topping country charts in the mid-1980s. His mother, Ruth Ann Rankey, provided the recipes for many of the country foods Yoakam remembers from his boyhood.

"And I'm proud to say that I've been blessed and touched By their sweet hillbilly charms."
"Readin', 'Rightin', Route 23" by Dwight Yoakam

Copyrights and Acknowledgments

PHOTO CREDITS

INDEX